PRAISE FOR
SOCIAL MEDIA STRATEGY

"This long-overdue book successfully combines the theoretical and practical, balancing real-life cases and interviews with a pragmatic and practical approach. Recognition of business purpose allied to customer/audience understanding provides a solid strategic base for successful social media activity. A strong read for anyone in the business."

Donald Lancaster, Director of Studies, Executive MBA Programme,
University of Bath

"Social media marketing is no longer optional, and those who use it without a clear underpinning strategy run the risk of losing ground to those who do. Julie Atherton carefully unpacks the winning formula for effective social media marketing in this engaging, stimulating and thought provoking key text. I strongly recommend that any marketer worth their salt should have a copy of this book on their shelf."

Rob Angell, Associate Professor in Marketing Research,
University of Southampton, and Co-founder, Angell Sloan Research,
University of Southampton

"This is much more than a social media 'how to' book. By showing where social integrates with the full suite of marketing tools and channels Julie has created a mini marketing handbook too. It's held together by her strong and simple ABC (audience, brand, campaign) model, and usefully covers social in the context of important marketing practices like brand purpose, behavioural economics, and customer journey planning. Interspersed with case histories and interviews with marketing leaders, it was a great read."

Mark Runacus MBE, Chair DMA Board and Co-founder and
Planning Partner, Wax/On

"This is a powerful and practical social media strategy guide to what makes truly great work, how to implement it and importantly how to measure it. An essential read for anyone who wants to implement successful social media campaigns. Highly recommended."

Pete Markey, Chi

"This book is the perfect guide to the contemporary digital culture that we are all now immersed in. Social media marketing is now such a huge influence within the consumers choice of brands and customer engagement, that this book is an essential tool in understanding it. On a personal note, Julie has been a huge supporter of our degree course and is a highly knowledgeable and informed person within the realms of social media."

Lee Thomas, Course Leader Advertising Design, University of South Wales

"Concise, insightful and action-orientated. Julie Atherton makes social media manageable."

Paul Armstrong, Founder, HERE/FORTH & TBD Conference

"*Social Media Strategy* brings together traditional models with the most current of social trends. This is a must read for established industry leaders to keep on top of their game as well as providing a great insight for those wanting to work in the sector."

James Eder, business coach and Co-founder, Student Beans

"A must for anyone engaged in social media. This book manages to be both at the cutting edge, forward thinking and a definitive reference of the best approaches to social. Frankly, it might put me out of a job."

Adam Fulford, Chief Strategy Officer, Proximity London

"Julie Atherton has done a great job in demystifying the world of social media to produce a practical, research-based guide to the successful creation and implementation of social media marketing strategies. Exceptionally she has linked this to wider marketing strategy and the book deals effectively with the difficult issue of the development of the brand in social media. The insights gained from her extensive experience in the field are supported and developed by interviews with a wide range of leading players in the discipline. I have no hesitation in recommending the book for all those interested in understanding and developing the opportunities for effective customer engagement in this fast moving and fascinating world."

Matthew Housden, Chair, DM Trust, Principal Lecturer, University of Greenwich, Visiting Professor, Grenoble Ecole De Management

"Clear and insightful. This book is the go-to guide for creating a far-reaching social media strategy for your brand, corporate campaign or cause."

Susan Walkley, Managing Partner, Havas Life Medicom

Social Media Strategy

A practical guide to social media marketing and customer engagement

Julie Atherton

Publisher's note

Every possible effort has been made to ensure that the information contained in this book is accurate at the time of going to press, and the publishers and author cannot accept responsibility for any errors or omissions, however caused. No responsibility for loss or damage occasioned to any person acting, or refraining from action, as a result of the material in this publication can be accepted by the publisher or the author.

First published in Great Britain and the United States in 2020 by Kogan Page Limited

2nd Floor, 45 Gee Street
London
EC1V 3RS
United Kingdom
www.koganpage.com

122 W 27th St, 10th Floor
New York, NY 10001
USA

4737/23 Ansari Road
Daryaganj
New Delhi 110002
India

ISBNs
Hardback   9781789660319
Paperback   9780749497071
Ebook   9780749497088

British Library Cataloguing-in-Publication Data

A CIP record for this book is available from the British Library.

Library of Congress Cataloging-in-Publication Data

Library of Congress Cataloging-in-Publication Data
Names: Atherton, Julie (Business strategist), author.
Title: Social media strategy : a practical guide to social media marketing and customer engagement / Julie Atherton.
Description: London, United Kingdom ; New York, NY : Kogan Page, 2019. |
  Includes bibliographical references and index. | Summary: "Social Media Strategy provides a simple, structured way to create integrated customer engagement and social media campaigns that work. Organizations often talk of digital planning but struggle to know which channels to invest in, how to integrate them with content marketing activity, or fail to develop measurable outputs that align with business objectives. This book provides a clear road map for efficient planning, deliverance and financial accountability of social media's contribution to the business. Social Media Strategy delivers practical guidance such as identifying and targeting audience segments, methods of two-way community engagement, reputation management, being present on the right channels, and driving action through influencers. It also identifies the relevant tools and platforms to audit, track and measure business impact and customer engagement. With example templates, interviews and global case studies including National Geographic, TUI, Dreams Beds and Tiny Giant, this professional guide delivers a long-term solution for maximizing social media led business development"– Provided by publisher.
Identifiers: LCCN 2019029613 (print) | LCCN 2019029614 (ebook) | ISBN 9780749497071 (paperback) | ISBN 9781789660319 (hardback) | ISBN 9780749497088 (ebook)
Subjects: LCSH: Internet marketing. | Marketing channels. | Social media.
Classification: LCC HF5415.1265 .A84 2019 (print) | LCC HF5415.1265
  (ebook) | DDC 658.8/72–dc23
LC record available at https://lccn.loc.gov/2019029613
LC ebook record available at https://lccn.loc.gov/2019029614

Typeset by Hong Kong FIVE Workshop
Print production managed by Jellyfish
Printed and bound by 4edge Limited, UK

*This book is dedicated to my husband and my boys
Rob, Jack and Luke, who assured me I could write a book and
kept encouraging me all the way through.*

*I also have a special thank you for Mandy Wood –
I couldn't have finished it without you.*

*And for Fi, who loved Twitter, and in whose memory I and
many others continue to push ourselves to do what seemed impossible.*

CONTENTS

06 Campaigns: A quick step guide to channel selection for your objective and audience 108

07 Measuring and benchmarking success: How and when do you know your social media strategy is working? 136

FIGURES

TABLES

TEMPLATES

Introduction: How to use this book

Who the book is for

Everyone who is either working in or studying digital marketing or public relations (PR), needs to understand the principles of social media strategy and its application to their business. This book aims to inspire and educate anyone with an interest in social media marketing and provide practical advice on how to create and deliver your own successful strategies.

Why I wrote this book

There are lots of social media books on the market but I have never been able to find one that combines both a strategic and practical approach. This book seeks to do that using my simple ABC approach to social strategy. This approach recognizes that social media is no longer a bit on the side, a place to play and experiment while the important channels get on with making money and building your brand; rather, it is an integral part of everyone's lives and should be an integral part of every business strategy. To succeed there are just three3 things you need to get right: A – your audience; B – your brand presence; and C – your campaigns. As long as your social strategy tackles these, you will be successful in social. My goal with the book is to give you the tools to do just that.

What the book contains

Social Media Strategy aims to provide a practical guide to social media marketing and customer engagement. Whatever your involvement with social media, the book explains how to create and apply a strategy to improve your business performance. Each chapter takes a key element of social media strategy building, explains the core concepts and provides tools and frameworks to help you apply them in practice. A comprehensive list of sources and resources will support your strategy creation, and relevant case studies and interviews demonstrate real world applications.

The book aims to help you:

- learn how to create a social media strategy;
- understand your audiences and their relationship with your brand;
- create a brand positioning and presence within social media and beyond;
- create successful social media campaigns;
- understand how to integrate social media with your other channels to market;
- use influencers successfully;
- measure social media performance;
- prepare for and manage a social media crisis.

How the book is structured

Chapter 1 – Understand how social media is utilized in business, marketing and interpreting customer expectations

This chapter looks at the role social media plays in business marketing and in setting and delivering to consumer expectations. It considers how social media is changing with the rise of private media and provides key facts and stats on the varied global levels of social media engagement and performance.

Chapter 2 – Integrated customer engagement: How to ensure your social media strategy is integrated into your wider marketing and business development

This chapter looks at the theory of digital customer engagement in order to understand how and why your social media strategy will enhance your PR and strategic business development. It explains key marketing concepts and tools, and provides useful practical templates that can be used as you create your own strategy.

Chapter 3 – Getting started: Aligning social media goals and KPIs with your wider business objectives

Any social media strategy needs to be aligned with your overarching business strategy. This chapter provides guidance on setting social media goals and key performance indicators (KPIs) for your PR and marketing campaigns that support your wider business objectives. Useful templates are provided to help you start building your own objectives and KPIs.

Chapter 4 – Audience: Using social listening to profile your audience and generate customer insights for a global social media strategy

Social media listening provides a wealth of information and insights to enable a detailed understanding of your different audiences and customer groups. This chapter considers global social media strategies and explains marketing segmentation and how to create profiles for fans and customers. You will explore the impact of psychology and generation on consumer behaviour and learn how to apply these insights to your own customers.

Chapter 5 – Brand presence: How to drive action and engagement through integrated content marketing on social media

This chapter looks at how to create a brand presence in social media, the second element in the ABC of social. It considers how you represent your brand in social channels and demonstrate your brand purpose. Integrated content marketing and the use of behavioural economics are explored and explained, showing how they drive engagement and impact customer loyalty. Interviews and examples provide demonstrations of award-winning social media campaigns in different sectors.

Chapter 6 – Campaigns: A quick step guide to channel selection for your objective and audience

Social channel usage varies by audience, location and market. This chapter introduces the campaign element of the ABC of social media and will help you decide which channels are the most appropriate for your objectives, enabling you to maximize your impact through digital integration. It is important to ensure that you are present on the most relevant channels both for building your brand presence and delivering specific campaign objectives. You may also need to use some niche social networks as well as the more popular favourites, and deciding which channels not to use are crucial decisions in any strategy. The chapter includes tips for selecting channels and insights for using different channels in both business-to-business (B2B) and business-to-consumer (B2C) environments.

Chapter 7 – Measuring and benchmarking success: How and when do you know your social media strategy is working?

This chapter explains the key social media metrics and how to measure social media campaigns. Top tips for measuring and benchmarking are included together with explanations of the most important calculations.

Chapter 8 – Customer or celebrity? Identifying and attracting the right influencers to advocate for your brand

This chapter explores how to identify and attract the right influencers to advocate for your brand. Case studies and examples are used to demonstrate how celebrities, experts, employees, fans and customers can be deployed for different influencer objectives and at various stages of the customer journey.

Chapter 9 – Crisis and reputation management for social media: A clear guide for the unpredictable

An essential part of any social media strategy is planning for the unexpected. A brand's reputation can be significantly improved or harmed in social media, and this chapter includes key learnings from examples of success and failure. Interviews with social media crisis consultants on their planning and reputational management recommendations complement real examples to provide practical insights and advice.

Chapter 10 – Thoughts on the future of social: What will happen next?

How do you stay abreast of the latest changes in technology and consumer behaviour? This chapter considers what might happen next in social. What will be the impact of artificial intelligence, virtual reality and voice, how will content be produced and what types of skills will marketers need to have? Interviews with leading practitioners bring an insight into their visions for social.

1

Understand how social media is utilized in business, marketing and interpreting customer expectations

This chapter looks at the role social media plays in business and marketing and in setting and delivering to consumer expectations. It considers how social media is changing with the rise of private media and provides key facts and stats on the varied global levels of social media engagement and performance.

Across the world, in every culture, social media has, for many, become a part of everyday life. It enables over 3.8 billion people, over 45 per cent of the global population (Hootsuite and We Are Social, 2019) to stay connected with loved ones and work colleagues, to share important memories or information, to tell stories and unleash their creativity, to run and manage businesses, to follow brands and celebrities, and capture not only what they have done, but how they feel. It is the natural extension of digitalization. Initially a digital replication of offline human social interactions, it has evolved to create its own social behaviours and ecosystems that are only possible online.

For businesses and brands, this means that social media can no longer be a bit on the side, a place to play and experiment, while the proper channels get on with making money and building your brand. Social media, like digital, is now an integral part of all marketing and branding, and as such needs to be embedded in any business or marketing strategy development. Social media marketers, like digital marketers are just marketers, and every person working in business should understand the role that social media plays.

As Bayindir says, 'today, we're experiencing a digital world with social media at the epicentre of a new reality where virtual personal impressions, possessions and choices are curated on social media profiles and truly becoming the digital self extensions' (Bayindir, 2019).

This book looks at social media strategy from a business marketing point of view. Over the last 30 years, I have been involved in running businesses and working with clients from both the brand and agency perspective. My career has spanned global publishing, building an award-winning digital agency from a start-up, partnering B2C and B2B brands from the automotive, travel, financial services, retail, luxury, utilities and digital sectors, advising charities and social enterprise businesses, and training marketing professionals and business leaders in digital, brand, social media and content marketing. This experience has given me a detailed insight into the different ways that organizations function, how brands are built and can decline, and how brand, reputation and marketing combine to build value into a business. This book uses this experience to demonstrate how to build a social media strategy that is embedded into your overall business strategy, the considerations needed and the advantages of this holistic approach.

In addition, while writing this book I have spoken to over 20 leading social marketers, leaders in their field who still work daily in social media. They work with brands across the globe in everything from audience research to social measurement, from social advertising to brand building, from community management to influencer marketing, and from crisis management to content creation. Many run their own businesses, work for global brands or work on international accounts at award winning agencies. All have a unique and insightful perspective on what makes social media work and how it fits into an overall business strategy, and thoughtful views on where social will go next. Their interviews are used to highlight different opinions and provide alternative ideas of how to practically implement your social media strategy.

Our social lives

One reason why it is important to embed social media strategy into your wider business strategy is due to the sheer level of variety and complexity involved when you consider all of the different social media options. The 2019 'internet minute' chart (Figure 1.1) shows exactly where our attention is and how our behaviour has changed.

FIGURE 1.1   This is what happens in an internet minute, 2019

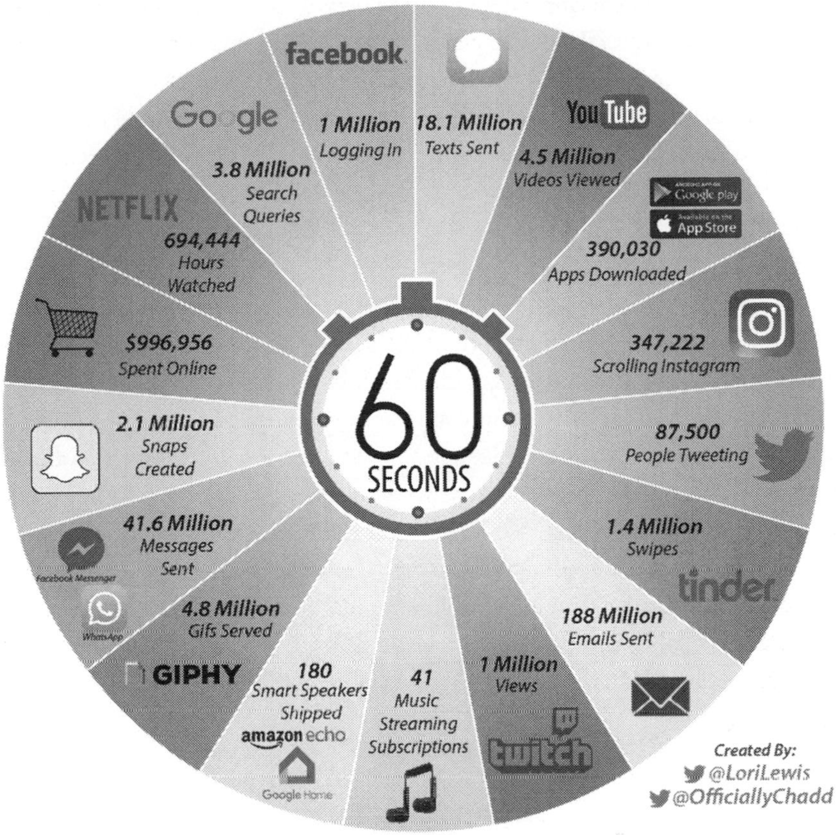

facebook

Go gle

NETFLIX

1 Million
Logging In

18.1 Million
Texts Sent

You Tube

3.8 Million
Search
Queries

4.5 Million
Videos Viewed

Google play

App Store

694,444
Hours
Watched

390,030
Apps Downloaded

$996,956
Spent Online

347,222
Scrolling Instagram

60
SECONDS

2.1 Million
Snaps
Created

87,500
People Tweeting

41.6 Million
Messages
Sent

1.4 Million
Swipes

Facebook Messenger

WhatsApp

tinder

4.8 Million
Gifs Served

188 Million
Emails Sent

GIPHY

180
Smart Speakers
Shipped
amazon echo

Google Home

41
Music
Streaming
Subscriptions

1 Million
Views

twitch

Created By:
@LoriLewis
@OfficiallyChadd

SOURCE Reproduced with kind permission of Lewis (2019)

Every minute, twice as many instant messages are sent as texts, almost a million more YouTube videos are viewed than Google searches are made and, despite the tales of the decline of and dissatisfaction with Snapchat and Facebook, they continue to generate significant activity (Lewis, 2019). Although many people are still involved in 'old school social', publicly posting the best versions of themselves for all to find and comment on, there is an increasing move to private, ephemeral social options such as messaging, snaps and Instagram stories. This trend is driven by younger audiences concerned about their digital footprint, mental health and well-being, and a need for more authentic, genuine and more personal conversations. But, where early adopters investigate the majority will eventually follow, and faster than they ever did before. So, as Instagram grows exponentially, it will soon be full of mums and granddads, and the social adventurers will find somewhere new to go.

In this book I talk about the ABC of social. This tripartite should be the lifeblood of your business in social media and the bedrock of your strategy. A is for audience, B for brand, and C for campaigns. Social media is where your brand meets your customer in a place where control is shared. Unlike other spaces, where brands tell the world about themselves, social is a place where brands and people converse.

Audience

So, social enables a brand to get closer to its customers or potential consumers either by providing unique and important insights into their behaviour, their views and how they feel about you, or by using sophisticated and accurate targeting techniques to ensure you are seen by them. When building your strategy, you need to understand the social life for your brand or business in relation to your commercial short- and long-term goals. Who your core audiences are, where they engage in social media, how and what they use it for, and how social is integrated into their whole life, as well as how you might fit into it as a brand.

Brand

Brands aren't built in one place;, the world's biggest brands exist in multiple spaces, some digital, some real world. Even previously pureplay digital brands such as Amazon are moving into bricks and mortar. As brands increasingly behave as cultural, purposeful ecosystems, and experience becomes the most important metric, social media ensures your brand has a presence wherever your audience spends their time. With no control over what people say about you in social, ensuring you have a strong brand presence there will support your wider brand and reputation building activity, and provide a narrative to encourage positive interactions.

Campaigns

All organizations want to encourage some form of action from their customers, consumers or supporters. That action might be to buy, visit, donate, volunteer, promote or a range of other activities, and these actions are core to the ongoing success of the business. Your campaigns will drive these actions; some will be created by you specifically for and in social, but you need to remember that 'all activity is social now' (Beament, 2019). Every experience an individual has with your brand has the potential to be filmed, photographed, commented on and shared, enhancing or detracting from your brand experiences and either driving or diverting the actions you would like them to take.

Social accountability

One reason for social to be slow to sit at the top table of organizational strategy has been the argument that it is hard to measure. In reality it is no harder to measure social than it is to measure your brand value – in fact, it is often much easier. Where measurement lets social down is when it is added as an after-thought, or only considers tactical social-only metrics such as engagement. If social measurement and KPIs are tied to the overall business objectives and KPIs then it becomes obvious where social media is demonstrating real value. In addition, as ad blocking continues to rise and content marketing and other inbound activities are recognized as important conduits to consumers, social becomes an even more important part of the integrated marketing mix.

Social futures today

Change is happening faster than ever before as technology increases the complexity and speed at which businesses need to respond. With the introduction and increase of CGI influencers, in-platform purchasing, voice and vertical video, marketers need to be ready to respond and capitalize on the opportunities they create. The book considers where we are now and what we can learn from the experts, innovators and early adopters on where we are going next. So, as we start on our strategy creation, Bayindir outlines the social landscape from a consumer psychologist's perspective.

INTERVIEW
Nisa Bayindir, consumer psychologist and digital strategy director

Background

An award-winning strategist and consumer psychologist who blends research, insights and consumer psychology to deconstruct consumer needs and motivations, Bayindir has a multidisciplinary professional background in social networks, start-ups, digital agencies and client-side global franchises. Regularly featured in various global news outlets and industry publications, Bayindir currently runs her own consumer psychology consultancy.

What is the appeal of social media?

Social media, naturally, has social at the core of its promise, or at least it did in its earlier days. It's such a game-changing phenomenon because it chimed right in with one of the primary needs of the social animals that we are. Being socially connected to *others like us* is how we actualize and nurture our existence, our identities. We grow and evolve as individuals, and become stronger as groups, through our social interactions. These platforms held a mirror to people to fulfil their individual and group needs and helped them validate who they are, or who they *aspire* to be. Gordon Allport, the father of personality and trait theories, is also the architect of the 'self extension' concept. It's the sum of possessions, values and interests that build or enhance the ego and one's sense of self. Today, we're experiencing a digital world with social media at the epicentre of a new reality where virtual personal impressions, possessions, choices are curated on social media profiles and truly becoming the digital 'self extensions'. As digital natives willingly go through the constant cycle of adoption of new platforms and interaction formats, we are witnessing the becoming of a new normal in human psychology.

How would you sum up the current social media landscape?

Social media is the melting pot of self extensions equipped with a previously unmatched reinforcement of human connections. As social media brought people/consumers closer, brands strived to get closer to consumers, and boundaries started to blur. *'Closed'* networks like Facebook turned into business platforms and open networks invented new formats to support targeted, innovative ads by brands. The social network landscape is now at a saturation point, with a lot of commercial and marketing noise overwhelming the consumers. We see an influx of choice and demand by brands for attention and purchases, up against the data privacy and content credibility concerns occupying the consumer psyche.

What trends are driving the near future of social media?

Two key trends we see in the evolution of social media today are actually brought on by social networks themselves – their competition to offer better, bigger, sponsored, 'influenced' content, entertainment and so on. With the ever-growing avalanche of choice and rich content, consumers are now pickier than ever. Social media is now age-agnostic and there's increasing discernment and savviness across all generations. They don't want to associate themselves, or their 'social media reactions', with just any brand or content – they know that the internet doesn't forget, and it's now almost a case of *personal brand management* on the consumer level.

How is consumer behaviour changing on social?

The saturation point brought on passive networking, account deactivations and committing to 'dark social' platforms (SMS, messaging apps, direct messaging). This was all brought on since consumers' self-perceptions seek individuality, privacy/familiarity and safety – almost all of these are not what social media can reliably offer any longer. The real life offline is where it all boils down to, so they are trying to find ways to mimic this level of intimacy and realness. Therefore, they are truly connecting with social circles in closed platforms, where brands are less welcome *unless* consumers proactively sign up for interaction. We are changing the way we use the social platforms: the light-hearted and entertaining side of social media, or the more ephemeral channels/interaction types, always come at the top of the list for usage motivations in most global surveys, for example.

What should marketers do next in social?

What marketers need to bear in mind is that they shouldn't ever give up on their learning quest to understand real human needs, real life/offline experience and psychological drivers behind consumer actions – and, to that end, remember that social media tactics or being omnipotent on all channels just because they are there are no longer the quick solutions to the problem. They should unlearn, even overhaul, their brand purpose, their vision, and what they stand for before creating a robust message to consumers that will naturally fit with some social networks but not all (and that's perfectly fine) and the human experience expectations of consumers on these channels. Social media is not the means to an end, it's just one of the tools to use to strike a chord with the consumer. Ultimately, whatever marketing channel is at play, only the human, relatable brand messages and online/offline experiences will go through the intellectual filters of the committal consumer interactions in the future.

(SOURCE: Bayindir, 2019)

References

Bayindir, N (2019) Consumer Psychologist and Digital Strategy Director [Interview] (1 May).

Beament, S (2019) Content Strategist [Interview] (24 March).

Hootsuite and We Are Social (2019) *Digital 2019: Global Digital Yearbook*, Hootsuite & We Are Social, London:

Lewis, L (2019) 2019: This is what happens in an internet minute. www.allaccess.com/merge/archive/29580/2019-this-is-what-happens-in-an-internet-minute (archived at https://perma.cc/F8ZU-TLT5)

2

Integrated customer engagement

How to ensure your social media strategy is integrated into your wider marketing and business development

This chapter looks at the theory of digital customer engagement in order to understand how and why your social media strategy will enhance your PR and strategic business development. It explains key marketing concepts and tools, and provides useful practical templates that can be used as you create your own strategy.

The traditional marketing funnel

For decades, businesses have built their marketing strategies based on the view that consumers start the buying process with a large number of potential brands in their consideration set. This set is continually reduced as choices narrow and finally the consumer makes a decision on which brand to select and buys.

Brands that adopt this view will also often apply the AIDA model to their marketing activity to drive sales and ensure conversion. The AIDA model was created in 1898 by Elias St Elmo Lewis, an American businessman, and has shaped advertising and marketing strategy for over 100 years.

The model describes the sales process and has four phases: awareness, interest, desire and action. Each phase has a part to play in convincing a potential customer to buy:

- **Awareness:** The first job of any marketing campaign is to ensure consumers are aware of a particular brand and the products and services

FIGURE 2.1   The AIDA model in action

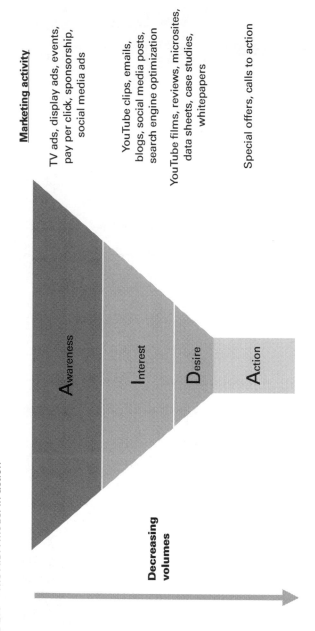

it offers. Awareness could be generated via display, social media or other adverts, word of mouth, or referrals. Often awareness adverts are disruptive, highly creative and targeted to specific audiences to ensure consumers notice them.

- **Interest:** Once the consumer is aware, the next phase seeks to generate interest in a particular product or service. At this stage, more detailed information is given either via the advert or on the company website. Consumer interest can be piqued with interesting or useful information, especially if it is unique to your product or especially targeted to your audience.

- **Desire:** Turning interest into desire is when your brand really needs to stand out from its competitors and create an emotional connection. What is the compelling reason to choose you? Is your brand the market leader, the most aspirational or the best value? Ideally the consumer will be persuaded to desire your product by the product itself or the initial advert, but often, and especially for B2B or high-value sales, this process will take time and require many different information and persuasion elements. For example, to stimulate and increase desire, car manufacturers use product configuration pages on their websites to encourage potential customers to visualize the exact colour and features they prefer.

- **Action:** This phase is the turning point, the conversion to the sale or the sign-up as a lead, depending on your marketing objective. Your marketing needs to be clear about the next step to take – 'buy here', 'book now', 'register'. Often the action will take place on your ecommerce site but it could be on your website, over the phone, in the physical world or on social media.

When the AIDA model is drawn, it is often shown in relation to the marketing funnel to demonstrate the process for a particular business and the reducing volumes at each stage (Figure 2.1). The examples below demonstrate the type of marketing activities that might be used at each stage.

Mapping the AIDA funnel

When reviewing your own purchase funnel, it might be useful to map your marketing and social media activity against the AIDA model. You can use Template 2.1 for this (download it at www.koganpage.com/sms (archived at https://perma.cc/L9GJ-P6FQ)). Here the template has been filled in with example content showing how a software company uses a

TEMPLATE 2.1   Mapping the AIDA funnel

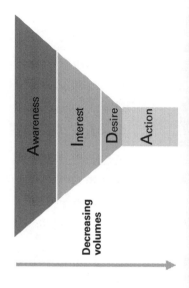

AIDA level		Marketing activity options for consideration				Volume by level	Conversion rate
Awareness	Activity	PPC clicks	Display ad clicks	Social media ad clicks	Event attendees		
	Volume	500	100	200	50	850	
Interest	Activity	Email opens	Social media post video views	SEO traffic	Blog post reads		
	Volume	100	80	150	60	390	46%
Desire	Activity	Case study views	Whitepaper downloads	Review reads	Microsite visits		
	Volume	20	40	10	30	100	26%
Action	Activity	Trials booked	Sales	Leads	Visits		
	Volume	50				50	50%

Key:

Example marketing activities are included. Actual activities shoud be selected and included in the tool

These numbers should be calculated or estimated and input into the tool

Excel will calculate the numbers to go in these cells automatically

variety of activities to encourage trials. The conversion rates are calculated at each level of the funnel to understand their impact on trials of the product. Social media activity forms part of an integrated mix.

The digital marketing customer journey

Over a decade ago, McKinsey began to explore the digital customer journey and how it differs from the traditional sales funnel idea. Known as the customer decision journey, the model enables the AIDA principles to be applied at each stage but is a more useful way to view customer–brand relationships in the digital environment than a standard purchase funnel. The customer decision journey has six elements that work together in the following way:

- **Consider:** Initially, potential customers are thinking about buying a product or service and one or more brands are in their starting consideration set. They may have been prompted to consider the purchase because they have seen some advertising, were recommended by a friend, or have a need to fulfil (for example, your vacuum cleaner has broken and needs replacing). In a traditional sales funnel this stage would include the largest number of brands. In the customer decision journey, the stage can start with just one brand.

- **Evaluate:** In this stage the potential customer starts to notice other competitor brands and moves through a process of adding and subtracting brands from the consideration set. Over time, the number of brands under consideration does not get smaller and smaller, as it would in the traditional sales funnel; rather, it can increase and decrease continually until the moment of purchase. In a digital journey, your customer is only a click away from your competitor, and techniques such as remarketing and the customer's own online research can add 'surprise' brands into the mix at a very late stage in the buying decision.

- **Buy:** In the traditional funnel this is the ultimate goal for a brand. The sale is made, the funnel has reached its successful conclusion. This stage is still important in the customer decision journey; it represents the brand's goal and does mean success. However, brands need to be very aware that this stage does not always represent success for the customer. Often, once a sale decision is made, the customer is wracked with indecision and insecurity as they wonder if they made the right choice.

FIGURE 2.2   The win–win customer decision journey

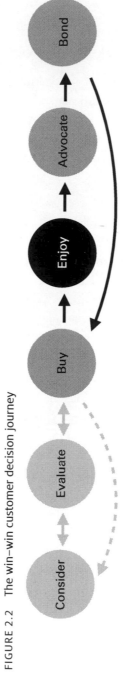

A development of the Edelman decision journey (Edelman, 2013)

- **Enjoy:** This is probably the most important stage in the customer decision journey. It represents the experience of owning and using the purchase and validates the reasons why the customer bought from the brand. Many brands neglect this stage and do not provide onboarding support or marketing materials to explain how to use and enjoy their products and services.

- **Advocate:** If a customer enjoys the purchase and the experience of using it then they have a high potential to become an advocate for the brand. Facilitating and encouraging advocacy can increase your brand's awareness and improve sales conversion, but is often a neglected stage.

- **Bond:** This should ideally be the ultimate brand goal. It describes the creation of a mutually satisfying relationship between the customer and the brand. If a strong bond is formed then the customer enters the loyalty loop, and instead of starting with a new consideration set next time they need a new product or service, they will prefer to go back to the brand and re-buy from them.

Visualized by Edelman (2013), the customer decision journey demonstrates the new way customers interact with brands in a digital environment. In Edelman's visualization, the 'buy' moment is highlighted as having primary importance, enabling the 'enjoy' and 'advocate' stages that lead to an ultimate bonded relationship. I prefer the visualization shown in Figure 2.2, which highlights the primary importance of 'enjoy' and the perpetual dilemma occurring from consideration to evaluation and between evaluation and purchase.

No potential customer has a goal to buy from your brand. They have a need or desire that buying from your brand could satisfy. By focusing on enjoyment, the experience of using the product or service, rather than the purchase itself you create a win for both the customer and the brand, and a much greater chance of advocacy and bonding.

Social media can be used at every stage of the customer decision journey to support and drive the process and offers the opportunity to improve the experience as well as encourage sales and bonding, as shown in Figure 2.3.

FIGURE 2.3   Social media usage in the customer decision journey (based on a revisualization of the Edelman customer decision journey)

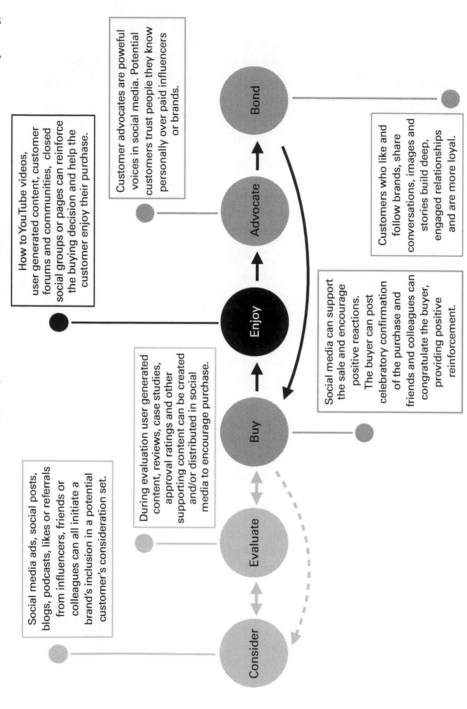

A revizualization of the Edelman customer decision jouney (Edelman, 2013)

The win–win purchase

Recognizing the insecurity of the 'buy' moment for customers is even more important in a B2B sale than a B2C sale. In general, the longer the consideration and evaluation phases and the higher the purchase price, the more likely the customer is to feel that they have made the wrong decision. If you have just bought a car you are more insecure about your choice than if you buy a hamburger, as the cost outlay is significantly higher and the impact on you and your family will be greater over a longer period of time. If you have just selected a new software tool for the company you work for, the insecurity levels will rise again as a wrong decision could impact your career.

Brands that focus on making the 'buy' moment a success by supporting an enjoyable experience create a win–win. The brand wins as it makes the sale it requires and the customer wins because they feel great about their purchase.

Social media is an important asset at the buy and enjoy moments as it provides an outlet for individuals to spread the news of their new ownership and receive reassurance and recognition from friends, family and colleagues. In addition, the opportunity to join and benefit from customer forums and communities can enhance the ownership experience and provide useful information on how to make the most of your new buy.

You can use Template 2.2 to decide on your own priorities for your brand.

The emotional connection between customers and brands

Many B2B marketers worry about their brand being 'boring' and find it more challenging than B2C marketers to identify interesting and engaging content to stimulate social media awareness and interaction. It is important to remember that for a B2B purchaser, the moment of purchase is a highly charged emotional experience. In research conducted for Google and CEB, Motista found that customers were much more likely to feel emotionally connected to B2B brands than B2C bands (CEB Analysis, 2013).

The reasons are simple but often overlooked. More people are involved in the B2B purchase than the B2C purchase, decision-making is more protracted and the ultimate decision has an impact not only on the organization but also on the career/reputation of the decision-maker. You may lose your job or miss out on promotion if you make the wrong choice on your next IT software solution for your firm, whereas making the wrong hamburger choice for lunch will not have nearly the same impact.

TEMPLATE 2.2   Mapping the customer decision journey

| Consider ⟷ Evaluate ⟷ Buy → Enjoy → Advocate → Bond |

Marketing objective:		Insert your objective here: Raise brand awareness, deliver qualified leads, etc		
	Stage objective		**Content elements**	
Journey stage	**Potential**	**Actual**	**Potential**	**Actual**
Consider	Decide which stages are relevant and then identify the appropriate content or campaigns using the potential content elements list as a guide		Social media ads, social posts, blogs, podcasts, likes or referrals from influencers, friends or colleagues	
Evaluate			User generated content, reviews, case studies, approval ratings and other supporting content	
Buy			Facilitate purchase notifications and image sharing	
Enjoy			How to YouTube videos, user generated content, customer forums and communities, closed social groups or pages	
Advocate			Influencer activation, review writing, recommendations	
Bond			Product co-creation,	

In social media, B2B brands can often miss the opportunities to create an emotional connection between themselves and their customers – recognizing this relationship and increasing the opportunities for engagement and support should be an important part of any B2B social media strategy. Brands that do this well, such as Caterpillar with their global Cat®#BuiltForItTrials campaign (Cat® Products, 2014) have created events, YouTube films and interactive content that can be seen and shared on a variety of social channels.

Although the ultimate decision to buy an expensive earth-mover or truck will be made at board level, the drama of giant Jenga or tug-of-war enables engaging content that can influence the consumers (digger drivers) and customers in social and other channels not normally utilized to target finance directors of large construction firms.

Customer engagement and social media

There are many different definitions of customer engagement, and in social media the term 'engagement' also has several interpretations. For clarity, these terms, as understood in this book are described as:

- **Customer engagement:** In marketing, this term is used to describe the depth of a customer-to-brand relationship. It denotes the level of trust and the frequency, length, and type of interaction. At its best, customer engagement is instigated and maintained by both the brand and the customer via multiple marketing, social media and experiential channels and experiences.

- **Engagement:** In social media, engagement is used to describe the interaction with social media content such as likes, shares and follows. Increasingly, brands have started to rank engagement in terms of meaningful interactions (comments and conversations) over passive interactions (likes and shares).

Meaningful interactions are more important than passive interactions, and the level of customer engagement increases the more often and the more diversely a customer connects with a brand. Therefore, social media can be used effectively to maintain positive levels before, during and after purchase. This can be particularly important when the decision-making process takes a long time (eg B2B marketing), or there are many years between repeat purchases (eg a new car or a new mattress), or the product benefit lacks tangibility (eg funeral or life insurance).

In addition, because social media is a collaborative, dialogue-based channel it is ideally suited to generating high levels of brand-to-customer, customer-to-brand, and even customer-to-customer interactions that enable the brand to maintain trust, awareness and usefulness over the long term. The shared interactions and real-time elements of social media are ideal for telling emotive brand stories and creating shared experiences. This is particularly important, as research by Gallup (2018) shows that fully engaged customers represent a 23 per cent increase in revenue, profitability and share of wallet.

What level of engagement should you expect?

We have established that engagement is important, but there are three engagement factors that need to be taken into consideration when building your strategy. First, people will differ in their propensity to engage in social media, and the make-up of your customer and follower audiences will therefore affect the amount and type of engagement you should expect. Second, individuals will have different levels of engagement in social media at different times in the customer decision journey. Third, engagement levels differ dramatically by different social media channels and therefore where your audiences engage and the channels and content you use for your brand will also affect your engagement levels.

Engagement by audience

One of the most useful ways to understand audience behaviours in social media is the Social Technographics Score (Liu, 2018), created by Forrester in 2014 and updated annually. Their analysis uses demographic and behavioural data and research to segment the US population into different groups according to the way they interact with brands and social media channels across the customer lifecycle. This three-stage approach provides detailed insights to help decide not only how much money to invest in social media for different audiences and brands, but where in the customer lifecycle to target that investment.

For example, Forrester breaks the US social media audience into four groups – Skippers, Snackers, Savvies and Stars (Figure 2.4):

- **Stars:** Make up 27 per cent of the US online population and are the youngest group. They are highly open to trying new product and brands, are very brand loyal and as well as accessing social media regularly are the most likely group to consume social ads.

- **Savvies:** Represent the average US online consumer. They are 50 per cent less likely to consume social ads but are just as likely to engage with social media. They are open to trying new products and brands.

- **Snackers:** Regularly access social media but rarely consume social ads and are less likely to try new products and brands.

- **Skippers:** Infrequent users of social media and almost never consume social ads. They are the oldest group and are the least likely to try new products and services.

Forrester summarizes their attitude to engagement as: 'Stars demand social interactions with your company..., Savvies expect..., Snackers appreciate..., and Skippers spurn' (Liu, 2018).

FIGURE 2.4   Forrester's Social Technographics Score classifications®

	SKIPPERS	SNACKERS	SAVVIES	STARS
Social Technographics Score range	0 to <10	10 to <30	30 to <60	00 to 100
Percentage of US online population	21%	23%	28%	27%
Female	45%	54%	57%	48%
Mean age	54	48	41	34
Brand loyal	69%	74%	74%	81%
Enjoy trying new brands or products	28%	38%	48%	74%
Read/watch/listen to social ads	3%	11%	29%	60%
Access social neworking sites daily on a smartphone, tablet, or computer	22%	76%	87%	83%

SOURCE Forrester Analytics Consumer Technographics North American Online Benchmark Survey (Part 1) 2018 (Liu, 2018). Reproduced with the kind permission of Forrester

Clearly, as a brand, it would be great to know whether your customers tend towards Star or Skipper behaviour, or even segment your customers base according to their social media behaviour. Customer segmentation and profiling is covered in Chapter 4 in more detail but the groups identified by Forrester above demonstrate clearly differentiated characteristics by segment, which enables a differentiated approach to marketing to them.

Engagement by stage in the customer decision journey

In the next stage of the analysis, Forrester considers the range of activities consumers undertake on social channels and look at where these are most likely to occur in the customer lifecycle. Forrester poses that by understanding

FIGURE 2.5　How consumers engage with content on social media

People can discover products and services via word of mouth and social ads.

People can explore products and services via social tools on brand sites.

People can begin (and sometimes complete) transactions on social sites.

People can engage with companies via branded profiles on social networks.

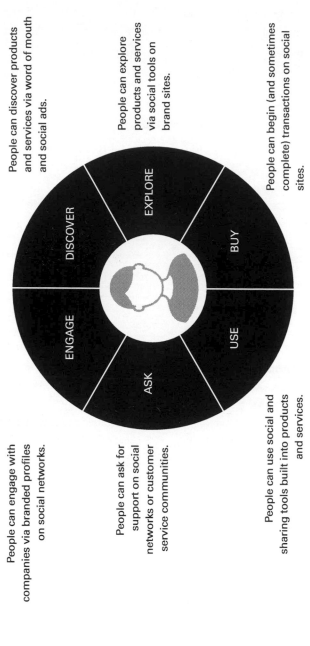

People can ask for support on social networks or customer service communities.

People can use social and sharing tools built into products and services.

SOURCE　Forrester Analytics Consumer Technographics® North American Online Benchmark Survey (Part 1) 2018 (Liu, 2018)

the consumers' purpose for being in social and the activities they engage in, it is possible to map that activity to parts of the customer lifecycle. Their lifecycle uses different definitions and has slightly different stages to the Edelman customer decision journey but it remains the same. It maps the progression of moving consumers from discovery (or consideration) via exploration (or evaluation) through buying and into using the product, asking questions to help improve the experience, and deepen engagement with the brand (the equivalent of enjoy-advocate-bond). In both the Forrester and Edelman models, the relationship with the customer doesn't end at the moment of purchase. Rather, what happens at this point and beyond is arguably even more important and essential in build a deep and engaged customer-brand relationship. Figure 2.5 shows how the behaviours map into a customer journey.

Forrester allocates scores to each types of behaviour and uses these scores to recommend the types of marketing activity you should invest in. For example, if your consumers are highly likely to use social media to discover new brands and products then as a brand you should invest in social advertising and advocacy and influencer programmes as your consumers would welcome finding out about you in this way.

Consumers with a high ask score (such as the Santa's Lapland mums discussed in Newton's interview in Chapter 4) expect their questions to be answered quickly and thoroughly in social. As a brand, you need to facilitate this perhaps with a dedicated Twitter profile or Facebook page, or by providing videos on YouTube that provide the support they need to enable them to have a positive and enjoyable customer experience.

By using Forrester's Social Technographics Score approach, each customer behaviour can be mapped to different channel and content plans. Although the score can only be generated when using Forrester's patented approach, you can apply the principles to your own marketing activity, and this is discussed further in Chapter 6.

Engagement by sector, channel and content

Content research from Hubspot in 2018 shows that, on social media, video is preferred to other content. When asked 'What kind of content do you want to see from a brand or business you support?' 54 per cent of respondents noted video, with emails and newsletters coming in with the second highest number of responses at 46 per cent.

This move to video has increased with increased capabilities and penetration of smartphone cameras and the rise of video based social media channels such as Snapchat. In addition, Rival IQ's social benchmarking report looks at how engagement rates vary by sector and social network and finds large differences for each (Figure 2.6).

FIGURE 2.6   Engagement rates by social media network

	Median engagement rate per post
Instagram	1.73%
Facebook	0.16%
Twitter	0.046%

SOURCE Table created using data from Rival IQ's Social Benchmarking Report (Rival IQ, 2018)

By knowing that your expected engagement rates are likely to move a percentage point, in the wrong direction, between Instagram, Facebook and Twitter you can predict relative engagement levels more accurately and manage internal stakeholder expectations. However, remember that lower engagement rates on Twitter may not mean your audience doesn't see or value your content. If the majority of your audience are spectators, they will be happy to absorb your information without sharing it or commenting on it.

Using social media to meet your wider marketing objectives

Social media is a powerful tool in the marketing arsenal and works best when it is completely embedded into the wider PR and marketing objectives.

For many businesses, social media is only considered at the end of the strategic process where it is added as an additional tactical channel. In reality, social media can be used exclusively, or as an integral part, to deliver a wide range of business and marketing objectives. Figure 2.7 details some key areas where social media can have an important impact on your marketing activity.

FIGURE 2.7   Social media's impact on marketing and PR objectives

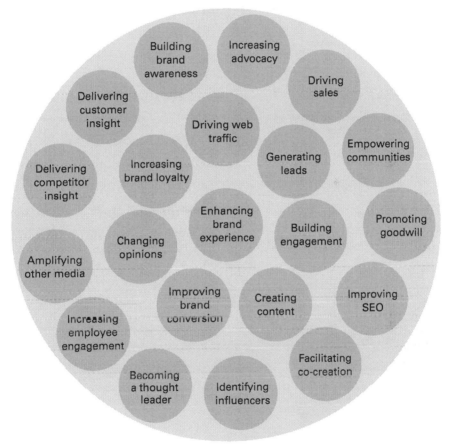

Putting customer engagement into action

When building your social media strategy identify a marketing goal you wish to meet and consider how the various elements discussed in this chapter, and shown here, will affect it:

- What is your marketing objective?
- What does a win look like for your business?
- What does a win feel like for your customer?
- Will you use a traditional marketing funnel approach or the customer decision journey?
- How will you apply the AIDA model to achieve the action you desire?
- What parts of the customer decision journey are you trying to affect with your strategy?
- Have you considered the length of the customer decision journey, the key touchpoints, the number of stakeholders and decision-makers and how important to the decision-maker their decision is?
- Do you know what type of social behaviours your audience exhibits – are they Skippers, Snackers, Savvies or Stars?
- Do you know the level of engagement your audience has on different social channels?
- Do you know the type of content they prefer to engage with?

The AIDA mapping and customer decision journey mapping templates included in this chapter will help you to structure your answers to these questions and focus your strategy in the most important areas. Most importantly, social should be integrated into your wider marketing and business strategy, enhancing your customers' engagement with your brand and supporting a strong brand story. Below, Sam Beament, an award winning social media strategist, shares his thoughts on integrating social media into your marketing strategy.

INTERVIEW
Sam Beament, content strategist and social media creative

Background

Sam is an award-winning content strategist with over 12 years' experience working with brands such as Dyson, Walkers Crisps, Evian, Microsoft, Danone, Barratt Homes and Lexus to fulfil their social media ambitions. Sam's breadth of knowledge spans from planning and executing social content for global advertising campaigns to using social channels for customer acquisition and retention.

Where does social media fit into the strategy development process?

It has taken a fair amount of time for many brands to fully integrate social media into their campaigns. For years, social media has been seen as an additional function that sat separately from everything else rather than an intrinsic part of the planning process. Social media often shares the same objectives as the overarching marketing strategy so the two are inherently linked. The main difference is the way the campaign is executed at the channel and format level.

If brands don't approach social as an integrated part of their marketing activity, it can lead to a disconnected experience for the consumer. Brands should always have one eye on social media and consider how their campaign may play out on social. For example, a company may design a press ad, but as soon as I take a photo and upload it to Twitter it becomes social content. It's important to break away from the old silos to deliver campaigns that are fully integrated and truly social.

How does a brand embed social media into their business strategy?

There is sometimes a requirement to educate people on what role social media can play. Social media is more than just paid advertising – it can work on many levels including supporting internal communications, driving employee advocacy, recruitment and, of course, customer service.

It is important at a brand level that everyone knows what the different social platforms can do and the roles they can play throughout the customer journey. Social is where people meet, play, talk about their lives and jobs, share their ideas and hopes. It's important to understand the role of social in people's lives – it is much broader and deeper than an advertising platform.

How you use social should come from your overarching business objectives and KPIs. Once you have decided the broader narrative of your brand, you can start to think what role social plays in telling that story, and meeting the targets alongside all the other channels.

What is your view on the balance of paid versus organic social?

I think organic social is making a bit of a resurgence at the moment. When I started my career, paid social didn't exist and brands had to work really hard to get people to notice them. To do this successfully, we had to really understand what made people tick and what drove them to engage with content, and hopefully share it with their friends. It was really challenging, but when it worked it really worked and the results were amazing.

Around 2011 the transition to paid social began and initially there was a real reluctance to accept that these channels were no longer 'free' for brands to use. Today there is full acceptance of paid social and for many years organic has been seen as 'dead', but I think many businesses are now beginning to see the benefit of a blend between paid and organic to tell a complete brand story.

Social platforms are flooded with paid content, and if your best customers hit all the top data points they will see a vast number of ads. Social advertising is often sales driven, which means it becomes hard for a brand narrative to cut through. Platforms such as Instagram and Pinterest still deliver pretty decent organic reach so I think there's an argument to move towards a better balance between organic and paid activity, although paid will always take up the lion's share of time and money.

How can an increase in organic social support a brand?

Whilst organic reach is low in comparison to paid, organic activity can be used to extend a brand story and therefore still has a role to play. I believe a blend of both is needed for success. For example, if someone wants to find out more about your business they will often visit your social channels – they won't seek out your ads. Social channels should be treated as a shop front, and it's crucial to create the right content to engage people who have actively chosen to find out more.

And it's not just about customers. Journalists, trade experts and potential employees will all look at a company's social channels to find out more about them. Of course, organic can no longer be used to drive high volumes of reach, but it still has a role to play.

How do you balance the need to tell your brand story and drive sales?

Social is incredibly flexible and highly targeted which allows brands to build sequential conversations with their customers. If you understand the journey your consumer will go on then you have an opportunity to tell your brand story and engage people before trying to make a sale.

Social media marketing should mirror how you would expect to interact with someone in real life. For example, it wouldn't be best practice to walk up to someone in the street and starting trying to sell them something straight away. Social media is no different. Brands should get to know their customers first, share an interesting story or tell them a joke. By separating the brand story from the conversion targets, it makes the job of creating great content far easier and more effective.

What's next for social?

I'm really interested in the impact of voice and virtual reality (VR) on social. Google Home, Alexa, Siri are all changing the way we search and seek out content. The instructions given to these devices are very different from a keyword search, and once we throw VR into the mix it will become a totally immersive experience. I think we will start to move towards frictionless transitions between the real and digital world and eventually the two will become indistinguishable.

The rise of social commerce is also one to watch. Platforms are keen to keep people within their ecosystems and I think it's only a matter of time before the likes of Facebook and Google fully embrace the retail experience. Very soon people will be able to click on an advert and buy something then and there, without ever having to leave the platform or close an app. Payments on social will soon be as normal as buying something on Amazon or eBay. You only have to look at China and WeChat to see where things are headed.

Do you think Facebook has passed its prime?

Definitely not. As an organization they have diversified so well and in January 2019 WhatsApp, Facebook, Facebook Messenger and Instagram made up four out of the five most downloaded android apps in the world; Tik Tok was the only non-Facebook app in the top five (Statista, 2019). In addition, Facebook know how to work with brands and are mature in terms of targeting and format diversity. They are not afraid to use functionality from other platforms too, such as Stories, which was originally developed by Snapchat. Facebook need to stay hungry, though, as the smaller platforms are catching up very quickly.

How will brands adapt to the new social media behaviours?

There has definitely been a shift towards more ephemeral content as people become more aware of what they've shared permanently sitting on social platforms. This has also led to a growth in dark social and messaging services such as WhatsApp, Facebook Messenger and direct messaging has grown rapidly on Twitter and Instagram too. I think there's a misconception that people are sharing less, when they are just sharing differently. People used to be comfortable publicly sharing their experiences online, but that is definitely changing as they become more aware of privacy issues and data breaches. This poses a challenge for brands that want to interact with people in these private spaces. Influencers can be useful introducers and, as platforms mature and functionality increases, I'm sure opportunities for brands will increase but no doubt they will cost more to implement.

(Source: Beament, 2019)

References

Beament, S (2019) Content strategist [Interview] (24 March)

Cat® Products (2014) Cat® #BuiltForIt trials. www.youtube.com/watch?v=DWc8dUl7Xfo (archived at https://perma.cc/SK29-92QU)

CEB Analysis. (2013) *The CEB/Motista Survey*, The Corporate Executive Board Company

Edelman, D (2013) Branding in the digital age, in *HBR's Must Reads: On Strategic Marketing*, Harvard Business Review Press, Boston

Gallup (2018) www.gallup.com/services/169331/customer-engagement.aspx?g_source=link_WWWV9&g_medium=TOPIC&g_campaign=item_&g_content=Customer%2520Engagement (archived at https://perma.cc/3A9U-S4ZG)

Hubspot (2018) Content trends global preferences research. https://research.hubspot.com/content-trends-global-preferences (archived at https://perma.cc/BTS2-UQNR)

Li, CBJ (2008) *Groundswell: Winning in a world transformed by social technologies*, Harvard Business School Press, Boston

Liu, JF (2018) Social Technographics® reveals who your social audience is – and how to approach them, Forrester®

Mintel (2018) *Social Media and Networks Research UK*, Mintel, London

Rival IQ (2018) 2018 social media industry benchmarking report. www.rivaliq.com/blog/2018-social-media-industry-benchmark-report/ (archived at https://perma.cc/5EAB-CK2A)

Statista (2019) www.statista.com/chart/8553/the-global-top-10-android-apps/ (archived at https://perma.cc/V6GA-HT8C)

3

Getting started

Aligning social media goals and KPIs with your wider business objectives

Any social media strategy needs to be aligned with your overarching business strategy. This chapter provides guidance on setting social media goals and key performance indicators (KPIs) for your PR and marketing campaigns that support your wider business objectives. Useful templates are provided to help you start building your own objectives and KPIs.

Business models in the digital age

There are many types of organizations, from hyper-local to global, from small and medium enterprises (SMEs) to large corporations, from non-governmental organizations (NGOs) to entrepreneurial social enterprises, from charities to public sector institutions, from B2B to B2C to B2B2C and even B2C2C. Whatever the size or type of your organization, there is one thing every business has in common – the need to understand its core purpose and vision, its strategy for continued existence and growth.

In the digital age, businesses face increasing and significant challenges as long-established brands are usurped by new start-ups, which are not only more agile and innovative, but also change all the rules of the game. Consider how Airbnb changed the hotel industry, Netflix changed TV and film viewing, Spotify changed music listening, ApplePay changed banking, Amazon changed shopping, Uber changed local travel, the list goes on and on.

Not only have these new organizations changed the industries that they operate in, they have also rapidly become powerful and valuable brands.

In the past, large, established businesses such as Coca Cola and Disney would always be at the top of the 100 most valuable global brands. Today, the top spots are in continuous transition and are dominated by innovators and tech brands.

According to the Brand Z report, only two brands, Microsoft and Google, remained in the top 10 most valuable brands between 2016 and 2018 (Kantar Milward Brown, 2018). The brands that dropped out, in the sectors of automotive, tobacco, confectionary, retail, etc were largely replaced with high tech, social media, sector disruptors and customer-focused brands (Figure 3.1).

FIGURE 3.1   Top global brand changes, 2016–18

	2016	2018
1	Microsoft	Google
2	General Electric	Apple
3	Coca-Cola	Amazon
4	China Mobile	Microsoft
5	Marlboro	Tencent
6	Walmart	Facebook
7	Google	Visa
8	IBM	McDonald's
9	Citi	Alibaba Group
10	Toyota	AT&T

SOURCE Adapted from Kantar Milward Brown, 2018

As Doreen Wang, Kantar Millward Brown's Global Head of BrandZ, comments:

> Brands that are winning in the intelligence-led marketing era include businesses such as Amazon and Tencent who put the consumer at the heart of everything they do. These brands use technology to understand the needs of their consumers and apply these learnings to create an ecosystem of services that fulfil multiple needs, enabling a seamless consumer experience between platforms.
>
> (WPP, 2018)

All businesses can learn from these global giants in terms of putting the customer at the heart of the business and using technology to facilitate a valuable customer experience. Your business model will impact your social media strategy, particularly in how you engage with customers and fulfil their needs. Therefore, it is important to understand your overall business model before embarking on your social media goals.

A simple way to understand different business models in the digital age is to use the value driver mapping model developed by Peter Fisk (2017). Fisk looks at the most important driver in each business, the one that most leverages the business's success, and uses this to define the type of business model. He identifies six types of model:

- **Maker models:** The business creates, owns and controls the products or services that are its greatest assets.
- **Channel models:** The channel to market is the essential driver of how the business operates.
- **Crowd models:** A level of cooperation or commitment is required from stakeholders to enable the business to function.
- **Payment models:** Traditional payment is not necessary in digital transactions.
- **Exchange models:** New forms of ownership and trade are established by the business.
- **Asset models:** Data and tech are at the heart of the business.

Some examples of the models are shown in Figure 3.2.

Deciding where your business sits in this model will help you prioritize the areas that drive your success and determine where you may want to focus in your social media strategy. For example, a business that is driven by what it creates, such as the knowledge and time maker model business Harvard will use its social media to demonstrate its excellence in this area, distribute content and build general brand awareness. A business that depends on its stakeholders' commitment, such as the crowdfunded venture Kickstarter, is more likely to use social media to find like-minded individuals and deepen engagement.

FIGURE 3.2   Mapping business models by value drivers

BUSINESS MODEL EXAMPLES					
MAKER MODELS	**CHANNEL MODELS**	**CROWD MODELS**	**PAYMENT MODELS**	**EXCHANGE MODELS**	**ASSET MODELS**
MAKE AND DISTRIBUTE Coca Cola, Microsoft	**SPECTRUM RETAIL** Amazon, Marks & Spencer	**MEMBERSHIP CLUB** Costco, Quintessentially	**SUBSCRIPTION PAYMENT** FT.com, Graze	**BUYER AND SELLER MARKETPLACE** Etsy, NYSE	**ADVERTISING AND SPONSORSHIP** Google, Metro Newspapers
MAKE AND SELL DIRECT BMW, HSBC	**NICHE RETAIL** ToysRUs, Wiggle	**CROWDFUNDED VENTURES** Kickstarter, Zidisher	**REGULAR REPLACEMENT** Gillette, Nespresso	**COLLABORATIVE CONSUMPTION** Buzzsar, Regus	**LISTED OR PROMOTED** Monster, LinkedIn
LICENCE TO MAKE Arm, Ed Hardy	**CURATED RETAIL** Fab, Positive Luxury	**OPENSOURCED COMMUNITY** RedHat, MySQL	**SHARED RENTAL** Zilok, Hilton	**BRANDED CONSORTIA** Cisco, Spar	**NETWORK BUILDERS** Hotmail, Twitter
DEMAND THEN MAKE ZaoZoa, Threadless	**AUCTION RETAIL** eBay, Sotheby	**MULTILEVEL MARKETING** Tupperware, Natura	**FREEMIUM PAY WITHIN** Angry Birds, Coursera	**TRADEABLE CURRENCY** Bitcoin, Airmiles	**REPUTATION BUILDERS** Tripadvisor, PaywithaTweet
KNOWLEDGE AND TIME McKinsey, Harvard	**FRANCHISED RETAIL** McDonald's, Subway	**GROUP BUYING** Groupon, Huddlebuy	**PAY AS YOU GO** AzuriTech, Techshop	**TRANSACTION FACILITATOR** PayPal, Visa	**CUSTOMER DATA** Facebook, 23andMe
CERTIFICATION AND ENDORSEMENT ISO, Verisign	**REMAINDER RETAIL** Saks, Vente Privee	**REVERSE AUCTION** Priceline, Freemarkets	**MICRO PAYMENTS** Flattr, Grameen Danone	**DYNAMIC PRICING** Expedia, Uber	**NON-PROFIT BUSINESS** Oxfam, Wikipedia

SOURCE   Reproduced with kind permission of The Genius Works (Fisk, 2017)

Business strategy in the digital age

Once you have established the type of business you are in, and perhaps the business model you operate, it is important to understand your overall business strategy. What are the vision, mission, goals for your business, and how do you plan to achieve them?

Your business strategy may take a very traditional approach or you could employ more innovative thinking that could help you succeed in a customer-focused, technology-driven digital environment, such as:

- challenger brand thinking;
- customer value ecosystems.

Challenger brand thinking

The term 'challenger brand' was coined by Adam Morgan in his book *Eating the Big Fish*. He defines a challenger brand as: 'a brand, and a group of people behind that brand, whose business ambitions exceed its conventional marketing resources, and in consequence it needs to change the category decision-making criteria in its favour, to close the implications of that gap' (Morgan, 1999). A challenger brand mentality can be applied to any type of business and it is a particularly useful approach in creating a single-minded focus for your business strategy.

In 2012 Morgan reviewed his initial thinking to explore the new challenger generation and understand what it means to be a challenger. His later book, *Overthrow* (Morgan et al, 2012), presents a new challenger model that poses that any brand can be a challenger. In this book he explores the narrative of being a challenger brand. The 10 narratives are:

1 **The People's Champion:** This type of brand defines itself by being on the side of the consumer. It often champions the consumer specifically against the market leader. This position has often been taken by airline brands – think Virgin versus BA and, more recently, the South African Kulula Airlines. The latter offered cheap airline tickets during the African World Cup even though they could have charged a premium as fans were desperate to travel to see the games.

2 **The Missionary:** A brand with a strong sense of purpose that it wants to share with the world. Lush embody this approach with their commitment to a more socially, politically and environmentally responsible world at the heart of their business.

3 **The Democratizer:** Driven by accessibility for all, the brand will make expensive things more readily accessible to the masses. Raspberry Pi created a small and affordable computer to enable more children to learn programming and other computer skills.

4 **The Irreverent Maverick:** Looks at the status quo and the safe approach and makes fun of it. Greggs, Paddy Power and Charmin all take the mantle for their category here.

5 **The Enlightened Zagger:** This brand takes the opposite approach to the current received wisdom of cultural or category thought. When Dove started using real women of all shapes and sizes in its advertising it took a completely different approach to rest of the beauty industry, which always featured perfect, slim and young women. Since Dove zagged, other brands have copied but the category still errs towards perfection over reality.

6 **The Real and Human Challenger:** By using real people as the face of the brand, the business is humanized in a potentially faceless category. Burt's Bees is a great example of this, with Burt's ethos and lifestyle central to the brand's positioning and communications.

7 **The Visionary:** Has a different view on what the category can offer. Mode Beds is a great example of this. They looked at the bed market and saw all the effort was going into mattresses. Instead, they have tackled the bed and created smart beds. AI enables the bed to learn how you sleep best and adjust accordingly, your phone gives you extra control and the ability to fine tune and adjust. You can even change your partner's position while they sleep and stop them snoring!

8 **The Next Generation:** This is a different time, so products and services need to be reconfigured or re-invented for the current age. The automotive industry is fast playing catch-up as consumers fall out of love with owning a car. New payment models and shared ownership such as Buzzcar and Zipcar are changing the category.

9 **The Game Changer:** A business that changes the category in which it operates, creating different relationships between business and customer and often inventing whole new services. Uber is a great example of this as it fundamentally changed the taxi model. Customers no longer wait hopefully for a random cab to turn up in the rain; rather, tech is used to link the nearest cab to them and enable them to monitor it, with positive effects on both convenience and safety.

10 The Feisty Underdog: Challenging loyalty to the market leader by introducing a real choice, as King of Shaves did to Gillette.

It may be useful to consider whether one of these narratives applies to your business strategy as they can vary in suitability depending on whether you are launching into an emerging category, re-launching in a crowded category or maintaining the momentum of an established position. In social media in particular, understanding your narrative can be useful in helping you differentiate your brand and develop a particular tone of voice. Greggs truly live the Irreverent Maverick challenger approach in their social media with their cheeky, opportunistic hijacking of current events, such as their #stayclassy Valentine's Day meal (Hosie, 2018). Promoted on Twitter and other social channels, the candle-lit meal included Prosecco and four courses.

Customer value ecosystems

This approach to business strategy enables an organization to increase its service and product offerings by understanding the value their customers place on their relationship with the brand and the broader needs the brand fulfils for them (Forrester, 2015). Nike probably has one of the most developed brand ecosystems, having developed its brand to partner its customers in multiple aspects of their lives from fitness to political agendas.

Scott Galloway, Professor of Marketing at NYU, predicted for 2019 that the strongest businesses will move to a 'monogamous recurring revenue relationship' (Galloway, 2019). Galloway calls this model the 'rundle' and believes that this focus on long term loyal relationships is both more commercially strong for the business and provides a more convenient and trusted solution for the consumer. This is the win–win of the enjoy-advocate-bond discussed in Chapter 2 in action. He cites that Nike has the opportunity to offer bundles that include every aspect of your fitness and health from what food you eat, to healthy hotels with better gyms and healthier restaurants, to doctor recommendations, and all because both you and Nike see yourself as 'a high performance individual' (Galloway, 2019).

This approach works for the behemoth brands. Amazon are already there, but, at a smaller level, it can also be an approach taken by all brands as they consider how they grow and deepen the customer loyalty relationship. The example in Figure 3.3 shows a young mum who has a gym membership. Her primary brand relationship is with the gym, which could decide to just have a membership relationship with her. However, by understanding both her needs and the areas where they could add value, the gym is able to offer a full ecosystem of support around the central gym membership. Some areas the brand can extend into actively enable participation at the gym, such as classes and a personal trainer; others create a deeper relationship that extend beyond gym attendance, such as support for events, including fun runs and community projects, a bar or restaurant and a crèche. If the relationship is strong enough the ecosystem could broaden to include clothes for the gym or nutritional advice and recipes. This ecosystem delivers a win for the customer, whose experience of getting fit and losing weight is enhanced, and a win for the brand, which builds a deeper relationship and higher revenues with more extensive engagement.

FIGURE 3.3   Customer value ecosystem example

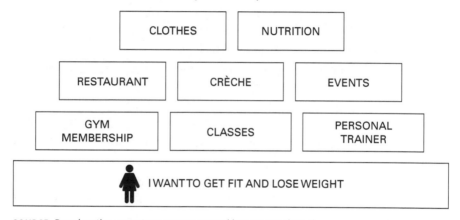

SOURCE Based on the ecosystem concept created by Forrester (2015)

Both of these different business strategy approaches – challenger brand thinking and customer value ecosystems – enable brands to grow and innovate within a digital environment. They also provide a strong launch pad on which to integrate and deploy an effective social media strategy. For example, the customer value ecosystem could be used as a basis for deciding the content pillars for your social strategy. Content pillars are discussed in more detail in Chapter 5, but for the gym example above it is easy to see how different content could be created to support events, working out and socializing in the restaurant.

Your business may use an alternative business strategy model but it is useful to understand what that model is before developing your social strategy.

Strategic planning frameworks

A strategic planning framework enables a business to understand the environment in which it operates and describe to all stakeholders how it is going to achieve its overall business goals. There are many different ways of articulating this information, but two uncomplicated approaches are PESTLE, for considering the external environment, and VMOST, for demonstrating what needs to happen internally.

PESTLE

Standing for political, economic, socio-cultural, technological, legal and environmental, PESTLE analysis enables a business to understand how external factors impact upon its ability to create and meet its overall strategic goals. PESTLE analysis is likely to have been an important factor in deciding on your business strategy as it enables an organization to understand its place in the wider world. It is also important for your social media strategic planning. Some examples of how these factors could impact your decisions in social media are:

- **Political:** For a global brand, the political differences between nations can affect access to consumers. One example of this is the restrictions on Facebook in China, which requires brands to use alternative channels to reach consumers there.

- **Economic:** The nature of payment is changing with the introduction of cryptocurrencies such as bitcoin and new ownership models funded by crowdfunding. Depending on your audience or sector, it may be important to take this trend into account in your strategic planning.

- **Socio-cultural:** Research and behavioural analysis of Gen Z shows that they are concerned about their digital footprint and ownership of their online identity. In the Gen Z research referenced by Cardona in Chapter 4, she notes that 'almost all have had privacy problems with either their account being tapped or having regrets over what they themselves had posted in the past and it continuing to be available for others to see' (Cardona, 2019). This will implicate the types of social media channel and content they engage with and therefore will affect the decisions of businesses who market to them.

- **Technological:** Social media is continually affected by technological change. Constant innovation from new technologies such as voice, AI and new social channels require brands to be alert and agile. For example, many brands now use chatbots to support their social and online activity.

- **Legal:** Changes in legislation can have a large impact on the way an organization does its business. In Europe, the introduction of General Data Protection Regulation (GDPR) and future changes to the EU E-Privacy Regulation have changed the way consumers view personal data and also affected businesses' ability to use data for targeting in social media or sharing with social apps.

- **Environmental:** These factors concern the physical environment your business operates in. Some businesses can be seen to have a detrimental environmental effect because of the products they create or the way those products are made. This could have an impact on how a business is perceived which will need to be considered in your social media strategic plan.

The PESTLE framework, when used in the context of social media, will help identify both opportunities and threats that exist for your business because of external factors within your market, sector or customers' world. Template 3.1 can be used to organize your PESTLE analysis. Some of the information will come from understanding your business model and value drivers, other information can be derived by analysing the context around your customer value ecosystem or by using the challenger approach. The social listening activity detailed in Chapter 4 will also help you add detail to your PESTLE analysis. Social media marketing, like all marketing, requires a thorough understanding of the context in which your business operates and the impact the wider environment and changing consumer behaviour will have on your future success.

TEMPLATE 3.1   PESTLE analysis template

POLITICAL	ECONOMIC	SOCIAL
TECHNOLOGICAL	LEGAL	ENVIRONMENTAL

VMOST

Standing for vision, mission, objectives, strategy and tactics, a VMOST approach to strategic planning can ensure that everyone in your organization is aligned in achieving the same overall goals. Normally visualized as a pyramid, with vision at the apex, each element is clearly linked to the core business goal in the following way:

- **Vision:** This describes what the future looks like for the organization. It should look at least five years ahead and set a real ambition to aim for.
- **Mission:** This is what needs to be achieved over the next strategic cycle in order to move closer to the vision. A strategic cycle is likely to be one to three years, depending on your organizational model.
- **Objectives:** These are the specific, measured, achievable, realistic and timebound (SMART) goals that enable an organization to measure its progress within a strategic cycle. The number of objectives at this level should be limited to about three to five.
- **Strategies:** These denote the direction to be taken in order to meet the mission and the objectives. The number and structure of the strategies will depend on the business, mission and objectives. Some strategies may be structured by department – product development, marketing, sales, etc; others may be structured by area of development, such as culture, innovation, customers, etc.
- **Tactics:** These are the specific actions that need to be taken to achieve the strategies. Each strategy will have a different set of tactics.

Figure 3.4 shows a table version of a VMOST pyramid for an automotive brand's social media activity. Template 3.2 can be used as a tool for creating your own VMOST table and ensuring that your social media objectives ladder up to meet your organizational vision and mission.

Creating SMART objectives

Objectives that are specific, measured, achievable, realistic and timebound are known as SMART objectives. They refer to goals that enable an organization to measure its progress within a strategic cycle.

In Figure 3.4, the objective is about increasing the number of electric vehicle sales from social media in order to support delivering the vision of

FIGURE 3.4   An example of a VMOST table for a brand's social media activity

V	Vision	The where to?	Where we want to end up in the next five years	Example: To be the market leader in electric vehicles
M	Mission	The what?	What we want to work towards the vison this year	Example: Sell more electric cars
O	Objectives	Another what?	The SMART goals we want to meet this year	Example: Increase electric car sales from social media by 20 per cent in the year
S	Strategies	The how?	How we will achieve our objectives	Example: Use social media to champion electric travel – become the thought leader in the category
T	Tactics	The doing	The implementation elements	Examples: Test a new creative route in social media. Test increasing the number of social media channels utilized. Test integrating the TV and social media strategies for improved overall performance
	KPIs	The measurement	The key indication for measuring performance	Examples: Increased brand awareness. Increased reach for branded content. Increased number of electric vehicle test drives from social media. Increased number of electric vehicle sales

SOURCE   Based on an example created by Adviso (2016)

TEMPLATE 3.2   VMOST template

V	Vision	The where to?	Where we want to end up in the next five years	Example:
M	Mission	The what?	What we want to work towards the vison this year	Example:
O	Objectives	Another what?	The SMART goals we want to meet this year	Example:
S	Strategies	The how?	How we will achieve our objectives	Example:
T	Tactics	The doing	The implementation elements	Examples:
	KPIs	The measurement	The key indication for measuring performance	Examples:

ultimately being the market leader in electric travel. The objective is SMART because it fulfils the following criteria:

- **Specific:** Increasing electric vehicle sales – we know exactly what we need to do.

- **Measurable:** We are going to ultimately measure the number of sales – we need them to increase by 20 per cent.

- **Achievable:** In this case a 20 per cent growth is possible, given the starting sales figure, the resources available and level of consumer demand predicted.

- **Realistic:** It is considered reasonable that the level of growth can be achieved in one year.

- **Timebound:** The objective has a defined time period in which it must be achieved.

Sometimes SMART objectives can become complicated and verbose. For complex objectives, it can be useful to use a tabular format to show objectives with the measurement and time elements shown separately from the core deliverable required. Figure 3.5 shows how this would work for the simple objective on the previous page.

FIGURE 3.5   A tabular presentation example for a SMART objective

Core objective	Timeframe	Measurement
Grow electric vehicle sales from social media	1 year	20% increase in sales

Introducing social media measurements and KPIs

Chapter 7 covers social media measurement in detail including the key social media measures and how to calculate the important KPIs.

KPIs are the most important measurements in any campaign or project. These measurements will determine the success or failure of any social media activity. KPIs can be set at a business, project or campaign level. Examples of social media KPIs include reach, sentiment, cost per lead, cost per sale, return on investment (ROI), and social equivalent advertising value (SEAV).

It is important to decide your KPIs at the start of a project and ensure you are able to track and measure performance against them. Measurement tools and examples are also included in Chapter 7.

References

Adviso (2016) How to define: Objective, strategy and tactic? www.adviso.ca/en/blog/business/definition-objective-strategy-and-tactic-infographic/ (archived at https://perma.cc/B8JK-E5H6)

Cardona, K (2019) Consultant [Interview] (15 January)

Fisk, P (2017) Innovative business models. www.thegeniusworks.com (archived at https://perma.cc/9ZR7-X6FR)

Forrester (2015) https://kloudrydermcaasicmforrester.s3.amazonaws.com/mcaas/Reprints/RES115784.pdf (archived at https://perma.cc/KK5D-SP2M)

Galloway, S (2019) DLD Munich 19: 'Nineteen' with Scott Galloway. www.youtube.com/watch?v=foCG9wX7eww (archived at https://perma.cc/38ZH-7VYZ)

Hosie, R (2018) IndyLife. www.independent.co.uk/life-style/food-and-drink/greggs-valentines-day-2018-candle-lit-dinners-romantic-couples-a8182996.html (archived at https://perma.cc/7ZJX-8SDH)

Kantar Milward Brown (2018) Brand Z: Top 100 global brands. WPP

Morgan, A (1999) *Eating the Big Fish: How challenger brands can compete against brand leaders*, John Wiley & Sons Inc, New York

Morgan, A, Holden, M and Devoy, M (2012) *Overthrow: 10 ways to tell a challenger story*, PHD, London

WPP (2018) Brand Z top 100 most valuable global brands 2018. www.wpp.com/news/2018/05/brandz-top-100-most-valuable-global-brands-2018 (archived at https://perma.cc/X38L-HL6Z)

4

Audience

Using social listening to profile your audience and generate customer insights for a global social media strategy

Social media listening provides a wealth of information and insights to enable a detailed understanding of your different audiences and customer groups. This chapter considers global social media strategies and explains marketing segmentation and how to create profiles for fans and customers. You will explore the impact of psychology and generation on consumer behaviour and learn how to apply these insights to your own customers.

Understanding your audiences

Your audience is the starting point of the ABC tripartite of social – audience, brand and campaigns. It is arguably the most important element, as your success in social will be dependent on your understanding, relationship and responsiveness towards your audience. It is important to remember that a brand's social media audiences can be very different from the traditional audiences found on your customer database or shopping in your store. Understanding who your social media audiences are is central to any social media strategy. First ask: do they vary from your traditional base? Are they different on each social network? Your social strategy will be built to meet the needs of your audiences and therefore it is essential to identify them and build up a detailed picture of who they are, and their preferences and behaviours.

As it is impossible to look at each person individually, the best way to understand your audiences is by grouping them into clusters by similar characteristics and behaviours. This process, used often in marketing, is known as audience segmentation and it can be applied in a social media context. Once the different audience segments have been created, a detailed picture or profile can be built up from a combination of social listening and other research and insight sources.

Customer, consumer, follower?

Social media audiences are not always made up of customers. For example, in 2017 National Geographic was described as being the 'number 1 brand in social media' (Mannarino, 2017) with over 350 million fans and followers across all its social networks. Clearly these are not all subscribers to the magazine, or viewers of the television series, but they are part of the National Geographic community and each audience segment will be considered in the National Geographic social strategy.

So, who are your customers, consumers and followers in social media? It is important to understand the difference and flex your strategy accordingly.

Your consumers are the people who ultimately use your products or services. Often, they are also customers, but if you sell baby food, for example, the customer is the mum and the consumer the baby. To be successful, your strategy will need to understand both the consumer's (baby) and the customer's (mum) needs. In a B2B environment the customer is very often different from the consumer. For example, a business selling technical services will typically sell to IT and procurement customers, but the end consumers will be everyone in the organization who ends up using the new tech.

Followers are different again. These are people or companies who are interested in your brand but may never buy or use your product. They can range from competitors to fans and can be very useful in building your reputation and increasing the visibility of your brand. They are also important as they may be your customers of the future or important generators of reach and engagement. Horry, in his interview in Chapter 10, reflects on the importance of reaching 'both customers and non-customers in generating the best effect on brand longevity' (Horry, 2019).

When building your audience segmentation, understanding whether you are talking to consumers, customers or followers is an important first stage of insight development.

CASE STUDY
National Geographic

National Geographic is an iconic US publisher, a global brand and often cited as being the #1 media brand in social media, with over 420 million followers globally and 7.6 content engagements per month.

Not all of their followers are customers of its magazine, film and charitable outputs, but social media has a strong part to play in the overall success of the business – building awareness, improving its reputation, driving traffic and advertising.

The brand was founded around the mission of helping people better understand the world around them and has had a longstanding focus on different cultures, environmentalism, diversity and amazing imagery and experiences. These attributes are well suited to the affinities of Gen Z, which bodes well for continued digital success.

As a global brand, National Geographic use different social channels in each regional market to make sure they are always visible and relevant. They also tailor the content to the different audiences on each channel and are quick to take advantage of new, interactive, visual social media opportunities such as Snapchat, Instagram, Facebook Watch and YouTube Live. National Geographic demonstrate that to excel on social media one size doesn't fit all.

To see National Geographic in action on social media follow them on your favourite social channel – they will be there.

SOURCE National Geographic, 2018

Understanding segmentation variables

Audience segments are created using a selection of criteria known as segmentation variables. The variables used will be dependent on the type of business you have, whether you are segmenting customers or followers, the social networks being used and the objectives of the project. You may decide to create your audience segments at the brand level and then interrogate how each segment engages with social media. Alternatively, you may start in each social network and investigate the profile of the audience you have there. A combination of both of these methods creates the best understanding of your audiences and provides stronger insights for strategy development. However, irrespective of which segmentation you use it will usually include some of the following types of variables:

- **Demographic:** These variables describe the quantifiable characteristics of a population.
- **Geographic:** These variables identify different aspects of an individual's location.
- **Psychographic:** These variables are based on an individual's feelings and interests.
- **Behavioural:** These variables describe the actions taken by individuals.
- **Firmographic:** Used for B2B marketing, these variables are based on the characteristics of the businesses you are targeting.

Demographic segmentation

Demographic segmentation is one of the most popular forms of segmentation and is useful in social media strategies because the variables are usually common across each social network and a brand's customer and prospect databases. This commonality means you can look at how the same group of customers behave on each social network and compare that to their behaviour and buying patterns in-store, on your ecommerce site and through other marketing channels. By combining variables such as age, income, gender and life stage, unique clusters of individuals can be created who have different relationships with your brand. For example, Burberry social media fans could include a demographic segment of professional women in their 40s with high levels of disposable income who regularly buy luxury brands, as well as a one made up of young fashionistas with limited disposal income who follow fashion designers and share the latest looks. The former could be customers of Burberry, the later are unlikely to be customers but could have an important role in promoting the brand.

Geo-demographic segmentation

This commonly used segmentation system combines both geographic and demographic information to provide classifications of groups of individuals based on their locality. Geo-demographic segmentation can be used to define small groups, around a particular store for example, or expanded to look at groups within a country or across regions. Global brands will often use geo-demographic segmentation to understand the different characteristics and behaviours of their customers and followers in different regions.

FIGURE 4.1   Segmentation variable examples

Demographic variables	Geographic variables	Psychographic variables	Behavioural variables	Company variables
• Gender • Age • Income • Generation • Marital status • Occupation • Life stage • Education	• Region • Country • City • Urban/suburban/ rural • Language • Climate • Time zone	• Hobbies and interests • Attitude and opinions	• Devices used • Apps engaged with • Ads clicked on • Content engaged with • Products bought • Time of day/day of week	• Industry type • Company size • Company revenue • Job titles • Number of employees

B2B segmentation

Demographic segmentation is also used in B2B marketing where information on the type and size of company can often be used as a filter before selecting the job roles and experience levels of the individual contacts. Some common segmentations based on the type or size of organization have descriptive names such as:

- SME: small and medium-sized enterprises;
- SOHO: small office, home office.

Lifecycle segmentation

There are also a number of commonly used demographic segmentations based on life stage. These include lifestyle segmentation. This segmentation is based on where a person is in their life stages, such as school leavers, retired couples, etc. Subsets of these life stage groups are often given descriptive names and acronyms by market research companies and brands, such as:

- DINKY: double income no kids yet;
- KIPPER: kids in parents' pockets eroding retirement savings;
- NEET: not in employment, education or training.

Generational segmentation

Based on the work of various sociologists and historians including Strauss and Howe (1992), the theory groups the population into generational groups spanning approximately 20 birth years each. The theories hinge on the fact that each group is defined by key events or technologies that affect their generation's attitudes and behaviours. This can be a very useful way of considering social media segmentation as it provides strong insights into how different generations use technology and social media channels.

The generational timeline shows that there is some overlap between each generation, rather than an absolute cut-off, and academics vary slightly in exactly where each cut-off should be (Figure 4.2).

In this book, in the light of the research by Strauss and Howe as well as more recent discourse, the different generations will be defined as follows:

FIGURE 4.2   The generations defined

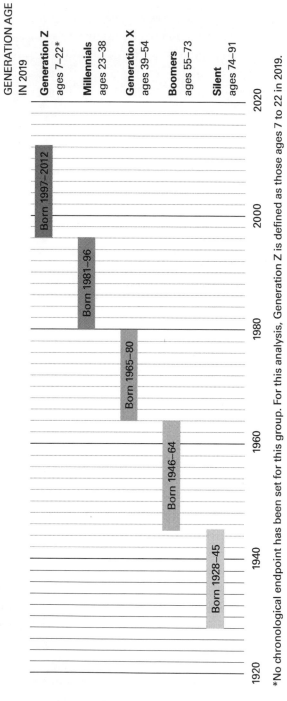

GENERATION AGE
IN 2019

Generation Z
ages 7–22*

Millennials
ages 23–38

Generation X
ages 39–54

Boomers
ages 55–73

Silent
ages 74–91

Born 1997–2012

Born 1981–96

Born 1965–80

Born 1946–64

Born 1928–45

1920   1940   1960   1980   2000   2020

*No chronological endpoint has been set for this group. For this analysis, Generation Z is defined as those ages 7 to 22 in 2019.

PEW RESEARCH CENTER

SOURCE Reproduced with kind permission of the Pew Research Center (2019)

- **Baby boomers:** Born after the Second World War, they have seen the invention of the internet, email, mobile and social. Wealthier than every generation that follows them, they are a mix of technophobes and technophiles.

- **Gen X:** Their formative years were the 1980s and early 1990s. Independent and entrepreneurial, they embrace tech and try hard to do it all, balancing work, friends and family.

- **Gen Y (Millennials):** Having grown up with technology, their lives are increasingly lived online and they understand the relationship between marketing, media and brands. Millennials are activists and use online communities to meet and share ideas with others passionate about the same causes. This generation includes the children born in China during the one-child policy.

- **Gen Z:** Known as the first digital native generation, they have never known a time without the internet. They expect individual digital experiences, watch programming when they decide, multi-screen and move seamlessly between online and real-world experiences.

- **Gen Alpha:** Born after 2010, AI, VR and driverless cars are likely to be part of their formative experiences.

Generational segmentation enables brands to understand where their customers or followers sit and the formative technological impacts that shape their attitude to social media (Figure 4.3). Gen Z have grown up in a

FIGURE 4.3   The generations and digital technology

	Gen Z	Millennials (Gen Y)	Gen X	Baby Boomers
Born	1995–2015	1980–94	1965–79	1944–64
Age in 2020	5–25	26–40	41–55	56–76
Generation size (US)	25% of population	95 million	82 million	76 million
Age when public use of email began	Always there	Max of 9	10–24	25–45
Age when Facebook launched	Max of 9	10–24	25–39	40–59
Age when iPad launched	Max of 5	16–30	31–45	46–65

world of mobile technology and social media. They are influenced by the global financial crisis and enter a global workplace of increased insecurity and perpetual change. As Millennials and Gen Z populations start to outstrip those of Baby Boomers, it is increasingly important for businesses to understand their behaviour, and particularly their changing behaviour on social media.

RESEARCH
Generation Z research 2016–19: Key insights

Background

Reed Brand Communications are a schools marketing agency that specialize in marketing to young people and their parents, providing research, strategy and brand design across the independent and state sectors.

They believe that research is the torch that lights the way for strategy and have been conducting longitudinal research to understand the Gen Z audience and their parents since 2016 to support their schools' marketing work.

Reed define Gen Z as those born between 1995 and 2005 (so in 2019 they would be aged between 14 and 24). The youngest are about to start their GCSEs and the oldest have finished university and just started work.

The research includes focus groups with pupils in years 10, 11, 12 and 13 (aged 14–18), desk research and telephone interviews with parents and opinion formers such as head teachers and tutors. The research focuses on Gen Z's attitude to social media and the wider cultural implications on their behaviour and openness to social media marketing. Reed have shared their key insights from their proprietary research here.

Key themes

Three words define this generation:

- relevance;
- authenticity;
- transparency.

These are their drivers, and what they want to see in everything in their lives. They access the world via their mobile (almost always a smartphone) and through video. Social media is a big part of this access, with social media usage beginning between the ages of 7 and 11 (years 5 and 7).

Social media usage

Gen Z use social media for a range of activities including:

- staying in contact with friends;

- sharing things with friends;

- keeping in touch with what their friends are doing;

- following celebrities;

- getting news – *Daily Mail* online is hugely popular;

- entertainment – games, music, etc;

- education – both for school work and informing themselves on issues or subjects of interest;

- inspiration – fashion, trips, ideas of places to visit and things to do;

- shopping.

Social media platform preferences

Gen Z use multiple platforms and have different relationships with each:

- **Facebook:** By 2016 Facebook was becoming popular with older generations, so was already perceived as 'uncool' by this generation. They have a mixed relationship with Facebook, believing it to be judgemental, and not kind to people. 'Facebook makes you hate the people you know, Twitter helps you like the people you don't' (16-year-old girl, focus group participant).

- **Twitter:** Accessed multiple times a day. Gen Z like the pace of Twitter and find it a good way to access news and follow celebrities.

- **Snapchat:** They like Snapchat as it is quick and then it disappears. They do not like to have a digital imprint, so they like Snapchat for this reason.

- **Instagram:** Less popular than Twitter and Snapchat. Instagram is seen as a showcase; it isn't authentic.

- **YouTube:** The most popular platform. Used for both social and educational reasons, it is even endorsed by teachers, who will recommend watching an experiment or documentary. 'YouTube takes the place of TV, it's a major part of my life' (15-year-old, male, focus group participant).

- **LinkedIn:** This isn't something school pupils engage with. They know about LinkedIn and understand they will need to get involved for networking and their career.

The positive aspects of social media

Social media is seen to bring some strong benefits:

- **Responsibility:** Young people are very connected and have a good understanding of the wider world. This has given them a sense of responsibility for the world they live in. They are growing up in a time of great instability (political, environmental and financial) and are very aware of this and take responsibility for change through sustainable shopping, veganism, etc.
- **Education:** Gen Z learn online, using social and digital channels to stay informed and learn about subjects that matter to them or are important for their education.

The negative aspects of social media

The negative aspects of social media are of concern to this generation:

- **Privacy:** Almost all interviewees have had privacy problems with either their account being tapped and someone posting content that they have no control over, or having regrets over what they themselves had posted in the past that continues to be available for others to see.
- **Mental health issues:** Social media gives the impression of having to live a perfect world, and this puts a lot of pressure on young people
- **Fake news:** This is seen as a real problem by Gen Z.

The cultural impact of social media on Gen Z

Social media is crucial to their leisure activities. They are their own brand manager and love using the platforms, but there is a growing reluctance to leave a permanent digital footprint because of privacy issues.

Identity is very fluid for this generation. Many will personally know friends and classmates who are gender transitioning, or others who have different combinations of race and ethnicity. In addition, many (as much as 80 per cent) claim to negotiate multiple online profiles or use alternative information on their profile so they cannot be tracked.

Friendship has a broad definition for Generation Z. They start to count vloggers such as Zoella as friends and go to vloggers for advice on relationships and what to wear because they don't perhaps have many real friends.

Using social media to market to Generation Z

Gen Z do not view social media as a way to market a business and particularly their schools. They see Facebook and Twitter as a way for their parents, not them, to access information about their schools. However, they love video and YouTube in particular.

They want to see authentic information. Social media marketing mustn't put pressure on this generation – the environment already feeds self-doubt, envy, feelings of isolation and the friction between your personal brand on social and the real person.

Emerging trends in social media for Gen Z

Social media connections may have peaked and real connections are making a comeback – phone calls or group video chats rather than broadcast posting.

There is an emerging rebellion against social media. Gen Z don't like fake news and are becoming less interested in Facebook and Twitter, which have been impacted by privacy and trust issues.

Interest is waning in role models such as the Kardashians and paid influencer promotions are seen quite sceptically – they know that they are being paid and this affects their impact.

AI and voice will have an impact but what that will be is hard to predict.

(Source: Cardona, 2019)

Younger generations are increasingly interested in private media over social media, ephemeral content over perennial content, and are drawn to newer and shorter format social channels. Instagram and Snapchat are increasingly the channels of choice for Millennials and their view of Facebook is very different from the older generations. In fact, research carried out with a US online audience in 2019 found that Gen Z was the only generation where Facebook wasn't the most popular network (Figure 4.4). YouTube is where they spend most of their time (McKeon, 2019).

Product segmentation

In some sectors, brands decide to segment by product rather than audience. For example, a travel brand that sells different holiday types from skiing, to

FIGURE 4.4   Preference for Facebook vs. YouTube by generation

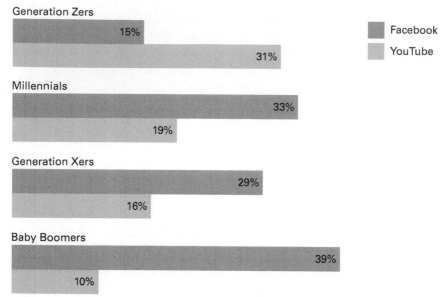

SOURCE Visual Objects 2019; Website UX Survey. Reproduced with kind permission from McKeon (2019)
Not all answer choices shown.
Percent of total respondents: N = 612 frequent website users.

sun, to safari may decide to look at its audiences from this perspective. This can be useful, as interest and behaviour rather than demographics might be driving the profile and the opportunity for previous customers to influence future customers is enhanced by this type of segmentation.

INTERVIEW
Louise Newton, Head of Sales and Marketing, Balkan Holidays, UK

Background

Louise is a stalwart of the UK travel sector, with wide experience in social, content and data marketing for multiple brands, including Inghams, Esprit Ski, Tui, Somak and Santas Lapland. During her career she has witnessed the digital transformation of holiday purchasing and been a leader and innovator in the use of social media to build engagement, create authentic experiences and drive sales. Here, she shares her thoughts on the current and future use of social media in travel marketing.

What are the biggest changes in social media marketing in the travel sector?

There has been a decline in trust between individuals and brands, with people much less likely to believe a brand than they are to believe what someone else in social media says. It's therefore increasingly important to the awareness and sales process to encourage people to talk positively about your brand in social.

When travel brands first used social media, the emphasis was on blasting out content and offers. Now, social is integrated into campaigns and has become the primary channel for storytelling and answering customer (and potential customer) questions.

What do you think will happen to travel brands in social in the next three years?

I think the best brands will get better and better at storytelling and finding interesting ways to engage their audience. They will do less volume, less broadcasting, but with better imagery and an increased use of video they will target content to specific audiences. They will move from preaching and telling to engaging and listening.

How did you differentiate between lots of different ski brands in social?

Our different ski brands all had very different audiences. For example, Esprit Ski is a family audience; often it's mums booking for the family. Conversely, Inghams appeals to the experienced skier; the average party size is smaller and they are more similar in age. Their needs differ widely in terms of resorts and amenities and their behaviour and use of channels also varies.

We changed our content and tone of voice to suit these different audiences and varied the way we used Facebook, Twitter and Instagram to reflect their different behaviour.

What is the role of organic versus paid social media?

A strong social strategy needs to think about using both paid and organic media. We used organic for inbound and paid for outbound marketing.

We used organic to build relationships through engagement. For example, Inghams' experienced skiers are like cyclists: they love to talk about the tech, the best runs, the new resort amenities and the snow quality. So, we support these interests and spark conversations between the brand and the skier, and skier-to-skier. Santa's Lapland customers are mums of young children booking a once-in-a-lifetime experience. They have lots of questions on safety, what to bring, or whether reindeer are dangerous, and so we need to reassure and answer quickly and comprehensively.

Paid social media is great for tactically driving web traffic. We used Facebook profiling and Lookalike Audiences to target cost-effective and relevant website leads.

What are your thoughts on the use of user-generated content?

User-generated content is really important in travel. We encouraged customers to share their photos for a chance to win a holiday next season. By incentivizing them to maximize shares to win, this had a twofold effect – maximizing reach and allowing our audience to authentically show how great our holidays are. We have also used the best images in the following season's offline magazine.

What are your top tips for using social media in the travel sector?

First, remember that social allows you to do things you cannot do in other channels. You can use it to build awareness and engagement by teasing out stories that aren't shared elsewhere. For example, locals in a resort sharing the best bars or trips, or the chef sharing new dishes they have created. These stories pique interest and then people dig deeper, searching for more and becoming convinced about the location.

Second, look at other sectors and take inspiration from how they use social, then give it a travel twist.

Finally, don't forget that you are selling something that is hugely aspirational so the images you select and the quality of those images is really important. Every picture needs to be brilliant.

(Source: Newton, 2019)

What is social listening?

Social listening is the active analysis and interpretation of any activity that happens on social media channels. It is used to provide insight into customer and follower behaviour. It can add a rich and informative layer of understanding to the information already provided by demographics, by considering additional variables such as behavioural, psychographic and geographic.

If demographic or geo-demographic segmentation is used to define and separate the individual audience groups, then social listening will add the detailed understanding and description onto each defined group/segment. The listening will identify how people feel and behave on social media in relation to your brand or business.

Social listening can be conducted within each social network using their own in-platform analytics tools. Alternatively, audiences can be looked at across multiple networks by using aggregated social listening tools such as Talkwalker and Fanpage Karma. Every aspect of social listening is conducted to add insights and understanding to each identified audience segment, which will help you understand their motivations and behaviours.

Social listening will complement the other insights and information you will probably already know about your audience from market research, store and ecommerce shopping habits, and information from other channels such as email, events, advertising and outdoor. Figure 4.5 shows how both social listening and other insights are used to build up a detailed understanding of each audience segment. Although information about all the insight areas can be gleaned via both social media and other means, social listening is particularly good at providing insights into:

- the content your audience loves;
- who your audience cares about;
- how your audience engages;
- what your audience thinks of your brand.

The content your audience loves

It is important to know the type of content that your audience finds the most interesting and engaging on social media. Content analysis is usually broken down into three different areas – media, context and topic.

MEDIA

Some types of content are specific to certain channels, for example Instagram stories. Others, such as images, gifs and links, can be used across all channels. In general, video content generates higher levels of engagement than other media, as demonstrated by Figure 4.6, but it can be expensive to produce and is unlikely to be the only type of content you choose to use. Remember also that some social networks prioritize video in their own algorithms. In 2018 Facebook changed its algorithm to prioritize peer-to-peer

FIGURE 4.5   Social listening and other insights

Key:
Social listening insights:
Research and digital insights:

sharing and meaningful interactions, such as commenting and conversations, over brand-to-follower posting and passive interactions such as liking and sharing (Tein, 2018). As live video content is known to spark more conversations and comments than some other types of content, brands have assumed that this type of content will be prioritized in the Facebook newsfeed.

CONTEXT

Your audience's content preferences will be dependent on their geo-demographic profile, their interests and the context in which the content appears, as well as being impacted by the product or service you sell. Because social media is a real-time environment that is continuously asking for feedback and interaction, it is possible to understand a great deal about the context in which content is served. With this information, brands can tailor their content to the audience's actual needs at a particular time and

FIGURE 4.6   Average engagements by Facebook type

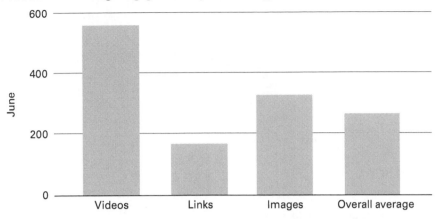

BuzzSumo analysis of 68 million posts in June 2017

SOURCE Reproduced with kind permission of BuzzSumo (Rayson, 2017)

in a specific environment. For example, social listening can tell you that your audience is engaging with your Twitter feed on mobile devices early in the morning and on LinkedIn on desktop during the day. As a B2B marketer, you may infer they are commuting to work while engaging with Twitter, and at work while engaging with LinkedIn. When deciding on your content for social media it may be better to ask for whitepaper downloads from the LinkedIn posts, and to share breaking news about your sector on Twitter. Testing these options would provide you with even more insight from your listening.

Focus your social listening on identifying which types of content generate the most interest, are shared the most, or your audience returns to again and again. For example, does one audience prefer the ephemeral content found on Snapchat and Instagram Stories and another long-form blogs and podcasts? What areas of conversation are more important than others? Do your audiences comment on or share your content? Are they happy to collaborate with you on new products or ideas? Do they like to enter competitions?

TOPIC

Social listening can provide useful insights into the topic areas and hashtags most interesting to your audience, and tools such as Talkwalker can visualize conversations and show how interest changes over time. Figure 4.7 shows the various topics of interest to airline travellers using Talkwalker's listening tool.

FIGURE 4.7   Issues affecting airline consumers

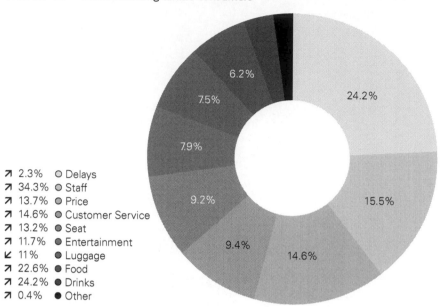

SOURCE Reproduced with kind permission of Talkwalker (2019)

By 'looking at the issues affecting airline consumers across the industry you can build a strategy that improves customer experience' (Talkwalker, 2019). Alternatively, by understanding the content your audience loves to engage with on social media you will be able to create more interesting, sticky content that deepens their relationship with your brand.

Who your audience cares about

Social listening provides information on the interests and hobbies of each audience. This can be shown in a variety of ways. For example, an audience segment may be interested in environmental issues, which could be seen not only from the brands, celebrities and hashtags they follow, but also from the topics they comment on.

Because your brand does not exist in a vacuum, your customers and followers will judge your brand based on their experience with your competitors, your brand neighbourhood and the recommendations of friends, families and influencers. It is therefore, important to use your social listening to understand each of these areas and the impact they have on your audience.

THE COMPETITION

Social listening will enable you to identify how your social media activity compares to that of your competitors. It can be useful to benchmark the content you create and the engagement levels you generate against other brands in your sector.

Your goal is to generate content that your audience really cares about and where you have the authority and authenticity to talk about the subject. If you can do this in a way that stands out from your competitors then you have an area of strength to take advantage of. By mapping your own content and your competitors' content against your consumers' interests, you will better understand your audience's needs and behaviours and be more likely to identify your strengths and avoid creating content that does not resonate. The findings from this mapping can be used as part of your PESTLE, as discussed in Chapter 3.

YOUR BRAND NEIGHBOURHOOD

Social listening can help you create an understanding of your brand neighbourhood. This insight into all the brands a particular audience follows enables you to gain a richer understanding of that audience's wider interests. For example, although you may be a fashion retailer, knowing that your audience follows Audi rather than Volvo, shops at Sainsbury's rather than Tesco, or loves Netflix rather than Prime, will provide you with useful insights into their views about themselves and their expectations of service and quality.

It is also important to remember that many of our brand experience expectations have been set by the super-brands of Amazon, Google and Apple. So much so, that no matter what sector you operate in your customers and followers will increasingly expect personalized, intuitive, rapid and often free services from all their brand relationships.

INFLUENCERS

The biggest influencers on our purchasing decisions are our friends and families. In a survey by YouGov, 42 per cent of US adults said that their purchasing decisions were most influenced by their friends while only 6 per cent said that influencer endorsements were the most important factor (Social Media Week, 2018). Social listening enables you to understand the number of connections your audiences have on each of the networks they use, as well as the celebrities and influencers they follow and engage with. Chapter 8 covers influencers in more detail.

How your audience engages

It is important to understand the different social networks your audience uses to engage with you as well as those where they connect with other brands or friends and family. Social listening identifies each network and provides behavioural data on when, where and how the audience interacts with your brand or other content. When creating a global strategy, the variations in social media networks and devices used, and timing of activity are particularly important criteria in ensuring relevancy across different regions.

VARIATIONS IN SOCIAL NETWORKS

Analysis by Cosenza (2018) shows variations in network usage across the world in early 2018. Facebook is globally dominant, but in China, where Facebook is banned, QZone is the largest social media network. In addition, WeChat 'has evolved to become an ecosystem' (Clay, 2019), containing within its messenger environment an important ecommerce platform supported by WeChat Pay. In Russia, Odnoklassniki is used to keep in contact with friends and VKontakte is the number one social media channel. Both of these channels support the Russian alphabet, helping them remain popular with Russian speakers worldwide.

VARIATIONS IN DEVICE USAGE

Mobile is increasingly the device of choice for social media but there are wide variations across the globe. In 2019 the global average was 42 per cent of individuals accessing social media via mobile, with Eastern Asia significantly higher than this at 70 per cent (Statista, 2018). This is an increase on the 2018 average of 39 per cent and 64 per cent in Eastern Asia. The North American rates remain unchanged year on year at 61 per cent (Statista, 2018).

VARIATIONS IN TIMINGS

Social media operates in real time, and therefore immediate reactions and responses can be monitored and used to understand a particular audience's feelings towards a brand or campaign at any one time. By analysing when an audience views and interacts with content you can decide when to schedule posts and also infer what else might be happening in their lives.

When reviewing device usage, consider the inferred insight that can be gleaned by combining time of day, day of week, location and device used. For example, restaurant brands can infer that someone is looking for a table now when they ask for recommendations of where to eat at dinner time, in central city locations and on their mobile.

When working on a global strategy the different time zones will need to be taken into consideration.

What your audience thinks of your brand

Social media listening can provide useful information on how your audiences feel about you at any given point in time and how their opinion compares to that of your competitors. Analysis of brand opinion on social media is known as sentiment analysis. Sentiment analysis is conducted using a social listening tool. The algorithm within the tool will categorize any comments about the brand as positive, negative or neutral. If most comments are positive then the brand has positive brand sentiment.

In reality, sentiment analysis is a rather blunt tool as algorithms find it difficult to identify irony, humour, slang, ever-evolving acronyms or brand names that have other meanings in normal speech. Some tools can be 'trained' by an analyst to recognize the context of certain words, but accuracy is likely to always be an issue with sentiment analysis.

However, sentiment analysis can be useful in three different areas – tracking brand opinion over time, alerting you to dramatic changes in your brand opinion, and identifying specific concerns with your brand.

TRACKING BRAND OPINION

If you have a social media listening tool that enables you to measure sentiment then you can generate a report showing your normal level of sentiment and the parameters of variance. In Figure 4.8 you will see that this brand began with a generally positive sentiment level but dropped dramatically in November 2018, recovered and then fell consistently into negative sentiment from mid-January 2019 onwards. The brand would be advised to investigate the reasons for these changes, which may be due to other external factors that are playing out in social media. If the brand were to conduct an awareness campaign or begin an influencer programme they might set a metric to measure improved brand sentiment. By tracking any change in sentiment they could analyse whether there had been any effect from the campaign.

BRAND OPINION ALERTS

It is possible to set up an alert in your social listening tool that will tell you if sentiment analysis suddenly spikes out of the 'normal' range, either positively or negatively. This can be very useful for social media managers, who like to be the first person in their organization to know if a campaign has gone viral, whether for positive or negative reasons. Using the example

FIGURE 4.8   Sentiment tracking graph example

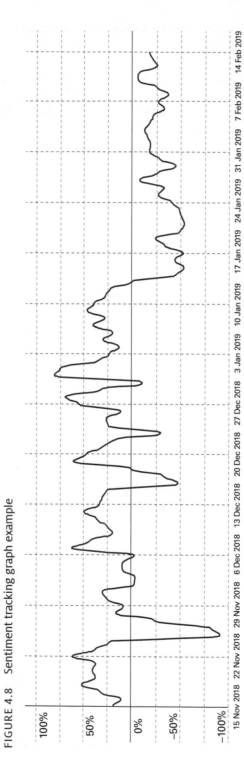

SOURCE Reproduced with kind permission of Talkwalker (2019)

in Figure 4.8, from January onwards the alert might be triggered if sentiment goes above zero or below 50 per cent (Talkwalker, 2019).

IDENTIFYING CONCERNS

The third area where sentiment analysis is useful is in indicating what your
customers are actually saying about your brand. Rather than looking at
scores, this insight looks at the topics and conversations included in the
positive and negative sentiment. The analysis here can inform you what it is
that your audiences love about your brand or the things that are not so
great. Famously, McDonald's used the negative sentiment they saw in social
media to address underlying customer concerns about their product quality.
They saw many comments suggesting they used poor quality meat, and
questions about animal welfare and nutrition, and decided to tackle them
head-on. Based on negative social media comments, McDonald's now host
answers to these questions on their websites, on YouTube, in their TV ads
and in social media. Proud of the quality of their products, they decided to
bravely answer all questions, truthfully (McDonald's, 2018).

Christophe Folschette of Talkwalker discusses his thoughts on the
importance of social listening below.

INTERVIEW
Christophe Folschette, Partner and founder, Talkwalker

Background

Talkwalker provides companies with an easy-to-use platform to protect,
measure and promote their brands worldwide across all communication
channels. Figure 4.9 shows an overview of their monitored data sources. Using
their AI-powered social media analytics platform, they turn this big data into
actionable insights, to enable brand monitoring, brand protection and brand
promotion. Folschette is responsible for building awareness of Talkwalker on a
global scale, and encouraging more businesses to embrace the opportunities
that its social listening platform can give them. They currently have over 2,000
global clients across a wide range of industries and sectors, including Duracell,
Ogilvy, Hong Kong Airlines and AccorHotels.

Why is social listening so important?

Social media is where consumer conversations happen. Although people may
not actively provide feedback to a brand, they will discuss brands online,

FIGURE 4.9   An overview of Talkwalker's monitored data sources

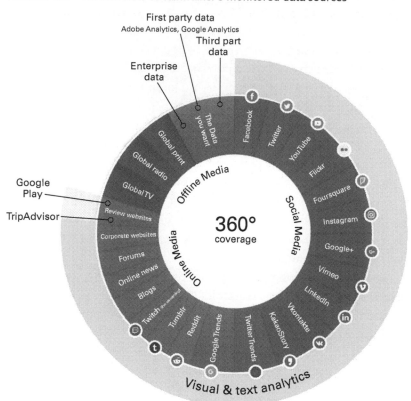

SOURCE Reproduced with kind permission of Talkwalker (2019)

provide reviews, and ultimately, raise issues about products. We also know that other consumers take these opinions very seriously, with 83 per cent of them trusting recommendations from their peers over brands. Social listening allows brands to be involved in those conversations, to understand exactly how each brand is perceived online, and help detect any potential crisis, brand sentiment, and to measure the impact of marketing campaigns.

What are the key insights social listening provides?

The insights for immediate action are the most important. No longer do marketing and communications personnel have to rely on gut instinct; they can make instant data-driven decisions.

There are too many examples to mention, but the important ones are:

- **Sentiment analysis:** This allows users to see not just the number of conversations generated by a brand, but also the sentiment behind those mentions. AI technology analyses the sentiment in the whole conversation, by context, not just keyword. For example, a marketing campaign could generate millions of mentions, and in the past that would have been deemed a success. Now, if we look deeper at that data and see that a significant percentage of those mentions were negative, you can easily see that the campaign didn't go as well as initially perceived.

- **Video and image recognition:** With Cisco predicting that 80 per cent of internet content will be video by 2021, we need an increased focus on visual media. Our research has shown that up to 80 per cent of pictures don't reference brands in the accompanying text, and up to 98 per cent in the case of video. If a brand doesn't monitor visuals, then they will miss at least half of their online conversation. Image recognition technology can detect brand logos, so brands can see exactly when and how images of their products are shared. Contextual data also shows the scenes, objects and other brand logos that are depicted in images alongside your brand.

- **Influencer marketing:** Influencer marketing is a hot topic for communication strategies. Talkwalker's *Global State of Influencer Marketing in 2019* report analysed the opinions of over 800 marketing and communication professionals around the globe, and discovered 69 per cent of brands list it as an important or top strategic priority for 2019. The Talkwalker Analytics and Influencer One platforms help brands find the ideal influencers for their brand, by identifying those with engaged, relevant audiences and those people that share brand content regularly.

(Source: Folschette, 2019)

Dark social

Dark social is social sharing that cannot be tracked and measured by traditional analytics. It typically happens in instant messaging apps such as Facebook Messenger, WhatsApp and WeChat, via Snapchat, email or SMS. It is sometimes known as copy-and-paste sharing.

Dark social is important because it accounts for the majority of all social sharing. It accounts for 82 per cent of social sharing globally and almost 90 per cent in Australia and South East Asia (Radium One, 2016).

Recognizing this sharing behaviour is an integral part of understanding the different behaviours of your global social media audiences. This is particularly important as the use of private media is increasing with the four largest private messaging apps (WhatsApp, Messenger, WeChat and Viber) surpassing the active monthly user figures for the top four social messaging

FIGURE 4.10   What's being shared via dark social platforms?

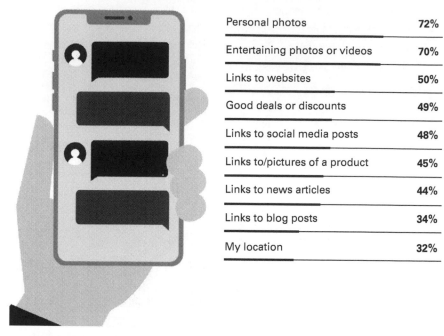

Personal photos	**72%**
Entertaining photos or videos	**70%**
Links to websites	**50%**
Good deals or discounts	**49%**
Links to social media posts	**48%**
Links to/pictures of a product	**45%**
Links to news articles	**44%**
Links to blog posts	**34%**
My location	**32%**

QUESTION What types of content are you most likely to share via private messaging apps?
BASE 2,155 internet users aged 16–44 in the UK/US
SOURCE Reproduced with kind permission of GlobalWebIndex January 2019

FIGURE 4.11   How are consumers sharing information or content?

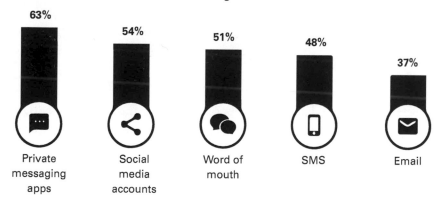

SOURCE Reproduced with kind permission of GlobalWebIndex

apps (Facebook, Instagram, Twitter and Linkedin) (Get Social, 2018). This trend for private media increases in the younger generational groups, with declining numbers of Gen Z signing up to Facebook and joining Snapchat and private apps instead (Abadi, 2018).

Creating profiles

Social listening can provide rich and detailed information helping you to understand the motivations, needs, behaviours and habits of your target audiences. This information is further enhanced by conducing market research, tracking shopping patterns and spend levels, mapping customer journeys and reviewing search and web behaviour. To bring this to life in a meaningful way it is useful to create profiles or pen portraits for each audience.

A profile is a description of the core differentiating attributes of a particular audience segment. It is often translated into a pen portrait and given a name that symbolizes the personality of the group. Figure 4.12 shows the ideal elements to include in a pen portrait, which includes all of the elements previously covered in social listening.

FIGURE 4.12   The pen portrait framework

Segment differentiators	Traditional segment descriptors	Social media segment descriptors
Geo-demographic informaton	Transactional, behavioural and psychographic information	Emotional, contextual, connected information
Who they are – defined by demographics such as age, income, gender, generation	What they buy – sourced from store, e-commerce data, competitor analysis and market research	What content they love – sourced from the networks they use, the type of media they interact with, the topics, conversations and brands they follow
	Where and how they buy – generated from customer journey mapping, commerce data, competitor analysis, market research	Who they care about – identifying their brand neighbourhood, their influencers and connections, competitor comparisons
Where they live – defined by locality, town, city, country, region	Why they buy from you – using customer feedback, brand positioning, consumer research (qualitative and quantitative)	How they engage – when, where and how they engage, the networks they prefer, time of day, day of week, device and location
	What channels they use – measured by Google Analytics, customer databases, media trends and research	What they feel about you – understanding sentiment, monitoring brand opinion, reviewing comments and themes, comparing to competitors

As discussed previously, if a demographic or geo-demographic segmentation is used to differentiate each audience segment then the insights about the segment's behaviour and attitudes can be created from a combination of traditional and social media sources. Figure 4.13 uses the pen portrait framework to build up a picture of an audience segment from a global cycling brand. This is just one segment the brand may have and other segments in other regions may be dramatically different.

FIGURE 4.13   Applying the pen portrait framework

Segment differentiators	Traditional segment descriptors	Social media segment descriptors
Geo-demographic informaton	Transactional, behavioural and psychographic information	Emotional, contextual, connected information
Who they are – affluent, professional men, Millennials, 45–55, married with teenagers at home or uni	What they buy – expensive branded road bikes, bike apparel and accessories	What content they love – news and major cycling events and races, local club news, local routes, tech info, their fitness/challenge comparisons to friends, videos, health info, podcasts, music
	Where and how they buy – online and in-store. Regular upgrades and multiple purchases	Who they care about – tech and cycling brands, fitness apps, famous riders, friends who ride
Where they live – urban/suburban – commutable to major cities, Northern Europe and US	Why they buy from you – you are a leading cycle brand. Your influencers are Olympic and Tour de France winners. Your products are cool.	How they engage – Twitter, YouTube, WhatsApp, on commute, lunchtime or at the weekend, when cycling
	What channels they use – email, social media, forums, events, clubs, search	What they feel about you – they love you and your products, want to be associated with the brand, hate any discounting and will regularly recommend you

Once you have identified the information using the pen portrait framework, you can create the actual pen portrait to share with your marketing, product development and social media teams. Figure 4.14 converts the information from Figure 4.13 into a pen portrait. This portrait shows the information in

FIGURE 4.14   A pen portrait in action

Tom
Successful, confident, healthy
Married
45
Company director in the City/ media/ creative industries
Works hard and exercises harder
Cycles 4–5 x a week
Goes to the gym
Shops designer
Always owns the latest tech and the latest gadget
Brand neighbourhood – Lexus, Apple,
Holidays with the guys – skiing, cycling
Holidays with the family – skiing, Europe, UK, US
Holidays with partner – city and spa breaks
Eats out – no red meat
Likes to buy the best – checks and gives reviews
Buys online to get a deal
Follows cycling and cyclists
Monitors and shares own cycling experiences and fitness levels
Early adopter – wants to be the first to know and try new things

TEMPLATE 4.1   Pen portrait template

Segment differentiators	Traditional segment descriptors	Social media segment descriptors
Geo-demographic informaton	Transactional, behavioural and psychographic information	Emotional, contextual, connected information
Who they are –	What they buy –	What content they love –
	Where and how they buy –	Who they care about –
Where they live –	Why they buy from you –	How they engage –
	What channels they use –	What they feel about you –

bullet points, but you could use a narrative or a short film. It is common to give the portrait a character or name and use an image to bring the portrait to life. Template 4.1 can be used as a framework for creating your own pen portraits.

B2B profiles

B2B audience segmentation and profiling follows the same principles as the B2C profiling covered above. However, in the B2B world the audiences may be segmented either by region, language, company size, value or a combination of these factors. The individual customers may well be known by name and their profiles will therefore be more individual and include more detailed motivational factors.

Global social media audiences

Global brands will often have different audiences in different regions and will need to take this into consideration when building global profiles. When creating profiles for global brands remember to:

- Make sure you know your audiences and how they differ by region.
- Segment using demographics and geo-demographics to maximize the opportunity to combine audience insights from multiple sources.
- Use social listening to really understand your audiences and their emotional and contextual feelings towards your brand.
- Build up pen portraits of your key audiences to share across the organization.

INTERVIEW
Ludovicia Fioravanti, content editor and copywriter

Background

Fioravanti works with a global luxury brand and oversees its social media strategy. The brand operates on a range of social channels including Facebook, Instagram, Twitter, Weibo, Line and VKontakte.

What is your overarching goal in social media?

Our goal is global awareness and particularly in our core and developing markets.

How do you manage a global social media strategy from Milan?

The core content is created or directed from *Milan*, which ensure that the brand's creative vision is consistent and all quality standards are adhered to.

Our strategy is based on mutual awareness and respect. Each region is different and so the region creates its own strategy, identifies local influencers and plans its own events and posts. Once the strategy has been written it is approved by head office and rolled out autonomously in the region.

Because of the different languages and audiences, it is important for the local regions to write their own copy for blogs and posts.

How do you make sure your content is suitable for all the regions?

Although we organize the content centrally, we liaise regularly with the regions to make sure we have the right content for them.

Do you have different audiences in different regions?

Yes. For example, In the US and UK our audience is much younger than elsewhere in the world. In Italy our audience is affluent older women from 30 to 40 years old.

What channel is the most exciting at the moment?

Instagram is the main growing channel for us in the US and the UK; it is very visually pleasurable.

What's the biggest challenge managing a global social media strategy for a luxury brand?

It is challenging to find a way to communicate haute couture one month and then follow up with ready-to-wear a month later. The range is so wide, but we have to remain consistent with our positioning. It's also important for us not to confuse our followers. We do a lot. Fashion week in Milan is followed by one in Dubai and another in China. We want to integrate all the cool stuff and keep the customer journey fluid, but not confuse our followers.

What is your top tip for operating a global social media strategy?

Keep in mind both the global and the local. It is very important to have a global vision and creative identity but trust that the local regions know how to share that content in the most impactful and positive way.

(Source: Fioravanti, 2019)

Having used a combination of social listening and other tools, you should have a rich and detailed understanding of your audience with relevant profiles that bring each segment to life. You are now well positioned to begin to address your social media objectives by creating a strong brand presence in social.

References

Abadi, M (2018) http://uk.businessinsider.com/generation-z-facebook-2018-1 (archived at https://perma.cc/RJ36-GZYT)

Ainsworth, J (2019) Head of Content, Prophecy Unlimited [Interview] (6 March)

Buzzsumo (2018) Content trends report 2018. https://buzzsumo.com/blog/content-trends-2018/ (archived at https://perma.cc/9W5W-4NEX)

Cardona, K (2019) Consultant [Interview] (15 January)

Clay, R (2019) Head of Influencer Marketing, Matter of Form [Interview] (6 March)

Cosenza, V (2018) World map of social networks 2018. http://vincos.it/world-map-of-social-networks/ (archived at https://perma.cc/974W-CPPW)

Fioravanti, L (2018) Content editor and copywriter [Interview] (3 October)

Folschette, C (2019) Partner and founder, Talkwalker [Interview] (15 February)

Get Social (2018) *Uncovering Dark Social: The essential guide to dark social in 2018*, Get Social

Horry, T (2019) Brand and Content Director, TUI UK [Interview] (15 January)

Mannarino, A (2017) How National Geographic became the #1 brand in social media. https://socialmediaweek.org/blog/2017/11/national-geographic-became-1-brand-social-media/ (archived at https://perma.cc/YJ27-JAXJ)

McDonald's (2018) www.mcdonalds.co.uk/mobile/food-quality/FAQ.html (archived at https://perma.cc/6V6L-EBKP)#

McKeon, K (2019) How different generations view and use top websites. https://visualobjects.com/web-design/top-web-designers/how-different-generations-use-top-websites (archived at https://perma.cc/BE34-P6MD)

National Geographic (2018) National Geographic press room. http://press.nationalgeographic.com/2018/04/24/national-geographic-ranked-top-social-brand-in-2017-by-shareablee/ (archived at https://perma.cc/D85V-2XGP)

Newton, L (2019) Head of Sales and Marketing, Balkan Holidays [Interview] (12 January)

Pew Research Center (2019) www.pewresearch.org/fact-tank/2019/01/17/where-millennials-end-and-generation-z-begins/ft_19-01-17_generations_2019/ (archived at https://perma.cc/KLJ7-3LCT)

Radium One (2016) *The Dark Side of Mobile Sharing*, Radium One

Rayson, S (2017) BuzzSumo. https://buzzsumo.com/blog/facebook-engagement-brands-publishers-falls-20-2017/ (archived at https://perma.cc/PEQ6-2YNR)

Social Media Week (2018) YouGov influencer marketing report, *Social Media Week*

Statista (2018) www.statista.com/statistics/412257/mobile-social-penetration-rate-region/ (archived at https://perma.cc/4SJW-8DVW) (archived at https://perma.cc/V2X5-NV4W)

Statista (2019) Social media and user-generated content. www.statista.com/statistics/412257/mobile-social-penetration-rate-region/ (archived at https://perma.cc/4SJW-8DVW)

Strauss, W and Howe, N (1992) *Generations: The history of America's future, 1584 to 2069*, William Morrow Paperbacks, New York

Talkwalker (2019) [Interview] (February)

Tein, S (2018) Hootesuite. https://blog.hootsuite.com/facebook-algorithm/ (archived at https://perma.cc/7UDN-CS65)

The Imagination Factory (2018) www.what-if.com (archived at https://perma.cc/R3JJ-YG7X)

The Imagination Factory Inc (2019) Site analysis. www.what-if.com/site-analysis/ (archived at https://perma.cc/J6LT-DNHT)

5

Brand presence

How to drive action and engagement through integrated content marketing on social media

---

This chapter looks at how to create a brand presence in social media, the second element in the ABC of social. It considers how you represent your brand in social channels and demonstrate your brand purpose. Integrated content marketing and the use of behavioural economics are explored and explained, showing how they drive engagement and impact customer loyalty. Interviews and examples provide demonstrations of award-winning social media campaigns in different sectors.

Why it is important to create a brand presence in social media

The previous chapter established how important audience identification and understanding are in creating any social media strategy. It is of equal importance to establish a strong and unique brand presence in social media that will increase the visibility of, and access to, your brand for customers and wider consumer audiences. In fact, because social is an intimate, conversational environment, it offers a unique space for consumers to connect with brands in a more human way than traditional advertising. It therefore can have a significant impact on establishing and maintaining your brand personality, increasing trust and building a bonded brand–consumer relationship. In short, social media enables brands to tell honest, authentic stories about their beliefs and values, and when their audiences share the same beliefs and values a stronger and more loyal partnership follows.

Chapter 6 will look in more detail at how to select the best channels to build and maintain your brand presence. This chapter will show how to define your brand identity in social and differentiate your brand from your competitors by starting with why your business exists and specifically what its purpose is on social media. The next step is to use integrated content marketing techniques to define content pillars, customer value exchanges and your hero, hub, help approach. Finally, behavioural economics principles will be applied to social media marketing to demonstrate how you can improve loyalty and engagement further.

How to demonstrate your brand purpose

As a first step, it is important to understand your brand purpose and be able to communicate this in a differentiated way. Your brand purpose is different from your vision; it is the passion within your brand, 'it outlines why you exist' (Couchman, 2017). In Chapter 3 we talked about an automotive brand whose vision was to be the market leader in electric vehicles. This vision gives the organization a clear understanding of what it needs to achieve, what success looks like, where it needs to go to ensure the commercial sustainability of its existence. However, this vision does not describe the purpose, the passion, the reason the brand exists. The brand purpose in this case could be 'to eliminate fossil fuels from travel'. The purpose may not be achievable in the conceivable future but it is an emotive ambition that differentiates you from your competitors and provides the bedrock of your brand values and behaviours.

Simon Sinek in his leadership book *Start With Why* (2011) explains his concept of 'the Golden Circle'. He believes that the 'why', the purpose, is how great leaders communicate ideas and sell products and services most effectively. The Golden Circle changes the way a brand talks about itself by prioritising 'why' the brand exists over what the brand sells.

Sinek argues that most businesses are good at telling people about what they sell and that some may also explain how they do it, but most do not consider why they are in business at all. For him, only great businesses start with why they exist, but the why is a significantly more compelling reason to buy. 'People don't buy *what* you sell, they buy *why* you do it' (Sinek, 2011). This reversed communication approach is both more effective and emotive because it appeals to our limbic brain which is responsible for our emotions and feelings and where gut feeling, trust, inspiration and loyalty are generated. Facts, figures, benefits and features are processed by our neocortex; these are what a business does, and are less interesting than a business's why.

This methodology is a useful tool for building your brand presence on social media because although your products or services may be very similar to those of your competitors, why your business exists and your purpose in social media is much more likely to be completely unique to you.

To determine your own brand purpose, ask yourself what your business's core beliefs are and why you believe them. This will help you define why your business exists, and this purpose should sit at the heart of how you tell your brand story on social media.

For example, there are many brands that sell bath and shower products that take care of the environment and do not test on animals. Body Shop, Simple and Lush would all fall into this category. If these brands talked only about the products they sell and the way the products are produced there would be little to differentiate them. Lush's beliefs are central to their business and range from freedom of movement, to making people happy, to organic ingredients (Lush, 2019). Lush believe that people, animals and the planet all deserve to be treated better and this purpose is brought to life across their social media and other marketing. Up until April 2019 they differentiated themselves with a range of social media content such as @LushTimesEN, their news Twitter channel reporting on ethical and human rights issues, their research and reports on sustainability, their #bathbomb films, and their annual #LushSummit.

What is content marketing?

This is a form of marketing that does not overtly sell products. Rather, it attracts consumers to the brand by providing relevant, useful and timely information that provides value to the consumer by answering a specific need. The value is generated by providing entertainment, education, support, inspiration or information. Content marketing is primarily an inbound or pull form of marketing as content is used to attract consumers to, and engage with, the brand rather than to send outbound, push marketing messages. Organic social media works alongside other inbound channels to drive brand awareness and increase engagement and loyalty. Having a close relationship with search, organic social media can have a very positive effect on search engine optimization (SEO) if your content marketing strategy is approached in an integrated way.

How to use integrated content marketing to represent your brand in social media

There are a number of techniques that can be used to help decide and structure your integrated approach to content in social media. The three most useful are content pillars, customer value exchanges and the hero, hub, help model. They work best when all three are used together.

Content pillars

Content pillars are a way of structuring different topics or themes of content into groups that appeal to specific audience segments (Barnhart, 2018). The content can be very varied in its type and include blogs, memes, vlogs, ebooks, case studies, reviews, videos, podcasts and many other elements, but the pillar is used to focus the purpose and theme of each different element. Content pillars are most effective when they unite an identified customer need with a specific business objective, which is in turn tied to your brand purpose.

So, once your business has identified its brand purpose, its *why*, and you have identified your core audiences and the specific reasons they want to connect and engage with your brand, then you can identify your content pillars. By selecting content pillars that support each element of the purpose, you will be able to present a consistent approach and message at every touchpoint that consumers have with your brand.

So, using the Lush example, if Lush's brand purpose, its why, is about creating fun vegan cosmetics without harming people, animals or the planet, then you would expect its content pillars to support the different elements of the purpose in order to present a consistent approach and message at every touchpoint a consumer will have with the brand. Lush are very open about what they believe in, and publish those beliefs on their website. Some of their beliefs are firmly embedded in political and sustainability issues, whereas others are more light-hearted. The Lush beliefs include:

> We believe in buying ingredients only from companies that do not commission tests on animals and in testing our products on humans.

> We invent our own products and fragrances. We make them fresh by hand using little or no preservative or packaging, using only vegetarian ingredients and tell you when they were made.

We believe in happy people making happy soap, putting our faces on our products and making our mums proud.

We believe in long candle-lit baths, sharing showers, massage, filling the world with perfume and the right to make mistakes, lose everything and start again.

(Lush, 2019)

It is apparent that not only does Lush create content to meet each of these different belief pillars, but also that these pillars fulfil the varied needs of different audiences. For example, if one audience was politically active Gen Zs, they might be particularly interested in a content pillar that focuses on the causes, campaigns and events that Lush supports, whereas, if another audience was motivated by organic luxury then they might be more interested in a content pillar that focuses on the quality of the ingredients and the enjoyment of an indulgent bath. The former audience might follow @LushTimesEN on Twitter, while the latter audience might post beautiful mages and films on Instagram under #bathbomb.

Customer value exchanges

Chapter 2 introduced Edelman's customer decision journey, which replaces the traditional marketing funnel thinking with a more fluid model that includes the six elements of consideration, evaluation, buying, enjoyment, advocacy and bonding in the brand relationship. In discussion of this model it was posited that although buying is often seen as the most important moment for the brand, the actual purchase is not what is important to the consumer. No potential customer has a fundamental need to buy a product or service from you. Their need will be the element that is fulfilled because the purchase has happened, or by other content during and after the purchase decision. For example, a consumer doesn't have a need to buy a burger from McDonald's; their need is to satisfy their hunger in a convenient, tasty and cost-effective way. If McDonald's can deliver this then there has been a positive value exchange for both the customer and McDonald's. If McDonald's doesn't deliver on all of the needs then, although a purchase has been made, the customer's needs have not been fulfilled and the opportunity to build a stronger and more bonded relationship between McDonald's and their customer has been lost.

Dave Chaffey (2019) talks about four customer needs in his gap analysis approach to content marketing. The needs he identifies are entertain, inspire, educate and inform. He maps these in a content marketing matrix, to demonstrate the relevant importance of each type of need fulfilment in the traditional purchase funnel. Chaffey demonstrates that entertaining and educational content are both most useful in the awareness part of the purchase funnel, but entertaining content is more emotional and educational content more rational. Conversely, he visualizes inspiring and convincing content as both being more useful at the purchasing stage of the funnel, but inspiring content is more emotional and convincing content more rational.

If we expand this thinking to include six types of need-based content, that will add real value to the consumers experience with a brand, then the content types can be mapped against the stages identified in the Edelman customer decision journey rather than against a traditional funnel. This is useful because when we include specific social media content in the matrix we can start to see how social media can help add customer value to every stage of the customer brand relationship.

The six types of need-based content are:

- **Entertainment:** Engaging content that is enjoyable to consume.
- **Inspiration:** Unusual and motivating content that that sparks something new.
- **Education:** 'How to' content that teaches the user.
- **Conviction:** Persuasive content that presents compelling ideas.
- **Information:** Sharing knowledge and leading thought.
- **Support:** Demonstrating care/providing a helping hand.

We know from research that entertaining and inspiring content is most likely to be shared and limited in longevity, while useful or helpful content, such as informative and educational content is more likely to be re-used over a longer period of time (The Webbys, 2017). Therefore, when planning how to build customer value into the content you use in social media it may be helpful to consider an amended version of the content marketing matrix as shown in Figure 5.1. The diagram is useful because it shows the most likely types of value needed to be delivered by content at each stage. However, it is not absolute as each type of content could be valued at every stage.

FIGURE 5.1   A development of the Chaffey content marketing matrix to enable it
to be mapped to the Edelman customer decision journey

Emotional

Entertainment	Inspiration	Support
Education	Conviction	Information

Rational   Consider and evaluate ⟶ Buy ⟶ Enjoy, advocate, bond

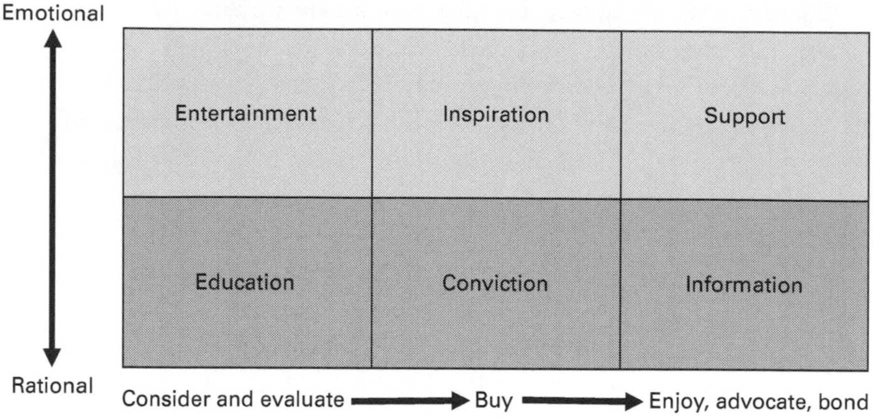

Up until April 2019, Lush social media content appeared to be built not only within specific content pillars, but also to meet particular customer needs, and therefore create real customer value. For example, Lush created different films for use on YouTube and other social channels. One range of films shows how the products are made (conviction), and another, how to use the products (support).

The hero, hub, help approach

Ideally, by now, your social media strategy will include a number of content pillars, usually between two and six, which directly relate to your brand purpose and your specific audiences' different needs. In addition, you will have identified where you might use different types of content to increase the value of your brand to your consumer at every stage of the customer decision journey.

The final element of the integrated content marketing approach is to look at how you prioritize and structure different types of content in your plan. This element is known as the hero, hub help approach, or sometimes the hero, hub, hygiene approach. The methodology was first defined by Google as a way to build better brands through video content (Noij, 2015), but has since been successfully used by many brands across both B2B and B2C businesses. The three types of content have very different but specific roles:

- **Hero content:** These are the large tentpole events around which strategies and campaigns are centred. This content is usually focused on supporting building your brand presence through building brand awareness and advocacy or by enabling brand repositioning or reputation management. Hero content may have a limited life span, as it could be tied to a specific date or event, but it is highly sharable, often entertaining, and certainly impactful. Examples of hero content in social media could be brand videos with high production values, original research outputs or product launches.

- **Hub content:** This is the regular content brands use to promote themselves, encourage engagement and introduce consumers to different aspects of the brand. Designed for your core prospects, this content uses owned or paid-for media channels and is often referred to as push or outbound marketing. The hub content will often use elements of the hero content that have been repurposed to suit different channels. In social media marketing hub content may use the channels' targeting options to identify customers and consumers the brand would like to engage with. The content is often informative or educational; for example, in a B2B process hub content might be used to provide case studies or pricing information to support a sale. It is particularly useful in the evaluation stage of the customer decision journey but can also be used to prompt advocacy, brand repositioning or support reputation management.

- **Help or hygiene content:** This is the pull content that is always available, easily found, and is created to fulfil particular customer needs. Designed for your core audience, this content is often used to support evaluation, build advocacy and in reputation management. In social media, customer reviews, how to videos, and customer service are all help content functions.

The hero, hub, help approach provides a structured way to manage the implementation of content within your social media strategy. When building your brand presence on social media you will need to use a combination of all three content types to be effective. A strong social media strategy will deploy the hero, hub, help approach for each content pillar and ensure that every element of content offers some additional value for the consumer.

The Lush 2019 Valentine's Day campaign (Garcia, 2019) can be understood using the hero, hub, help model as demonstrated in Figure 5.2. New products were created for Valentine's Day that were cheeky and highly sharable. The emoji-based aubergine, peach and banana bath bombs and massage bar created a stir on social media with fun announcements and short films to celebrate each one. This hero content was supported with hub

FIGURE 5.2   An interpretation of the Lush 2019 Valentine's Day content allocation

The Lush brand purpose	Creating fun, vegetarian cosmetics without harming people, animals or the planet.		
Content pillars	**Pillar 1:** Happy people making people happy.		
Hero content	Sexy emoji-based aubergine, peach and banana bath bombs and massage bars. Fun films and posts to launch.		
Hub content	Videos explaining how each product was made. Posts to drive sales.		
Hygiene or help content	Customer reviews, ingredient lists and UGC bath bomb experiences.		

SOURCE Content is based on observations in social media

content videos explaining how each new product was made and information on how to buy them. Finally, customer reviews and UGC bath bomb experiences supported other help content such as ingredient lists and where to buy. It seems likely that the whole campaign sat under a content pillar about making people happy.

You may wish to use Template 5.1 to detail your content pillars and the specific types of hero, hub and help content you will use for each.

CASE STUDY SYLVIA PLATH AI
Hero, hub, help content in action

Background

Tiny Giant, the creative marketing practice, take the hero, hub, help approach to content creation to maximize impact, brand awareness, engagement and new client generation via social media.

Objective

Use an innovative idea to demonstrate what the agency delivers for clients, highlight its skills and maximize brand awareness through social media.

Strategy

A creative marketing practice. Tiny Giant wanted to show how they could combine bold ideas and the smartest technology to augment creativity and deliver ideas in an engaging way. They used AI to generate Plath-inspired poems for a World Poetry Day event in order to maximize social media impact.

The AI/human creative process

The poems were created by training a neural network on Sylvia Plath's original work. Her poetry was chosen because it is dystopian, troubling but beautiful, and has no rhyme. The neural network learned from the input and over time was able to generate new lines of poetry that captured the essence and themes of Plath. Creative writers then shaped the output into five Plath-inspired poems.

To further enhance the creativity, the team partnered with a robot handwriting company that learnt how to mimic Plath's handwriting and write the poems by 'hand'. An actor also performed the poems for audio and video at the event.

Audience

An audience of potential new clients who are interested in creativity, ideas and tech.

TEMPLATE 5.1 Hero, hub, help content template

Content pillars	Pillar 1	Pillar 2	Pillar 3
Hero content			
Hub content			
Hygiene or help content			

The hero, hub, help content

The idea has enabled content that met a range of audience needs and created a high level of reach, brand awareness and engagement.

- The hero content was the poetry inspired by Sylvia Plath and released on World Poetry Day.

- The hub content was the films and recordings that kept the idea alive and teased the launch. These included the film of the robot hand learning how to write like Plath.

- The help content included all the answers to the questions about AI – how were the poems created, what is unique about the relationship between Plath, the neural network and the creative writers? This content was hosted on a project microsite plAIth.com, plus the Tiny Giant website to support lead generation and conversion.

The social media channels

The channels were selected in order to reach potential new clients in the target audience and showcase the agency's work. They included the agency's own channels on Twitter, Instagram, YouTube and a campaign microsite and the agency website. The two founders used their own LinkedIn and Twitter profiles to boost engagement and reach.

Results

The integrated approach was highly successful at driving new business leads and increasing brand awareness within and outside social. It resulted in: a well-attended event that created new leads, including meetings with three potential new clients; coverage in *AI Insider* magazine; and an invitation onto an AI Twitter chat and a podcast interview to discuss Tiny Giant's projects.

(Source: Harrison, 2019)

Using content marketing to drive action and engagement

The combination of content pillars, customer value exchanges and the hero, hub, help approach provide a strong framework to drive action and engagement. This is because they ensure that your social media content is focused on the important areas of your brand that differentiate you from your competitors and demonstrate your personality. The focus on a value exchange encourages consumers to get involved as the benefits are targeted to meet their specific needs. The hero, hub, help approach ensures a consistency of messaging about a specific content area across every touchpoint, increasing the impact and maximizing SEO and other media channel results through planned integration.

INTERVIEW
Ian Atkinson, Marketing Director, SunLife

Background

An award-winning strategic marketer, author of three business books and twice voted among the top 10 marketers of the year at the Financial Services Forum, Atkinson leads the strategy for brand, advertising, content and PR for SunLife and has previously worked on a range of global brands including Alfa Romeo, Barclays, Jaguar, Nando's, Oxfam and Zurich.

What is the relationship between content marketing and social media?

There is a strong relationship between social media, PR, content marketing and SEO. All four support each other, and they can be especially important for brands that have a limited above the line presence. Relevant, interesting content is a great way of attracting people to your brand and your social media channels can be a good way of distributing your content.

Engaging content gives people a brush with a brand, it helps make a brand famous even with those people not yet in the market to buy from you. It can create 'word of mouth' – people sharing your content, which increases brand familiarity; it can create 'pull' advertising because you're front of mind when someone then has a trigger to buy a product you offer, and it can increase their receptiveness to your 'push' advertising, your direct response marketing.

It's well established that if you spend your marketing budget in more channels it can be more effective than putting it all in just one or two channels, and content can be a cost-effective way of increasing the number of channels you can be in with some level of authenticity and scale.

How does social media fit into the hero, hub, help content marketing model?

I like thinking about a Venn diagram of content creation with three circles: where can you be authentic as a brand, what would engage your audience (either for its informational or educational value) and what doesn't already have amazing content out there. Where these three circles overlap, that's your sweet spot for content creation.

Then:

- Help content is primarily focused on search – being the best answer to someone's question, whether an article, a video or a tool.

- Hero content is your big ticket content – bold, unique items designed to get PR and for your audience to talk about and share. It creates word of mouth – which remains one of the most powerful forms of marketing there is. Psychology tells us we believe what someone else tells us more than we believe the advertiser – even if we don't know the 'someone' from Adam. So social shares feel like a recommendation... even if you don't know the person who is sharing.

- Hub content is where you regularly post episodic content on your social channels and is great for building a following where your target audience will keep coming back because they know what kind of content you do and it's content they like. So instead of trying to think of something new every time, you're deliberately creating a repeated format. This content should be a mix of organic and paid to maximize the impact and ensure it is seen – putting a bit of paid promotion behind it can actually see it favoured by the platform so it performs better organically too.

How much does content have to change by channel?

Video is key on every channel, but it is important to think laterally as well as within each channel. For example, include transcripts for video to maximize search as well as social media impact.

Social media isn't about re-purposing advertising from other channels. It needs to be different for each channel, because the channels all have different elements and the audiences will also differ. Advertising created specifically for a platform and audience works best.

Where does social sit in the purchase funnel?

It really depends on your brand and product. If you are selling something that requires a big decision – equity release, for example – no one will buy off an ad. However, social media can be used really effectively to alert them about your brand, generate opted in leads and enable them to request more information.

Social also works really well when it is combined with other channels. The more places your consumers, and potential future consumers, see your brand, the higher your impact and credibility.

How does social media fit into a marketing strategy?

You can, of course, 'do social' as a brand, either just for customer servicing or also to engage an audience. But you can also use social media platforms as a straight-up advertising medium; once you know what audiences are on each platform, if they match your target audience, it can be a very effective channel outperforming, for example, display.

In fact in some cases the platforms are becoming segments in themselves now. Facebook is very different from Twitter, and YouTube from Instagram. This is a real benefit to brands as they can clearly identify, based on their audience, where they need to be and where they don't, and what purpose each channel will have.

Each channel is so different from the others, they cannot be treated in the same way, so it makes more sense to talk about a Facebook strategy or an Instagram strategy than a 'social' strategy – you can't just copy-and-paste your campaign from one to the other wholesale.

Why is Facebook such a great channel for older audiences?

Facebook has an ageing demographic; the audience of new older people on Facebook is increasing and the average age of existing people on the channel is also getting older. In addition, this older demographic is highly engaged on the platform. Many use it as the best way of keeping in touch with family and as a way of getting access to the family photo album.

Their level of engagement is often much deeper, too – older audiences, for example, often write much longer, more personal comments than younger audiences, so you learn more about them.

Because of the vast amounts of data that Facebook has, it is easy to identify your audience and measure the effectiveness of any paid activity.

What's next for targeting on Facebook?

Although Facebook targeting can be very detailed and effective, they charge a premium for audience segmentation, often more than it is cost effective to do. Which means what could be precision targeting is often mass marketing, just because it's cheaper.

What's interesting is Facebook has more data points on a customer than the advertiser probably has. If we could access the thousands of data points at an anonymized level we might start to include some interesting elements in some of our ads to leverage this. This means that we could use the insights not only from a targeting point of view, but also as a way of thinking differently about the actual content.

(Source: Atkinson, 2019)

Using behavioural economics to drive action and engagement

In marketing, behavioural economics is the study of psychological, emotional, cognitive and social effects on consumer behaviour. It is based on the work of the Nobel Prize winning psychologist Daniel Kahneman and outlined in his book *Thinking, Fast and Slow* (2011). Kahneman talks about the brain in terms of two different systems, System 1 and System 2.

System 1 is our automatic reaction and the way we make decisions the majority of the time. It is subconscious; we don't know what we are about to say or do, we just do it without thinking. This behaviour is hard-wired into us all. It is great in the main because our brains don't have to get tired trying to figure everything out and we can react quickly to dangerous situations, such as pulling our hand away from a fire. However, because it is automatic behaviour it can sometimes fool us, because our brains make assumptions about things that aren't true. A great example of this is the visual illusion of two equal circles that appear to be different sizes because of the circles around them. Our brain assumes they are different sizes because one is surrounded by bigger circles, and therefore must be small, and the other is surrounded by smaller circles, and therefore must be big.

System 2 is our considered response. It takes longer and our brains have to work much harder because they carefully work out the answer or decision. System 2 is often referred to as logical decision-making while System 1 is considered to be more emotional. Kahneman argues that our brains are lazy and will try to use System 1 for most decisions. When we are making important decisions, it might be necessary to force our brains to engage in System 2 thinking to make sure we consider all the implications.

Kahneman identifies hundreds of different patterns of System 1 thinking, which he calls heuristics or biases (Kahneman, 2011). These heuristics have been tested in behavioural experiments and shown to be true across different

FIGURE 5.3   Behavioural economics System 1 in action

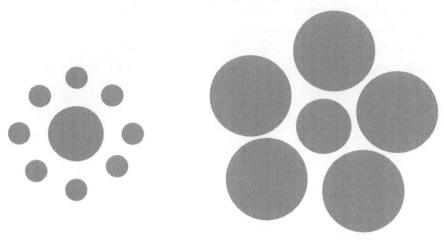

cultures and communities because they are the way the human brain has evolved to behave in certain situations.

Over the last decade, marketers have started to explore and use behavioural economics to improve the performance of advertising and build deeper, more emotional connections between brands and consumers. Behavioural economics is ideally suited for this purpose because it explains how human beings naturally behave, and, in marketing, we want to encourage natural behaviour, not force unnatural behaviour. For example, most demographic groups are represented on Facebook but just because they are registered as a user doesn't mean they will behave in the same way. Older age groups, Baby Boomers, are much more likely to use Facebook to post photos of friends and family, share news, tag people they know and be regular and frequent visitors to the site. Younger demographics who have a Facebook profile may only use that profile to access Messenger or to watch what is happening in their network. They may not post at all, or post very little, preferring to share content on other platforms such as SnapChat or Instagram. Knowing this information, a brand should use this insight to encourage their consumers to interact on the platform of their choice in the way they feel comfortable.

Behavioural economics can help us understand how people in general are like likely to respond to certain types of information and circumstances. Once you understand how behavioural economics works you can start to deploy it in your social media campaigns to increase response and engagement.

Although Kahneman wrote the seminal book on behavioural economics, probably the most useful and succinct application of the theory to marketing and advertising is Richard Shotton's *The Choice Factory* (2018). Shotton selects 25 heuristics that he believes are most useful in marketing and advertising and explains both the theory behind the heuristic and its practical application. Figures 5.4–5.7 explain four heuristics (social proof, loss aversion, the endowment effect and the power of the group) that are particularly useful in increasing loyalty, engagement and action in social media.

FIGURE 5.4   Using behavioural economics heuristics in social media: social proof

Social proof bias	The evidence of social proof bias	How to use social proof bias in social media
People make decisions based on social norms. They like to behave as others do and will feel more comfortable doing something that they know is popular.	The Cialdini experiment: Three new messages were placed in hotel rooms to encourage towel re-usage – an environmental message, a social proof message stating that other peole re-used towels, and a relevant social proof message that stated that most people in that room had reused towels. 35% of visitors responded to the environmental message. 44% to the social proof message. 49% to the relevent social proof message.	Strategically, brands should never assume that consumers know how popular they are. Large fan and follower communities demonstrate this popularity and could be promoted more by brands. Tactically, social ads for Facebook and other platforms enable brands to state how many people have already taken up an offer. The social proof can be made even more relevant by specifying the number of people in your local area who have already taken up the offer.

SOURCE Based on content in Kahneman (2011) and Shotton (2018)

FIGURE 5.5   Using behavioural economics heuristics in social media: loss aversion

Loss aversion bias	The evidence of loss aversion bias	How to use loss aversion bias in social media
People are more willing to take risks to avoid losing something than they are to gain something.	In head-to-head tests, marketing offers that state 'Stop wasting £xxx' perform better than those that state 'Save £xxx'.	Many brands use social media campaign to offer discounts on their products and services. Positioning your brand as helping your consumer, so they do not waste time or effort, is an opportunity to differentiate your brand and increase margin.

SOURCE Based on content in Kahneman (2011) and Shotton (2018)

FIGURE 5.6   Using behavioural economics heuristics in social media: the endowment effect

Endowment effect bias	The evidence of endowment effect bias	How to use endowment effect bias in social media
People value things that they own more than things that they do not.	Once people feel that they own something they attribute a greater value to it and often the attributed value is signifiantly higher than the actual value.	Social media offers opportunities for crowd sourcing, co-creation and shared ownership, all of which help people feel a sense of ownership about goods and services, which help increase loyalty to your brand.

SOURCE Based on content in Kahneman (2011) and Shotton (2018)

FIGURE 5.7   Using behavioural economics heuristics in social media: the power of the group

The power of the group	The evidence of the power of the group	How to use the power of the group in social media
Experiences that happen as part of a group deliver heightened levels of emotion.	Throughout history humans have been dependent on others for survival and so are very attuned to the emotions and feelings of the group. Experiments conducted by the University of Tennessee demonstrated that viewers of ads and videos in groups had more extreme reactions to the content. They were happier, sadder or more scared than viewers watching alone.	Many social platforms show heightened engagement rates for live content. Even though the group may not be physically watching togther, they are commenting and sharing in real time. Group chats on messaging apps are also working on this bias. The increased sharing of funny or entertaining content is probably also related to this bias.

SOURCE Based on content in Kahneman (2011) and Shotton (2018)

Increasing customer loyalty through social media

Loyalty to a brand occurs when the relationship has deepened into a mutually beneficial bond. For this to occur, the experience at every touchpoint needs to add value and deliver a positive outcome for the consumer. By understanding your brand's purpose in the context of fulfilling your customer needs you have an opportunity to deliver stronger and more emotionally driven experiences across your social media activity. Furthermore, as many social media interactions are brand rather than sales orientated, they offer insights into your business and spaces where you can tell authentic stories to build trust.

Brand communities and loyalty

Communities in social media can exist for both customers and consumers and are a strong way to support bonded and loyal relationships. In fact, many of your most important social media communities may be fans rather than customers. For some sectors, such as entertainment, there are no direct customers per se, but the brand's social spaces can be used to create excitement and engagement, share stories and increase the closeness of the fans to the brand's purpose. For these fans, the existence of a brand social space with unique content enables 'fans looking for a more personal feeling... to make connections with the shows they love' (Williams, 2019).

In April 2019, Lush decided to 'switch up social' (Whatley, 2019) and turn off its UK social channels, closing down @LushLtd in favour of #LushCommunity. Lush can still be found on social media but they are focusing more on direct conversations with their followers rather than having to pay to be seen in their fans' social feeds.

INTERVIEW
Sophie Williams, Chief Operating Officer, Social Life

Background

Williams is the COO of Social Life, a creative social media agency for entertainment brands. They connect the world's biggest broadcasters with their most important fans. Social Life is a different kind of agency based on the founding principles of innovation and reward for their team, clients and the fandoms they work for. Their work is fans focused, listening to and responding to what the fans want, and as real fans of the shows they work on, each person at Social Life is well positioned to understand what the fans want.

By being respectful of the shows and their audience, working with team members who have relevant lived experience, or bringing in consultants if needed, Social Life are able to speak authentically to audiences and to help them get the most out of the shows they love.

How would you describe the work you do at Social Life?

We create social spaces that fans can use to get closer to the shows they love. Fans are looking for more personal-feeling ways to make connections with the shows they love and we give them a space and platform to be able to do that.

We're in the very lucky position of being able to make content that people actively want. We're not spamming people's timeline. People seek out the content we make, such as a sneak-peak at behind the scenes content, or interviews with their favourite actors. It's a very lucky position to be in.

How do you approach a social strategy for the shows you work on?

Every show is unique, we tailor the channels and the team to suit the fans but we do follow some guiding principles.

We only work on shows that we are genuinely interested in. When you work with fandoms you have to have something to add to the conversations. If we cannot speak authentically in that place, the fans would see through us and we wouldn't be authentic.

The fandom is a community and we are part of that community, so we pick a team who love the show to work on it, and make sure they have lived experience of the issues raised. For example, for Pride, we wanted to makes sure the show we associated with the movement had a right to be there. So, we picked the best-fit show for Pride and the artists and teams we used were all from the LGBTQA community. Statistically, minority groups have a harder time accessing larger, more corporate, better paying work, and so although it wasn't in our remit it was important to us that we were able to guide them in skills to negotiate and make sure their work was valued as it should be.

We don't promote the network or use paid advertising to promote our social spaces. We create an environment where the show lives and our audience seek us out. The network benefits because the fans are talking about the show and sharing the unique content.

How quickly does a typical community build on social media?

If the show is good the community will build really quickly. The show does most of the heavy lifting but we make sure it is amplified and continued. It's not unusual for a high-performing show to have over half a million followers on Instagram a month after launch.

What techniques do you use to select the channels you use?

We work in terms of interest groups rather than demographics to decide the channels. Values and interests are the most important factors in determining the community and where they want to engage. So, depending on the theme of the show, we can gauge where and how people might want to be. We would usually stick to the main social channels of Instagram and Twitter, but for shows with audiences with communities that are active on other spaces we might suggest other platform like Reddit or Facebook to reach people in the spaces they naturally use.

We don't always recommend owned channels for every account – for something more short-term or one-off we may suggest having those assets live on a brand channel.

What type of content do you use?

We have built a reputation on being conscientious and authentic. We know what the issues are and make sure that we represent them authentically. Although we might have an initial content calendar, and an expected pathway by channel with ideas on how things might progress, we will be quick to understand and respond to the mood and interests of the fans. For example, pre-launch, we might start with a strategy to introduce and break out each character, and, because we have access to the scripts and our producers visit the show, we will have our own view on who might be the favourite character, key theme or moment and be ready with extra content. However, after the launch of the show, a catchphrase or character might become really popular and so we will respond to that by creating new content and building the meme. We can have good guesses in the pre-launch about what elements, characters and lines the audience will resonate with – but there are always surprises we didn't see coming. These social accounts take on a life of their own when we begin interacting with fans.

How do you make sure you have the right tone of voice?

We build up trust by demonstrating how well we know and love the characters and the show. In all instances we make sure that people who work on the show's social are fans, they know they shows inside out and better than anyone. They know the in-jokes, they get the tone of voice perfectly and often need to write in it. On some show we have worked closely with the show's writers over the course of several years to gain their trust and confidence so that we can take on the characters to a level of accuracy they, and the fans, would be happy with.

The show's producers act as brand guardians. They need to be trusted because although some content can be checked before it is posted, in a Twitter takeover, or Instagram Q&A, for example, the content is written in the moment.

What are your top tips for creating and managing social spaces for fans?

I have three:

1   **Be authentic.** Consider the communities you are working with, make sure you have an authentic and in depth understanding of them. If you don't, then let someone else who does work with that community. We have recently turned down briefs around sports, and the black American college experience – we don't have the knowledge to speak authentically here and so we know these aren't accounts for us.

2   **Diversity is essential for creativity and commercial success.** Disadvantaged groups find it difficult to get roles in advertising so we make sure that we reach out to people from different backgrounds and actively create a diverse and safe creative environment.

3   **Be inclusive.** Remember that different fans are at different stages of their relationship with the show. We need to balance keeping the elements that the existing fans have already enjoyed, while elevating the content to reach a new audience. The existing fandom have grown to know and love the show, but the challenge is not to make the social too exclusionary or too full of in-jokes that people who are only just discovering the show are intimidated or feel they're not part of the club. The joy of social is its ability to build communities, so the balance is rewarding the existing fandom without scaring away or being unwelcoming to new people.

What do you think are the next steps for social?

Stories and interaction are king. Already Instagram polls, their questions feature, giphy stickers, and other genuinely interactive pieces of content are really exciting. Over the next few years every innovation that helps people interact and feel like something is made just for them will be a winner.

(Source: Williams, 2019)

This chapter has shown how important your brand purpose is; its relevancy to your primary audiences will be important in developing your social media strategy. The next chapter will demonstrate how different social channels can be used to build your brand presence and deploy effective social media campaigns.

References

Atkinson, I (2019) Marketing Director, SunLife, UK [Interview] (13 March)

Barnhart, B (2018) Hello social. http://blog.hellosocial.com.au/blog/social-media-basics-what-are-content-pillars (archived at https://perma.cc/P6KV-R27U)

Chaffey, D (2019) Smart Insights. www.smartinsights.com/content-management/content-marketing-strategy/the-content-marketing-matrix-new-infographic/ (archived at https://perma.cc/4FLM-HNKR)

Couchman, H (2017) What's the purpose of brand purpose? Everything you need to know. http://fabrikbrands.com/whats-the-purpose-of-brand-purpose/ (archived at https://perma.cc/4MML-B48N)

Garcia, T (2019) Lush to release emoji-themed bath bomb collection for Valentine's Day 2019. www.teenvogue.com/story/lush-emoji-themed-bath-bomb-collection-valentines-day-2019 (archived at https://perma.cc/L6HT-PX2X)

Kahneman, D (2011) *Thinking, Fast and Slow*, Penguin, London

Lush (2019) We believe statement. www.lushusa.com/story?cid=article_we-believe-statement (archived at https://perma.cc/FQC9-KELR)

Noij, M (2015) SlideShare. www.slideshare.net/MichielNoij/google-a-better-way-to-build-brands-through-content (archived at https://perma.cc/9WFJ-YMRJ)

Shotton, R (2018) *The Choice Factory*, Harriman House Ltd, Petersfield

Sinek, S (2011) *Start With Why: How great leaders inspire everyone to take action*, Portfolio Penguin, London

The Webbys (2017) *Internet or Die: 2017 trend report*, The Webby Awards

Whately, J (2019) What Lush did next... on social media. www.thedrum.com/opinion/2019/04/17/what-lush-did-next-social-media (archived at https://perma.cc/DXY8-LQ5N)

Williams, S (2019) Chief Operating Officer, Social Life [Interview] (5 February)

6

Campaigns

A quick step guide to channel selection for your objective and audience

Social channel usage varies by audience location and market. This chapter introduces the campaign element of the ABC of social media and will help you decide which channels are the most appropriate for your objectives, enabling you to maximize your impact through digital integration. It is important to ensure that you are present on the most relevant channels both for building your brand presence and delivering specific campaign objectives. You may also need to use some niche social networks as well as the more popular favourites and deciding which channels not to use are crucial decisions in any strategy. The chapter includes tips for selecting channels and insights for using different channels in both B2B and B2C environments.

Getting started with channel planning

It can feel daunting to select the social media channels to use for your business. Choose too many, and you may not have the time and resources to manage them effectively and could detrimentally affect your brand. Choose too few, and you may miss important opportunities to connect with customers and increase sales. Choose the wrong channels, and time and money are wasted on irrelevant activity.

To make the right decision, a structured analytical approach is needed that puts the win–win for your brand and your customers (discussed in Chapter 2) at the centre. By making sure the channels you use are the right channels for your customers and that they are best placed to meet your commercial objectives, you will successfully select the right ones.

As discussed previously, social media can be used across all your marketing activity, from brand building, to product development, to lead generation, sales and advocacy. This broad range of applications can make channel selection feel ever more daunting. Following the ABC approach simplifies this.

The ABC approach

The ABC approach is a simple and effective way to plan your social media strategy. Its three elements – audience, brand and campaigns – form the bedrock of your strategy and enable your social media to be integrated with other marketing and PR activity and focused on core business objectives. In previous chapters we have discussed audience and brand and they are recapped here.

Audience

It is important to start with your audience. Who is your audience? Where and how do they engage in social channels? Is your social media audience the same as your customer base? Do you have a number of different social media audiences? Chapter 4 highlighted how to use social listening, and additional research, to identify and understand your audience(s) and create useful segments and personas to articulate their unique characteristics. Some of these characteristics will determine how they engage with social media itself; for example, as discussed in Chapter 2, are they social Stars or social Skippers (Liu, 2018)?

Brand

At the next level, you need to establish why your brand exists on social media and develop a social media presence for it. This is primarily the 'pull' of marketing, your inbound social activity. It demonstrates your brand values and talks about issues where you and your customers or followers have a shared passion. The fandoms discussed in William's interview in Chapter 5 are a good example of this. This social content ensures that your brand is found and retained in social media by meeting your customers' needs. As with all inbound marketing, it takes time and investment to build up inbound impact but the channels selected here will provide the foundation on which all other social media channel usage is built. This chapter will discuss how to select the channels to build your brand presence on social and also go on to look at channel selection for specific campaign objectives. The marketing practice, Tiny Giant, used a variety of social channels to launch their brand and build a presence on social. Their integrated approach has enabled them to go from start-up to success in just a few months.

CASE STUDY TINY GIANT
New international business launch

Background

Tiny Giant is a marketing practice founded in 2018 by two award-winning advertising creatives, Kerry Harrison and Richard Norton. They work with a team of creatives and computer scientists to fuse technology and ideas to deliver engaging content, chatbots, voice-first campaigns, creative AI projects and AI workshops. Their work is bold and challenges the interaction of what happens when creative ideas meet AI and smart technology. They have already used this magic combination to create AI-conceived cupcakes and cocktails, Plath-inspired poetry, and AIDA, the first ever AI guest curator at the Cheltenham Science Festival in 2019.

Tiny Giant launched in October 2018 from a standing start. Like many small entrepreneurial businesses, there was no real budget for marketing, but the agency had to make an impact, it had to build a brand and reputation, and it needed to generate leads and sales for its creative AI work. The founders decided to use social media as their channel to market because it is fast, cost effective and easy to manage.

Objective

The objective was clear – launch a brand and position it in a new space: creative AI. Build brand awareness and credibility, and become the thought leaders. In addition, although Tiny Giant works internationally, Harrison and Norton wanted to make a big impact in the South West of the United Kingdom, as they are based in the region.

The audience

Tiny Giant is a marketing practice. Their prospective clients are innovative brands that they can work with directly, or other agencies who may partner with them to add Tiny Giant's specialist skills into specific projects.

The individuals who might buy their services are senior decision-makers, board directors or owners in agencies, or senior clients. Whether client or agency, they will need to be brave, interested in tech and innovation and appreciate the value of ground-breaking creativity.

Strategic approach

The strategy focused on impact, ownership and engagement. From the launch onwards, Tiny Giant has owned social media in the creative AI space using a combination of channels, events and podcasts that work together to build and maintain brand awareness and generate leads.

The channels

A combination of real-world events and social media create a valuable engagement platform with their audiences.

Social channels

LinkedIn is the primary channel, as this is highly visible with brand and agency decision-makers and an ideal place to demonstrate thought leadership. Tiny Giant does have a company page, but the strategy focuses on building the profiles, levels of visibility and engagement around the two founders, Harrison and Norton.

The secondary social channels are WhatsApp and Twitter. Although the audiences on these channels are relatively passive, each act as a great way to share news and information about the creative AI space, and provide an opportunity for direct conversations as leads are generated. Twitter, in particular is very effective for reaching the AI community.

Instagram and YouTube act as tertiary channels. The former is the backstage pass; it is used to host behind the scenes moments, and the latter hosts their video content.

Other channels

A range of other channels are used to directly engage with prospects, influencers and clients, and to provide content for the social channels and thought leadership.

Tiny Giant holds a monthly event, I'll Back South West, #IBBSW, which hosts talks from industry leaders and creative experimenters in AI and advertising. This is a spin-off of the London event with whom they share an additional WhatsApp thread.

The two founders also regularly speak at other AI-related events, which gives them access to other followers and visitors. These include CogX, Future Sync, MAD fest and I'll Be Back London.

A weekly podcast, Tiny Giant Jams, is used to nurture potential leads and create content for the other channels.

Finally, an Alexa skill has been developed to provide a daily flash briefing with updates on the latest AI news.

LinkedIn, WhatsApp and Twitter are all used to promote and support the speaking opportunities, case studies, the podcast and #IBBSW.

Key learning

There is a real difference in interaction between different types of post. For example, video is the most effective type of content on LinkedIn, while gifs work better on Twitter.

In addition, each channel works best at different times. For WhatsApp, it's the evening, for Twitter it is direct messaging (DM) at the weekend, with recipients responding immediately. LinkedIn works day and night; it is very effective, with Thursday and Sunday being the best performing days. This is probably because people in the start-up space work days, nights and every day of the week.

(Source: Harrison and Norton, 2019)

Campaigns

Finally, you can think about campaigns. How do you ensure that you can meet your business and campaign objectives in social media? The social media activity at a brand level will be a continuous presence but, at this level, you can add channels purely for the length of a campaign or start to mix paid and organic social to boost or reduce volumes. This is primarily 'push' marketing, your outbound social activity, used to guarantee volumes and re-ignite conversations. Each campaign is unique but your audience is primed to receive each new campaign if you already have a strong social brand presence and utilize the knowledge and engagement gained there. The Sylvia Plath campaign for Tiny Giant featured in Chapter 5 is an example of this type of additional activity layered onto their established brand presence to drive awareness of a particular event and ultimately new business leads.

Let's now look in more detail at how to apply the ABC of channel selection.

Understanding your audience

As we have discussed before, understanding your audience in social media is vital and you can use a combination of tools and methods to gain this information. This is discussed in detail in Chapter 4, but to recap: you may use traditional market research methods such as a quantitative questionnaire or qualitative focus groups, either offline or through digital and social channels: you could analyse your customer database or monitor web journeys using tools such as Google Analytics; and you could use social media listening and in-platform analytics to understand engagement, context, social behaviours and demographics. All of this information will enable you to really understand who your audiences are, and break them into different groups either by demographics, or behaviours, or a combination of the two.

Once you have identified your segments you may want to dig deeper into their behaviours and think about which channels they engage with and how they act on those channels in relation to your brand. If you work with Forrester, then they will be able to calculate the Social Technographic Scores for your various audiences (Liu, 2018). However, every brand can apply Lui's principles to their audience analysis. Ask yourself, what channels do my audiences engage with, what do they do there, are they asking questions to enjoy my product more or looking to find new products and services to solve a particular need? Is my audience an eager and regular contributor to social conversations or someone who rarely visits social sites and doesn't respond to social advertising?

With your audiences clarified you can start to think about each channel and its suitability for each of your objectives and their specific audiences. For example, a cycling brand may identify that it has three core social media audiences: audience 1 – keen amateur cyclists; audience 2 – families; and audience 3 – professional cyclists. The demographics of each audience are very different, but so is their aptitude and desire to use social channels and the purpose they use those social channels for.

Audience 1 correlates to the pen portrait for Tom from Chapter 4 (Figure 6.1). This audience is 'socially savvy' in Lui's terms, and 'expects' to engage with your brand on social media. The audience also uses different social media channels at different points in the customer decision journey. For example, they are keen to have the best kit and tech and want to be aware of new products and enhancements that they can discuss and share. In addition, they will read reviews and investigate several options before deciding to buy. Finally, they are enthusiastic tech users and share their times and routes with other cyclists. This means that this audience is mostly involved with the brand in social media at the discover, explore and use parts of the customer lifecycle.

FIGURE 6.1   Pen portrait for Tom

Tom
Successful, confident, healthy
Married
45
Company director in the City/ media/ creative industries
Works hard and exercises harder
Cycles 4–5 x a week
Goes to the gym
Shops designer
Always owns the latest tech and the latest gadget
Brand neighbourhood – Lexus, Apple,
Holidays with the guys – skiing, cycling
Holidays with the family – skiing, Europe, UK, US
Holidays with partner – city and spa breaks
Eats out – no red meat
Likes to buy the best – checks and gives reviews
Buys online to get a deal
Follows cycling and cyclists
Monitors and shares own cycling experiences and fitness levels
Early adopter – wants to be the first to know and try new things

Analysis and social listening also show that the audience is using social channels in different ways. Fitness apps drive their daily engagement with Facebook, Twitter and Instagram, whilst YouTube is primarily used to view great rides. In addition, they are influenced by tech and innovation brands and by following professional cyclists and tech blogs.

Setting the brand stage

So, we know who our audiences are and how they might engage with us. The next step is to create your brand presence in social media. Many brands have a corporate level element to their social strategy that typically creates and deploys content that is generic, safe and focused on what the brand wants to say about itself rather than what their core audiences want to hear. If a brand's strategy works in this way, it is likely to have social feeds full of announcements about subjects such as new offices opening, mergers and acquisitions, videos featuring corporate messaging and references to the company vision statement. Often this corporate-style content will be used across multiple social channels with little variation and it is unlikely to give a genuine impression of the brand's personality.

The ABC approach asks you to think of setting the stage for your brand in terms of what your audiences need rather than what the brand wants to say. By doing this you put your audiences first. You ask yourself, what is the most important aspect of my brand in terms of its social media presence? How will my audience find my brand when they are engaging in social, and, most importantly, what impression do I want to give? All of these will be answered when you explore your '*why*' and decide on your content pillars, as discussed in Chapter 5. By answering these simple questions, you can decide on the core channels you must operate in social in order to survive – the channels that, if you didn't include them, would detrimentally affect your brand performance.

In the case of the cycling example discussed here it is apparent that, for audience 1 (Tom), corporate information on the cycling market, the company offices and global expansion are not of interest to them. Investors and share-holders may be interested in this information but they are unlikely to engage with it in the same channels as those where Tom is active. For Tom, the brand needs to be active where he is active. This could mean creating a Facebook page as a cycling community, hosting a cycling channel in YouTube or facilitating a tech discussion forum. In Barthram's interview later in this chapter he reminds us of some of the niche social channels that work for specific sectors or audience segments. 'The gaming brand Zwift pairs with your indoor bike and connects you with your mates so you can ride with them and race them when you're cycling in the garage' (Barthram, 2019). Because you know that this audience is addicted to fitness apps and moni-toring their performance and length of rides, you will need to investigate where and how they like to share this information and ensure your core brand channels are compatible with easy sharing and integration with the most popular apps.

It is important at this level to keep the number of channels at a level where you can continuously maintain them with high-quality content and interactions.

Delivering campaigns

By building a strong brand presence you ensure that your audience regularly encounters your brand in the social channels they most visit. This activity generates a stable level of interactions, web visits, shares, leads and other actions that build up over time, ensuring your brand awareness is maintained and your brand personality and content is recognized as fulfilling your core audiences' needs. Although the core brand activity in these channels is focused on building a brand presence and much of it will be organic, you may still need to pay for some activity to ensure that you are visible in your audiences' social feeds. 'Without paid social you can be in danger of creating a content echo chamber where only your most ardent fans see your content' (Barthram, 2019). At the campaign stage you can start to think of specific marketing objectives. Perhaps you want to support a new product launch, a new store opening, drive sales or integrate social with an event to amplify its impact. Each different campaign objective will have a different budget and timescale allocated to it. Some may be seasonal, another may last only a few days, such as the clearing campaign for the University of Gloucestershire in the case study later in this chapter. Whatever the objective or length, your campaigns offer the opportunity to add additional social channels specifically for that campaign or to add additional and different activity into the core channels selected at the brand level. For example, in the University of Gloucestershire clearing campaign, Facebook Live was an additional campaign that was added on top of their usual Facebook activity and ran for just five days.

INTERVIEW
Nick Barthram, Strategy Director

Background

Shift Media is part of the Play Sports Group. As a full-service marketing agency, it offers everything from brand development to PR, social and media planning. Its unique difference is that it is 100 per cent dedicated to cycling and so brings unparalleled expertise to its clients in the bike world. Nick is the Strategy Director at Shift. He shares his thoughts on using social media for cycling brands.

What are the biggest challenges cycling brands face in social media?

First, don't be blinded by coolness. Cycling marketing is cool – we recently shot an ad with Christopher Walken! But most bike brands are cool and use similar content so it's really hard for them to differentiate themselves and stand out in social. If they do create differentiated content then it does connect with the audience and we see engagement and reach increase exponentially. For example, last year YT Industries, a mountain bike brand, released an 11-minute horror film on YouTube, and are now smashing their targets because they have created something truly different.

Second, focus on changing perceptions of non-customers, not just speaking to your fans. Social channels are really good at keeping fans engaged with the brand but it's also important to change the perceptions of people who buy from your competitors and encourage them to buy from you. This means that paid social is really necessary to ensure your brand gets seen not only by your customers who follow you on social, but also by potential customers who are following your competitors.

What are your views on social media as part of the marketing mix?

It is essential to be present in social, but different elements are important for different reasons. Video views are only useful if they contribute to brand salience and/or sales. Most brands don't have a massive reach on their own social channels, and at best only a third of their followers will even see any posts, so organic alone won't have the impact needed. Paid social is an important addition to make sure content can be used to change the perceptions of, and drive sales from, non-followers.

Without paid social you can be in danger of creating a content echo chamber where only your most ardent fans see your content, they always like and engage with the same types of content and so the brand continues to produce only the content they engage with. This can stifle creativity and obscure your brand from new audiences.

How important is social media in community engagement?

It's important to know what your audience wants from every channel. A bike brand's social pages are great for sharing content and news about the brand with people who already love it. It keeps them engaged and makes sure they know about anything new.

It's also important to keep an eye out for disruption in the market that changes behaviour. The gaming brand Zwift pairs with your indoor bike and connects you with your mates so you can ride with them and race them when you're cycling in the garage because it's too cold to go out. As it's a digital platform, it has its own communication and peer-to-peer channels through which Zwift do a great job of keeping people involved.

What are your top tips for brands in social media?

1 Lock in customers and fans by serving them the content they like – in cycling that means heavily stylized products from bikes to parts, to apparel, to tech. Product shots win for bike brands (when talking to engaged customers).

2 Welcome them to the club and keep their interested by continuing to create and share the content they love – but don't blow your budget on this; your media budget should be focused on driving up penetration, not talking to existing customers.

3 Therefore, consider social media in the mix with all of your other channels and allocate budget based on performance. A larger brand may focus on TV, with social media as a support. A smaller brand may prioritize paid social and pay per click (PPC).

4 Be aware that tighter targeting can sometimes increase the cost per impression. Reach is really important in creating cultural meaning for a brand and this will normally need to be paid for either in social or in other channels.

(Source: Barthram, 2019)

Channel selection criteria

Not all channels are created equal and so it is important to understand not only which channels your audience is present on but also how they engage with the channel and the different characteristics of each channel.

There are a number of different terms used to describe social media channels, including app, platform and network. In this chapter, these terms are used interchangeably to refer to channels. The website for each social channel mentioned in this book can be found in Appendix 2. In this chapter it is important to understand how the characteristics of each channel varies against some key criteria including:

- audience volume opportunity;
- audience quality profile match;
- audience behaviour match;
- audience engagement rates;
- available advertising opportunities.

Audience volume opportunity

Audience is the most important criteria of all in deciding which social channels to use. The social media landscape is dominated by the larger players. Outside of China, this is essentially Facebook and YouTube, with 85 per cent and 80 per cent respectively of online adults having an account with them (GlobalWebIndex, 2019) (Figure 6.2). In China, where Facebook is restricted, audiences use channels such as WeChat and Baidu Tieba (Figure 6.3). These large audiences provide significant opportunities for marketing teams by providing access to high volumes of consumers and the additional ability to target specific groups, at volume, through paid advertising.

When considering your audience size on a specific channel, however, it is important to look further than just the number of accounts they have. Your audience may well be signed up to Facebook but may not be actively using the channel. The research by GlobalWebIndex shows that active Facebook users are lower than their number of live accounts, whereas more people engage with YouTube every month than there are people with a YouTube account. In China, Baidu Tieba, Weibo and Youku also have a higher number of active users than accounts.

This behaviour is in part due to the platforms themselves. You do not need a YouTube account to watch YouTube, but you need a Facebook account to visit Facebook. But it is also affected by changing consumer behaviour. Facebook is becoming less popular with younger age groups and increasingly popular with the over 55s. This is partially due to the natural aging of the platform; many people who joined Facebook in their 20s are still using Facebook and are now older, and partly due to an increase in new older joiners coinciding with a decline in new younger joiners. In the UK this latter group grew by over 2 million users between 2016 and 2018 (Figure 6.4).

So, when selecting channels for your audience, consider not only the volume of the existing audience but also whether this is a growing channel for them or one in decline. If it is in decline, look at other channels where they are showing an interest. The volume might not be high enough today but could be within the next year or two. As Figure 6.5 shows, in the UK, Snapchat's popularity with 25- to 34-year-olds has now surpassed that of younger audiences, and is still growing rapidly. As the volumes get closer to the volumes on Facebook it starts to become a realistic marketing option for this group.

FIGURE 6.2   Top social platforms excluding China

Question: On which of the following services do you have an account? // Which of the following sites/applications have you visited in the past month via your PC/laptop, mobile or tablet?

Base: 123,832 internet users aged 16–64 from outside China

% outside of China who are members or visitors/users of the following services

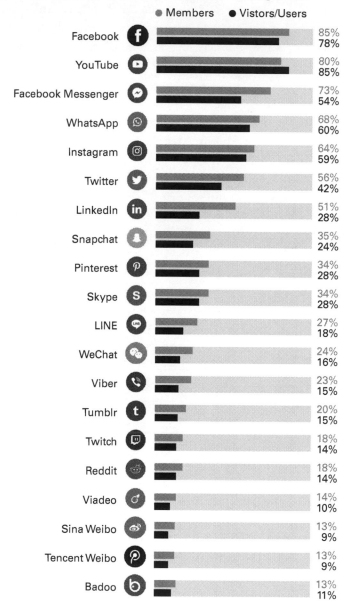

● Members   ● Vistors/Users

Platform	Members	Visitors/Users
Facebook	85%	78%
YouTube	80%	85%
Facebook Messenger	73%	54%
WhatsApp	68%	60%
Instagram	64%	59%
Twitter	56%	42%
LinkedIn	51%	28%
Snapchat	35%	24%
Pinterest	34%	28%
Skype	34%	28%
LINE	27%	18%
WeChat	24%	16%
Viber	23%	15%
Tumblr	20%	15%
Twitch	18%	14%
Reddit	18%	14%
Viadeo	14%	10%
Sina Weibo	13%	9%
Tencent Weibo	13%	9%
Badoo	13%	11%

SOURCE GlobalWebIndex Q4 2018. Reproduced with kind permission of GlobalWebIndex (2019)

FIGURE 6.3   Top social platforms in China

% in China who are members or visitors/users of the following services

● Members   ● Vistors/Users

	Members	Visitors/Users
WeChat	78%	74%
Tencent QQ (China only)	68%	66%
Qzone (China only)	56%	55%
Youku (China and Hong Kong only)	52%	61%
Sina Weibo	51%	59%
Facebook	38%	25%
Tencent Weibo	35%	40%
Tudou (China only)	33%	35%

SOURCE GlobalWebIndex Q4 2018. Reproduced with kind permission of GlobalWebIndex (2019)

FIGURE 6.4   Number of UK visitors to Facebook by age, March 2016–March 2018

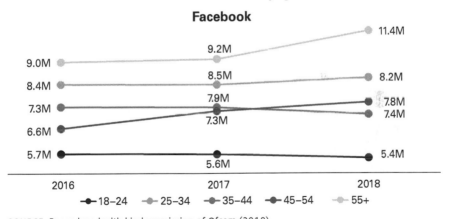

Facebook

●— 18–24   ●— 25–34   ●— 35–44   ●— 45–54   ●— 55+

SOURCE Reproduced with kind permission of Ofcom (2018)

Audience quality profile match

Once you have developed an understanding of the volumes available on each channel that match your audience, you may want to refine this by looking at how closely they actually match your audience profile. For example, if you are a B2B marketer in the tech industry you may be able to

FIGURE 6.5   Number of UK visitors to Snapchat by age, March 2016–March 2018

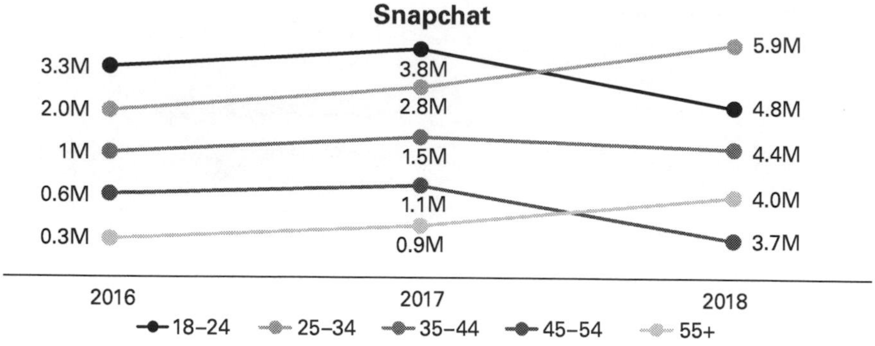

Snapchat

	2016	2017	2018
	3.3M	3.8M	5.9M
	2.0M	2.8M	4.8M
	1M	1.5M	4.4M
	0.6M	1.1M	4.0M
	0.3M	0.9M	3.7M

●— 18–24   ●— 25–34   ●— 35–44   ●— 45–54   ●— 55+

SOURCE Reproduced with kind permission of Ofcom (2018)

find a reasonably large number of individuals that match your audience profile on LinkedIn. However, if you were to look at a niche social network such as Dzone, you would find perhaps a smaller number of individuals, but those individuals would be there to actively engage with the types of content you are producing and actively seeking the information that you could provide. The volume may be lower but the quality will be higher, and this may elevate the channel above a higher volume channel in terms of its importance to your business.

An additional criterion to consider when assessing the quality match would be the suitability of the channel for different global audiences. This may be because of restrictions on certain channels in specific markets. For example, in China, channels such as Weibo or WeChat are likely to replace Facebook. Language suitability can also affect this quality decision as some channels have been developed to accommodate particular alphabets and are therefore more suitable for reaching those audiences. Vkontakte, which uses the Russian alphabet, is highly popular in Russian speaking countries and therefore may become a priority channel for this reason.

Audience behaviour match

Social media behaviour has undergone a considerable change since 2016 with the growth of instant messaging and ephemeral content. This change has been led by younger audiences who are increasingly concerned about their digital footprint and privacy issues, as highlighted in the Reed research in Chapter 4, but it has also affected other demographic groups. It is therefore, very important when selecting channels to identify the types of behaviour your audience engages in and where this occurs in terms of your customer lifecycle.

For example, does your audience use social media to ask questions about how to use specific products and services, or do they tend to follow brands for inspiration? If they are interested in the former activity, YouTube might be an important channel for you to feature how-to videos. If they are focused on the latter, Pinterest might facilitate their desire to create inspiring boards to shop from, or Instagram might drive focused leads to your website. Each different social media channel has characteristics that make it suitable for certain types of behaviour and if this behaviour is important to your customers and important for you to facilitate for your business objectives, then the channel will increase in priority for your brand. The AIDA case study shows how a Twitter poll was used to find, engage and activate interest in the Cheltenham Science Festival.

CASE STUDY USING TWITTER POLLS
AIDA, an AI guest curator, Cheltenham Science Festival

FIGURE 6.6   The AIDA avatar

SOURCE Reproduced with kind permission of Tiny Giant (2019)

TABLE 6.1 Example of a social media channel comparison chart

Social media channel	Facebook	WeChat	Twitter	Snapchat	WhatsApp	TikTok
Best markets	Global excluding China	China	Global excluding China	Global excluding China	Global excluding China	Global including China
Content type	Increasingly video based, high photographic content.	One stop shop microblogging, video, image and post sharing and ecommerce platform.	Microblogging supported by images, giphs and short videos.	Ephemeral images and videos with fun stickers and lenses.	Private messaging app supporting video and voice.	Music videos for lip syncing and comedy karaoke.
Great for individuals to...	Share photos, videos and posts with family and friends. Find popular news stories and follow brands.	Do all they need in terms of shopping, sharing and influencing in one platform.	Find out news and gossip. Follow celebrities and personalities. Complain about brands.	Share short fun moments with friends.	Share information with small private groups in an encrypted space.	Create crazy karaoke and fun music videos for friends.
Great for brands to ...	Reach large numbers of consumers via paid advertising. Build a strong brand presence and drive sales.	Reach Chinese consumers using influencers and posts to drive engagement and sales	Respond to customer comments. Hijack popular events and stories.	Engage with a younger demographic to build credibility and brand engagement.	Reach highly engaged special interest groups with targeted content. Manage customer conversation.	Reach a much younger demographic. Explore what might be next on Facebook and Instagram.

Background

AIDA was the Cheltenham Science Festival's first ever AI guest curator, named after Ada Lovelace, reputed to be the first computer programmer.

A neural network, AIDA learned from 10 years of Science Festival talks and generated dozens of potential talks for the Cheltenham Science Festival in 2019. AIDA not only came up with the titles for the talks, which included Introvert Narwhals, Aliens What What? Space Dinosaurs and Everest Spoon Science, she also devised a foreword for the Festival brochure.

Driving engagement

A Twitter poll was used to select the actual talk for the festival and share the news about which topic won the poll. This encouraged attendance of the event at the festival and spread awareness to a science and tech audience.

Increasing engagement

To support the festival's AI content, and to ensure AIDA could sit alongside her human guest curators in the brochure, an avatar was created. This gave AIDA a personality and a visual identity, which maximized engagement and sharing on social media.

At the festival, an academic spoke on the subject of Introvert Narwhals, a panel debated AI creativity and culture, and BBC radio 'interviewed' AIDA as part of the Festival's launch. All of this continued to be amplified on Twitter.

(Source: Harrison and Norton, 2019)

Appendix 2 describes all of the social channels mentioned in the book. Many channels are banned in China. However, they may still be available there via work around VPNs. Table 6.1 provides a quick comparison of a few key channels.

The channels you will be considering are likely to vary from those shown here, but it may be useful to use Template 6.1 to identify the core channels your audience engages on.

Remember, some audiences, such as the Skippers mentioned in Chapter 2, will not purchase on social media but they may use certain channels for watching how-to videos, looking at reviews or making complaints. Others, such as Stars, will 'demand social interactions with your company' (Liu, 2018). In marketing, we are not trying to change natural behaviour, rather we want to encourage that behaviour on behalf of our brand. It is therefore

TEMPLATE 6.1   Social media channels for consideration template (part 1)

Social media channels for consideration			
Is my audience here?			
Is this a primary or secondary channel for them?			
What behaviours do they exhibit here when engaging with friends and family?			
What behaviours do they exhibit here when engaging with brands?			
Do my social media objectives have a good fit with the way my audience behaves on social media?			
Is this a social channel I should consider using for my brand?			
Is this a primary or secondary social channel for my brand?			

very important to understand how your audience behaves in each channel you are considering using and to match your usage to this behaviour. For example, if your audience wants to address customer service issues on Twitter, don't force them to do so on Facebook; if they are more likely to enter competitions on Facebook then run your competitions there; and if they follow Instagram Influencers and share content more widely here than elsewhere make sure this is part of your brand awareness strategy.

Audience engagement rates

Different channels have different levels of engagement. Instagram has much higher levels of engagement than Facebook, and Twitter's rates are lower than both of the others. Knowing that you will see different levels of engagement by channel is important when deciding on which channels to use. Engagement levels will also vary depending on the sector your organization operates in. News and entertainment brands see more engagement on Twitter, whereas design and creative brands work better on Pinterest.

When selecting the social media channels to use for your brand or business, do also consider how your audience interacts with itself and other audiences on that channel. Peer-to-peer engagement is an important part of social media and will help increase reach and conversion rates. For example, the University of Gloucestershire uses Facebook because even though its usage is in decline with their younger primary target audience, this audience's older parents are active on the channel, and both audiences have a Facebook presence, so content can be tagged and easily shared between them and the brand.

CASE STUDY UNIVERSITY OF GLOUCESTERSHIRE CLEARING CAMPAIGN

Background

The University of Gloucestershire is a mid-sized UK university with specialisms in industry-ready subjects such as teaching, health and social care, cyber security, and creativity and design. The year 2018 was a low birth-rate year for prospective students in the UK and there was a degree of uncertainty about the prospective international student population due to Brexit.

Clearing is concentrated into the few days after the A-level results, when students who did not achieve the grades they needed, and those with higher than expected grades, try to find a university place. Universities compete to fill all their places on each course and often attract students who hadn't initially applied or heard of the university before.

This case study looks at how the University of Gloucestershire tackled clearing in the highly competitive environment of 2018.

Objective

The campaign had four phases, beginning with a pre-campaign teaser, building through increased brands awareness and culminating in driving action to call the clearing hotline or visit the website. Finally, the campaign continued beyond the clearing peak, keeping potential students interested in the University of Gloucestershire and continuing to recruit students in the clearing tail period.

The audience

UK A-level students who wanted to go to university in September 2018 and received their results in August 2018.

The channels

Facebook, Instagram and Twitter were selected because this is where both the students and their parents engage. In addition, the campaign was primarily organic and used only a minimal amount of post-boosting paid media. Rather, live video was used to increase engagement and optimize visibility via the platforms' algorithms and peer-to-peer engagement.

The timing

Initially planned for the Thursday (A-level results day) and Friday, the campaign performed so well that two additional days were added on Saturday and Sunday.

Strategic approach

The strategy focused on using four student ambassadors to create powerful peer-to-peer engagement with potential students. These students were recruited from the university's ambassador scheme. They represented different subject areas and worked together as a team with strong on-air chemistry.

Because most universities offer similar courses, the university wanted to highlight their difference in terms of location and personality. They also wanted to provide content in social that wasn't being delivered via other media channels.

Facebook Live sessions were chosen as the media opportunity, with two per day on Thursday and Friday and one on Saturday morning.

The sessions took the form of a Town Tour and lasted about 20 minutes. There were lots of opportunities for the ambassadors to answer questions live, but a one-hour walk-through prior to the tour ensured the ambassadors had lots to talk about if questions were sparse (University of Gloucestershire, 2018).

Call to action

During the live videos the ambassadors regularly mentioned the number and web address to contact if you were considering the University of Gloucestershire in clearing. Their genuine love of the university and local knowledge made the call to action (CTA) feel natural and impactful.

Campaign optimization

The audience were encouraged to ask questions using the Instagram Questions feature and additional content was filmed in between the live sessions and grabbed to answer them. They also filmed additional content for use after clearing, such as a video of five things to pack when going to university. After each live session, the team self-critiqued and built the learnings of what worked and didn't into the next session. The team also dropped elements of the campaign that didn't work, such as a live chat group on the website, which failed to grab attention.

Results

The results were outstanding, with over 44,000 video views and 150,000 unique impressions in just five days. On Instagram the Insta Stories had between 800 and 1,050 views, which is 300 times higher than normal.

Why it worked so well

Although clearing only lasts for a few days, the team started planning for it well in advance by setting up a pre-clearing working group. This group coordinated the strategy, and made sure a strong brand identity was created for the campaign and seeded socially prior to clearing. This meant their audience was primed to hear from the university before clearing began.

The group also tested different content types. For example, they found that organic visuals performed much more strongly than corporate visuals on Instagram and these pre-campaign tests increased the impact of the actual campaign when it went live.

Next steps

The campaign was so successful it is being rolled out to increase the performance of open days in 2019.

Source: Fitzgerald, 2019

Available advertising opportunities

The final criterion you may want to consider in channel selection is the availability of paid advertising opportunities. Paid social ads are useful for increasing volumes at speed and enabling targeting to specific audiences on high-volume channels with broad audience demographics such as Facebook and WeChat.

One way of categorizing the media opportunities is to use the converged media model approach created by Lieb and Owyang (2012) (Figure 6.7). This approach breaks down the media opportunities into three core categories:

- **Owned media:** The media you own and control such as your website, email newsletter, podcast and blog.

- **Paid media:** Traditional paid advertising, much of which now occurs on social platforms or as in-video display ads.

- **Earned media:** Organic social sharing or PR.

When media converges as it does in social media, the lines between different types blur and an amplification effect takes place. Channels that support advertising enable strong posts to be boosted and targeted at new audiences, and channels with high engagement rates will enable significant organic reach, maximizing the benefits of the converged media model.

FIGURE 6.7   The convergence of paid, owned and earned media

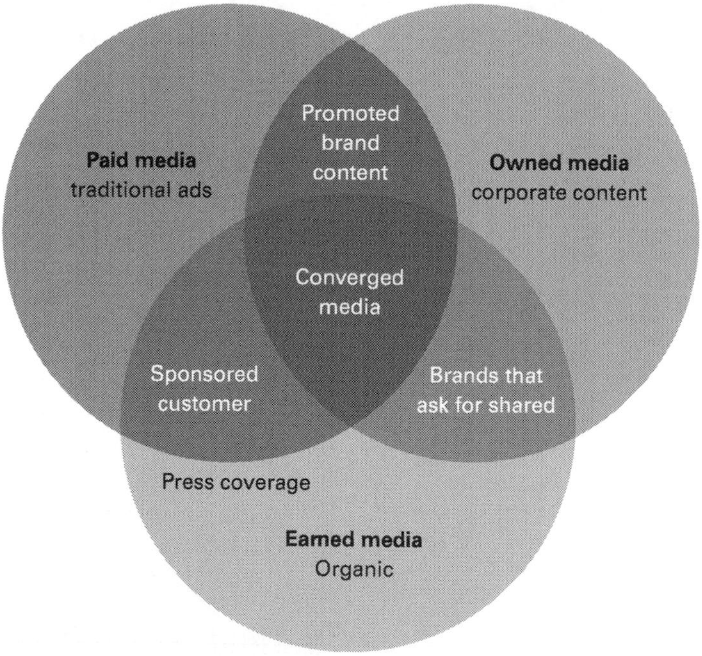

Paid media
traditional ads

Promoted
brand
content

Owned media
corporate content

Converged
media

Sponsored
customer

Brands that
ask for shared

Press coverage

Earned media
Organic

SOURCE Reproduced with kind permission of Lieb and Owyang (2012)

Using the social media channel selection templates

By using the criteria of audience volume opportunity, audience quality profile match, audience behaviour match, audience engagement rates and the advertising opportunities available you are able to compare each available channel and its suitability for your audience.

Some channels will be so important you will decide to have a continuous brand presence there, where you make sure you fulfil the needs your audience has in social media. These will be your primary social media channels. Other secondary channels will be useful for specific campaigns and you will decide to use them in a more tactical way. You do not need to have a continuous presence on these channels. You may also use aspects of your primary channels for specific campaign purposes. For example, in the University of Gloucestershire case study the brand has a continuous presence on Facebook and Instagram but only used Facebook Live and Insta Stories for its clearing campaign. Their resources aren't sufficient to enable continuous use of these tools but they were ideally suited to the short-lived clearing campaign.

When making final channel selections, identify the primary and secondary channels for your audiences using Part 1 of the channel consideration template (Template 6.1). Then, once you have identified the channels and the behaviours your audiences exhibit there, use Part 2 (Template 6.2) to

TEMPLATE 6.2   Social media channels for consideration template (part 2)

	Social media channels selected			
Brand	Which channels should I have a continuous presence on?			
	What need will they fulfil for my audience?			
	What tools will I use from the platform to build my brand presence?			
	What paid advertising opportunities will I use?			
Campaigns	Are there any channels that will help me meet specific campaign goals?			
	What tools will I use to support each campaign?			
	What paid advertising opportunities can I use?			

decide which channels and which tools in each channel you will use for building your brand presence and which for specific campaigns.

Whether you are working in B2B or B2C marketing, it is important to select and use only those channels that are important to your audience and enable you to utilize the behaviour they exhibit there to bring them closer to your brand. You do not need to be in every social channel and should be clear about why you do exist in the ones you have selected. Fewer channels managed well will be much more effective than many channels managed poorly. Also, remember that 'because there is so much noise out there, people go to channels for very specific purposes' (Sweales, 2019) and you will need to understand why your audiences visit each of their channels. In the following interview Lynsey Sweales provides some important insights on channel use for B2B social media marketing.

INTERVIEW
Lynsey Sweales, CEO, SocialB

Background

SocialB is an international award-winning digital marketing agency that works with global brands, such as Nissan, TSB, United Nations, and ASDA, in training, consultancy and implementation. Lynsey is a recognized leader in digital, a previous Vice Chair of the DMA Social Media Council and a Google Digital Academy Partner and Trainer. She supports both B2B and B2C brands on their digital strategy creation and delivery.

How important is LinkedIn in B2B marketing?

The targeting possibilities on LinkedIn make it a very powerful platform for B2B marketing. LinkedIn can fit into a customer journey that leads directly to purchase by targeting based on job title, company size, sector, location, etc, to generate awareness. By understanding your customers' wants and needs you can add value by creating truly useful and interesting content for them. Once a prospect shows interest in the content, then this interest can be followed up with lead generation activity.

Ideally, it is best to use ads in the main news feed, as inmail can be very annoying. It is much better to take a personal approach. Once someone likes your post you will see lots of information on them and can follow up with a connection request or ask for a call.

How can you increase the effectiveness of LinkedIn as a B2B marketing channel?

You may have a very good understanding of the general benefits of your product or service but often you will need to communicate differently about them on social media. It is important to start with the audience and understand what they want and where social fits in their decision-making journey. It could be to generate awareness, convince through reviews and case studies or anywhere in between.

It is really important that your company page and the core people in your business have their profile page set up and use it professionally. Sales teams may need training to give them the confidence to use LinkedIn effectively. However, done right, it is a powerful networking opportunity that can build and grow businesses very cost effectively.

Do you have any tips for B2B marketing across different global markets?

It is very easy to forget the small things when building global campaigns. For example, people have different job titles for the same roles in different countries and the spelling might vary even if the language is the same.

It is really important to set up a test and learn approach and work with people who understand the cultural differences of each market. For example, in Mauritius, Facebook is a very important channel and needs to be included in any campaign, and in Oman people only update their LinkedIn profile if they are looking for a new job, so care needs to be taken on this channel. They also prefer to do business face-to-face, so this, rather than telephone, needs to be the next step in the journey.

How important is measurement on social media for B2B?

Social media needs to be embedded into the whole sales process, with clear KPIs, such as a certain number of leads per month, that demonstrate where it has added value. For some businesses, it is possible to report on the user journey from social through to their website and build up a conversion picture all the way through. If we can add in lead quality to the analysis, the value becomes even more transparent.

What is happening to behaviour on the different social media channels?

There has been a real change in how people are using different channels. LinkedIn has changed dramatically from a CV site to a really useful place to meet people and create business. As video has been introduced it has become more engaging but it is still behind the other social platforms in terms of functionality. Interestingly, as there is a general move on other platforms into private conversations in special interest groups, the popularity of the LinkedIn Group function has waned. This feels like a lost opportunity for the channel.

Because there is so much noise out there, people go to channels for very specific purposes. There is much less just looking around. For example, LinkedIn is great for me to see what my connections are doing and to look for potential opportunities for business. Twitter, which used to be used for sourcing information, answering questions and reaching out to new audiences, is a more passive channel than ever, with re-tweets of information and news more common than the initiation of investigations. Facebook feels like it is declining, with Instagram being the more engaging and innovative platform.

What effect will tech have on social media?

As voice takes steps to replace search, and watches and lenses replace mobile, social will need to take a transformational leap. Once you have an Apple watch the time spent on your mobile decreases (at least I have found this, along with speaking to other people who have mobile watches). Will the mobile disappear? How will the social media experience change through a watch or smart glasses?

Currently the ad targeting on social is very powerful, but with the mobile devices that we use ever-evolving this feels like it will get harder. The answer is likely to be increasingly integrated experiences – a 'cathedral experience' like Nike. Their stores exist primarily to create experiences rather than sell product. They integrate with their other channels and people are more likely to talk about the experience rather than the product on social. Influencers will still be important, but those with fewer followers will be more important, as they are more likely to have closely aligned interests and therefore create closer, more authentic connections with their followers.

Source: Sweales, 2019

References

Barthram, N (2019) Strategy Director, Shif Media [Interview] (25 January)

Edelman, D (2013) Branding in the digital age, in *HBR's Must Reads: On strategic marketing*, Harvard Business Review Press, Boston

Fitzgerald, D (2019) Director of Communications, Marketing and Student Recruitment, University of Gloucestershire [Interview] (7 January)

Gallup (2018) www.gallup.com/services/169331/customer-engagement.aspx?g_source=link_WWWV9&g_medium=TOPIC&g_campaign=item_&g_content=Customer%2520Engagement (archived at https://perma.cc/37J5-UTNN)

GlobalWebIndex (2019) *Social Flagship Report 2019*, GlobalWebIndex, London

Harrison, K and Norton, R (2019) Co-founders, Tiny Giant [Interview] (13 March)

Hubspot (2018) Content trends global preferences research. https://research.hubspot.com/content-trends-global-preferences (archived at https://perma.cc/AC74-LR3A)

Li, C and Bernoff, J (2008) *Groundswell: Winning in a world transformed by social technologies*, Harvard Business School Press, Boston

Lieb, R and Owyang, J (2012) Altimeter – the converged media imperative: How brands must combine paid, earned and owned media. www.slideshare.net/Altimeter/the-converged-media-imperative (archived at https://perma.cc/S5HV-KG2Y)

Liu, JF (2018) Social Technographics® reveals who your social audience is – and how to approach them, Forrester®

Mintel (2018) *Social Media and Networks Research UK*, Mintel, London

Ofcom (2018) *Communications Market Report*, Ofcom, London

Rival IQ (2018) 2018 social media industry benchmarking report. www.rivaliq.com/blog/2018-social-media-industry-benchmark-report/ (archived at https://perma.cc/N7AZ-V2UK)

Sweales, L (2019) CEO, Social B [Interview] (15 March)

Tiny Giant (2019) www.tinygiant.io (archived at https://perma.cc/9Y4S-6EYK)

University of Gloucestershire (2018) Facebook live video. www.facebook.com/uniofglos/videos/2810560226941037/ (archived at https://perma.cc/2KHS-4HB8)

7

Measuring and benchmarking success

How and when do you know your social media strategy is working?

This chapter explains the key social media metrics and how to measure social media campaigns. Top tips for measuring and benchmarking are included, together with explanations of the most important calculations.

Why measure social media campaigns?

Many organizations still measure only limited elements of social media campaigns, but with some planning it is possible to understand the true impact social media is having on your business. By measuring social media activity, in the same way as other marketing activity, priorities on investment, content creation and resource allocation can be made through informed comparisons and judgements. As Folschette (2019) says in his interview later in this chapter, 'forget vanity metrics. These are the numbers that look nice, but are pretty fluffy, and aren't directly related to impact... they're not important to your CMO'.

The measurement levels

In Chapter 3 we talked about setting KPIs that aligned with the social media objectives and the overall vision and mission of the organization using the

VMOST framework. In this chapter we will look at ensuring your social media measurement ladders up through your business to add value at every level. To do this it is useful to look at social media measurement based on three decision-making levels:

- business impact level;
- social media strategy level;
- social media tactics level.

Business impact level

These are the measurements that will demonstrate the impact your social media activity is having on meeting the overall business objectives. They are the measurements that are reviewed by the C-suite at their monthly board meetings and are the KPIs that show whether the overall business is on target and successful. C-suite measurements often include KPIs such as sales revenue, leads, brand reputation and net promoter score (NPS). It is important to understand the metrics that drive your business and track your social media activity in order to demonstrate the impact it has on the overall business priorities. Often your brand presence on social media will contribute to metrics such as NPS and brand reputation, and lead generation or sales campaigns will contribute towards the revenue based KPIs.

Social media strategy level

These measurements will demonstrate the overall effectiveness of any social media campaign. The measurements will usually be reviewed by the social media manager, the brand or marketing manager or the head of marketing or sales. Typical measurements that are important at this level are organic versus paid comparisons, return on investment, social equivalent advertising value, sentiment, sales, leads, engagement, followers, impressions and reach.

Social media tactics level

These measurements are used to optimize and improve social media campaigns in real time to ensure the social media activity delivers the best results. The metrics enable the social media analyst or executive to tweak the campaign and improve overall performance. Typical areas of measurement are day of week to post, time of day to post, creative and content tests, media tests, channel comparisons and social advertising tests. Because social media campaigns operate in real time there is a significant performance improvement opportunity if ongoing optimization is built into campaign delivery.

The relationship between the roles and the measurement levels are shown in Figure 7.1.

FIGURE 7.1   The three levels of social media measurement

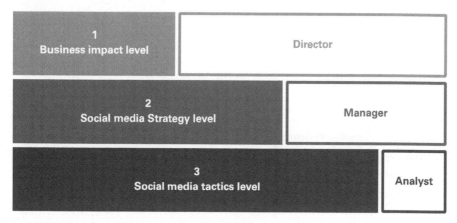

The key social media metrics at a tactics level

Before exploring social media measurement further, it is useful to clarify the meaning of some of the most important metrics.

The most commonly used metrics are:

- **Impressions:** The number of times your content is displayed.
- **Reach:** The number of people who have seen your content.
- **Engagement:** The number of people that have interacted with your content. This could be video views, shares, likes or other activities that demonstrate some form of interaction.
- **Click-through rate:** The number of people who have clicked on a link to your website or other content compared with the number it was displayed to.
- **Conversions:** The number of people who have completed your desired action – for example, signing up to your newsletter or buying your product or service.

In Chapter 6 we discussed the University of Gloucestershire clearing campaign. They used a variety of different measurements to determine the success of the campaign. Ultimately, at a business impact level they were looking to generate an increase in student numbers for September 2018. However, at a strategy and tactics level they were able to optimize the campaign by looking at shares, views, reach and impressions as shown in Table 7.1.

The team monitored these results as they happened and used them alongside a discussion of what had worked well or badly during the Facebook Live filming to make continuous improvements. When Live Chats weren't well attended on the first day they were dropped in favour of stronger activity.

Assessing the importance of different metrics

Figure 7.2 shows the most commonly used social media metrics and their relative importance. For example, while the number of impressions can be large and impressive, it may give no indication of whether anyone in your target audience has actually seen your content. Conversely, the conversion rate is an accurate measurement of the effectiveness of your social media activity at a business impact level as it shows the number of people who have acted (eg buying your product or signing up to your newsletter) in relation to the number who have seen your content.

FIGURE 7.2   Key social media metrics

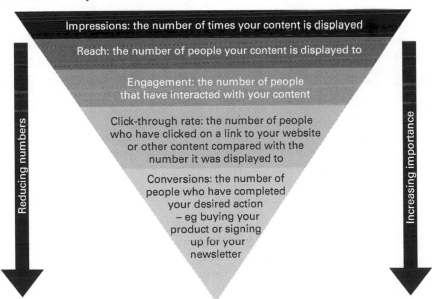

TABLE 7.1 Extract of Facebook results for the University of Gloucestershire clearing campaign

Date	Video description	O (organic) / B (boosted)	Comments	Shares	Reactions	Video views	Reach (unique impressions)
15 Aug	What to expect over the next few days video	O	3	19	45	2,900	5,800
16 Aug	A level results day welcome – call us now from Conor	B	10	7	50	3,900	16,100
16 Aug	FB Live tour of Quays and Upper Quay accommodation	O	16	8	45	2,100	5,600
16 Aug	FB Live tour of Cheltenham town centre	O	17	9	52	2,500	7,700
16 Aug	End of day message	O	0	1	13	794	3,000
17 Aug	Friday welcome – call us now from Jade	O	1	4	6	904	3,000
17 Aug	FB Live tour of Pittville Park/Student Village	O	13	2	33	1,600	6,200
17 Aug	FB Live from Gloucester Cathedral	O	11	2	24	1,700	6,000
17 Aug	End of day message from Conor	B	0	5	30	22,000	79,700
18 Aug	FB Live from the Brewery and FCH Campus	O	21	1	24	1,500	4,700
18 Aug	End of day message from Conor and Jade	O	0	1	13	917	2,700
19 Aug	Tour of the new Business School	O	14	29	54	3,400	9,900
	TOTAL		106	88	389	44,215	150,400

SOURCE Reproduced with kind permission of the University of Gloucestershire (Fitzgerald, 2019)

In addition to these volume metrics, it is important to understand how much your social media activity is costing. The following metrics are important in understanding the relationship between the volume of activity and its cost. They are:

- **Cost per click (CPC):** The cost of a social media post divided by the number of people who clicked on the link within that post.
- **Cost per lead (CPL):** The cost of your social media activity divided by the number of leads that activity generated.
- **Cost per thousand impressions (cost per mille, CPM):** The cost of your social media activity divided by one-thousandth of the number of impressions that activity generated.
- **Cost per view (CPV):** The cost of your social media activity divided by the number of views that activity generated.

In social media there is another level of measurement that is important because it gives an indication of the impact your social media activity is having on your audience. These measures are:

- **Frequency:** This is the number of times the same person sees your post. If the frequency is too high it can cause people to become annoyed and unfollow your page or hide your posts.
- **Relevancy score:** This score is allocated by Facebook to your social ads and indicates how relevant your ad is to your audience. The score ranges from 1 to 10, where 1 is irrelevant and 8–10 is highly relevant. The higher the score, the more likely Facebook will serve the ad to that audience. By increasing your relevancy score you can effectively improve the performance of your posts and reduce the cost of your ads.

The most important measurement calculations at a strategy and business level

There are many measurements that are possible in social media, but there are perhaps three stand-out calculations that enable you to compare your social media activity across other marketing channels, are easily understood and highly valued by the C-suite, and demonstrate the impact your social media is having on meeting core business objectives.

These calculations are return on investment (ROI), social equivalent advertising value (SEAV) and net promoter score (NPS). The following sections show how to calculate these measurements.

Return on investment/return on marketing investment

This is most important metric of all, as it demonstrates the value of each £ of marketing spend. It is often the most difficult measurement for organic social media campaigns but if it can be measured it enables social media activity to be directly compared to all other marketing in order to prioritize investment and assess channel impact.

ROI can be calculated using five steps.

STEP 1: DECIDE ON THE SOCIAL MEDIA OBJECTIVES FOR YOUR BRAND

There are many social media objectives. For some brands it will be to generate sales or leads, for others to improve brand awareness or improve customer satisfaction. Whatever the reason, it is important to decide each social media objective and make sure it is SMART.

STEP 2: ALLOCATE SOCIAL TACTICS WITH SPECIFIC GOALS TO YOUR ACTIVITY

Once you have decided on your social media objectives, the next step is to allocate some specific social media goals to your activity. These goals need to be realistic and measurable. For example, if your purpose in social media is brand awareness then your social media goal might be website visits, enquiries or email sign-ups. If your objective is to improve customer satisfaction then your social media goal might be to reduce product returns or improve net promoter scores. If your objective is to generate sales then your social media goal might be to increase purchases or product trials.

It is important that each goal is set at a campaign level in order to assess the success of each activity. In addition, the goals need to be tangible activities that will impact business success. Tracking likes and shares can be useful but will not enable you to measure ROI.

STEP 3: TRACK AND MEASURE YOUR PERFORMANCE AGAINST YOUR GOALS

Google Analytics is usually the easiest way to track and measure a campaign's performance against your goals. It allows you not only to look at which social channels are driving traffic, but also on a more detailed level at each goal individually and, if desired, its impact on conversions later in the funnel.

In order to calculate ROI you will need to assign a monetary (revenue) value to each goal.

- If your goal is to increase sales then the value will be the average sale value.
- If your goal is to increase email sign-ups then you can assign a value by multiplying your average customer lifetime value by your email subscriber to customer conversion rate.
- If your goal is to reduce product returns then the value can be calculated by using the cost of an average product return (this will probably include the revenue lost from the sale and the cost of facilitating the return).

STEP 4: DETERMINE YOUR SOCIAL MEDIA SPEND

Your spend calculation should include all of the costs of running your social media activity, such as content creation, social media listening tools, social ad costs and employee time per campaign.

STEP 5: CALCULATE YOUR SOCIAL MEDIA ROI

With steps 1 to 4 completed the ROI calculation can be applied to each campaign:

ROI = (revenue – costs) / costs

By using this methodology you can compare performance across both social media channels and non-social media activity. You can also prioritize investment into successful areas and identify campaigns to target for improvement where negative ROI is adversely affecting your overall success.

If a negative ROI is calculated then the activity can be cancelled or adjusted and monitored until a positive ROI is achieved. In acquisition, a negative ROI is often acceptable because the ongoing lifetime value will more than compensate for an initial loss.

The following examples show how to set up, track and calculate ROI for three different social media purposes – raising brand awareness, improving customer satisfaction, and driving sales.

SETTING UP A CAMPAIGN TO MEASURE ROI FOR BRAND AWARENESS

Step 1: Social media objectives

A UK computer software company wants to expand into the US market and decides that its purpose in social media is to increase its brand awareness.

Step 2: Social tactics and goals

The company will measure increased brand awareness using the number of email sign-ups. Other metrics such as reach, impressions and engagement will also be tracked but not used in the ROI calculation.

The company sets up an awareness campaign to run on Twitter and LinkedIn. A range of content is produced to support the campaign, such as free research, whitepapers, tools and events. In each case an email sign-up is needed to access the free content.

In order to track the campaign activity, Google's URL Builder is used to enable the results to feed into Google Analytics. bitly is also used to shorten the URLs using Google Analytics and enabling them to feature the brand name. By using different branded links for each piece of content and channel, the effectiveness of all activity can be measured as well as the overall ROI for the campaign.

Step 3: Tracking and measuring

Google Analytics is used to measure performance by setting up the email sign-up goal in the acquisition/social/conversion section of the dashboard (Figure 7.3).

The goal is set for email sign-ups and a thank-you page added as the destination (Figure 7.4). The number of thank-you pages accessed will enable the number of email sign-ups to be accurately calculated in the Google Analytics.

Using the Google Analytics data and other information and data from the sales and marketing analysis, the following calculations enable revenue to be attributed to the campaign.

The lifetime value of a customer is calculated as:

Average sale value = £2,500 per annual licence
Average lifetime of a customer = 2.4 years
Average lifetime value per customer = 2.4 × £2,500 = £6,000

FIGURE 7.3   Google Analytics dashboard campaign set up

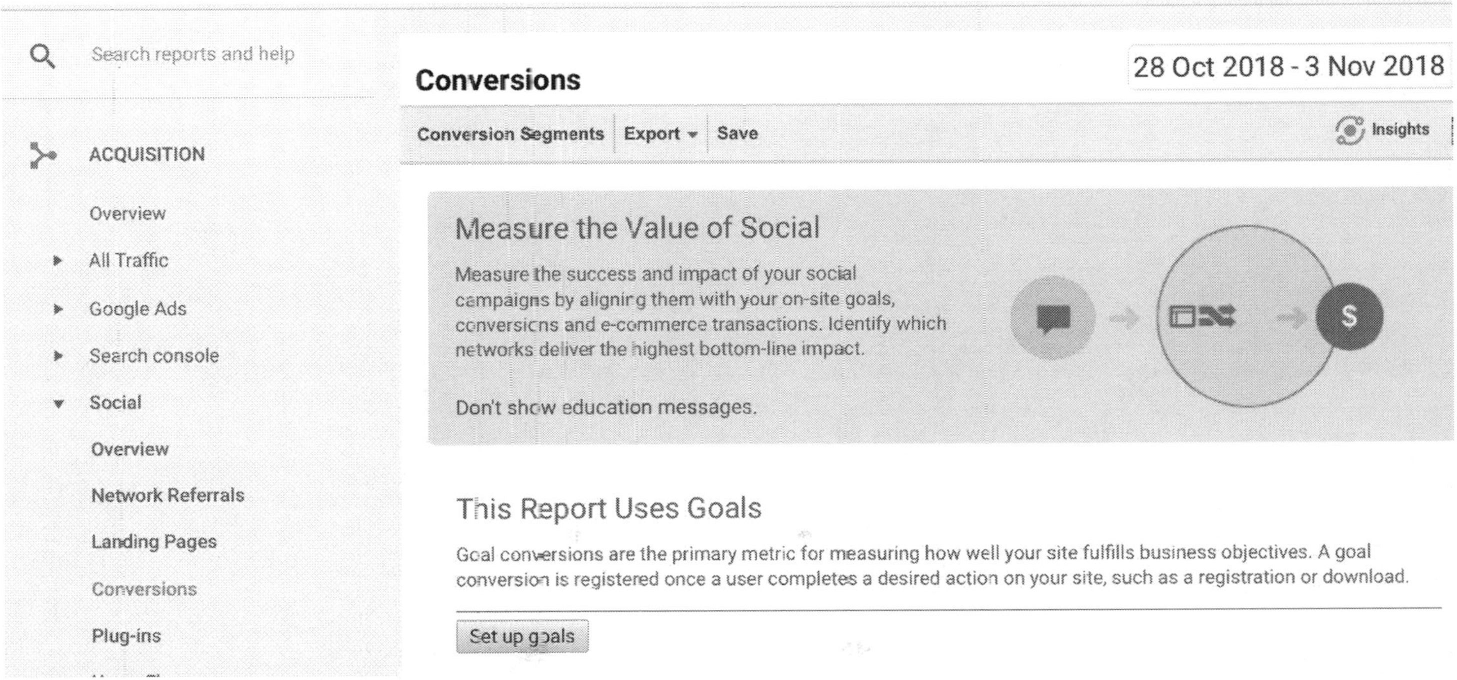

SOURCE Google Analytics screenshot reproduced with kind permission of Google (2018)

FIGURE 7.4   Google Analytics dashboard goal set up

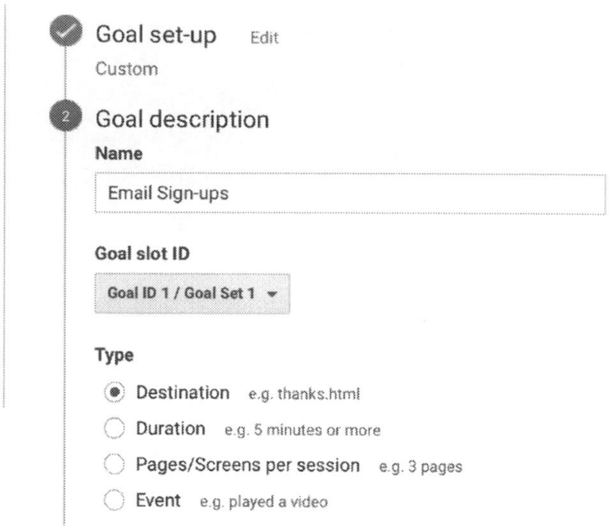

SOURCE Google Analytics screenshot reproduced with kind permission of Google (2018)

The value per email sign-up is calculated as:

> Conversion rate of email sign-ups to customers = 5.2 per cent
> Value per email customer = £6,000 × 5.2 per cent = £312

The total revenue generated is calculated as:

> Total number of email sign-ups = 400
> Total email sign-up revenue = 400 × £312 = £124,800

Step 4: Social media spend

Social media spend for the campaign is calculated by allocating a proportion of the social media team time and social tools budget to the activity and adding this to the cost of any social ads and campaign specific content creation.

Total campaign cost is calculated as:

> Team resources cost equates to 10 per cent of team time = £10,000
> Social tools cost equates to 10 per cent of annual licence fee = £1,500
> Content creation spend = £20,000
> Social advertising spend = £15,000
> Total costs = £10,000 + £1,500 + £20,000 + £15,000 = £46,500

Step 5: Social media ROI

By using the ROI equation, the ROI of the software company's brand awareness campaign can be calculated as:

(Revenue − costs) / costs = ROI(£124,800 − £46,500) / £46,500 = 1.68ROI = 1.68

SETTING UP A CAMPAIGN TO MEASURE ROI FOR CUSTOMER SATISFACTION

Step 1: Social media objectives

A flat-pack furniture company currently has a 20 per cent returns rate on a new line of bedroom furniture. It has monitored its social media channels and customer feedback surveys and has realized that customers find the current instructions confusing and customer service response times poor, and have started to complain regularly about the brand on social media. The company has set a social media objective to improve customer satisfaction.

Step 2: Social tactics and goals

The company will measure improved customer satisfaction using the number of product returns. Other metrics such as sentiment analysis, the number of customer complaints on social media and engagement will also be tracked but not used in the ROI calculation.

The company creates a series of how-to videos, Instagram story instructions and a specific Twitter channel to help anyone currently building a piece of their furniture and to direct them to the videos.

In order to track the campaign activity, Google's URL Builder is used to enable the results to feed into Google Analytics. bitly is also used to shorten the URLs using Google Analytics and enabling them to feature the brand name. The effectiveness of all activity can be measured, as well as the overall ROI for the campaign, by using different branded links for each piece of content and channel.

Step 3: Tracking and measuring

Google Analytics is used to measure performance by setting up a video views event goal in the acquisition/social/conversion section of the dashboard (Figure 7.5).

FIGURE 7.5   Google Analytics dashboard goal set up – video views

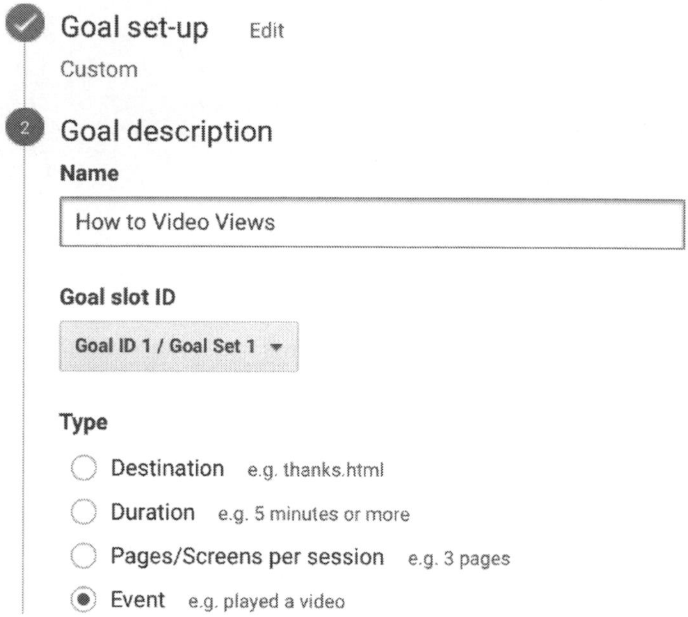

Goal set-up   Edit

Custom

Goal description

Name

How to Video Views

Goal slot ID

Goal ID 1 / Goal Set 1 ▾

Type

○ **Destination**   e.g. thanks.html

○ **Duration**   e.g. 5 minutes or more

○ **Pages/Screens per session**   e.g. 3 pages

◉ **Event**   e.g. played a video

SOURCE Google Analytics screenshot reproduced with kind permission of Google (2018)

Using the GA data and other information and data from the sales and marketing analysis, the following calculations enable revenue to be attributed to the campaign.

The value of a product return is calculated as:

Average sale value per product = £120
Average number of product sales per month = 250

The value per video view is calculated as:

Product return rate prior to customer satisfaction campaign = 20 per cent
Product return rate post the customer satisfaction campaign = 5 per cent
Cost of product returns prior to campaign = (250 × 20 per cent) × £120 = £6,000
Cost of product returns post campaign = (250 × 5 per cent) × £120 = £1,500
Number of video views in month 1 = 100
Value per video view = (£6,000 – £1,500)/100 = £45
Video views total 3,000 for the full year.

The total revenue generated in year 1 by the customer satisfaction campaign is calculated as:

Total number of video views = 3,000

Total video view revenue = 3,000 × £45 = £135,000

Step 4: Social media spend

Social media spend for the campaign is calculated by allocating a proportion of the social media team time and social tools budget to the activity and adding this to the cost of any social ads and campaign specific content creation.

Total campaign cost is calculated as:

Team resources cost equates to 20 per cent of team time = £15,000

Social tools cost equates to 10 per cent of annual licence fee = £0

Content creation spend = £15,000

Social advertising spend = £5,000

Total costs = £15,000 + £15,000 + £5,000 = £35,000

Step 5: Social media ROI

By using the ROI equation, the ROI of the furniture company's customer satisfaction campaign can be calculated as:

(Revenue – costs) / costs = ROI

(£135,000 – £35,000) / £35,000 = 3.86

ROI = 3.86

SETTING UP A CAMPAIGN TO MEASURE ROI FOR GENERATING SALES

Step 1: Social media objectives

A fashion brand wants to use social media to increase sales.

Step 2: Social tactics and goals

The company will measure the number of sales generated by its social media channels. It uses Instagram and Facebook as its primary social media commerce channels.

The company uses the Instagram LikeToBuy function from Curalate to generate a link in its Instagram Bio and the Facebook pixel to track the performance of its Facebook ads.

Step 3: Tracking and measuring

Google and in-platform analytics are used to measure performance. The social media campaign links directly to the ecommerce site with a purchasing CTA. The goal is set to measure the value of purchases from social media so the destination page in your tracking will be the page after a customer makes a purchase.

Using the Google Analytics data and other information and data from the sales and marketing analysis the following calculations enable revenue to be attributed to the campaign:

The average value of a sale is £25

The total revenue generated per month is calculated as:

Total number of sales = 2,100
Total sales revenue = 2,100 × £25 = £52,500

Step 4: Social media spend

Social media spend for the campaign is calculated by allocating a proportion of the social media team time and social tools budget to the activity and adding this to the cost of any social ads and campaign-specific content creation.
Total campaign cost is calculated as:

Team resources cost equates to 5 per cent of team time = £3,000
Social tools cost equates to 10 per cent of annual licence fee = £0
Content creation spend = £5,000
Social advertising spend = £2,000
Total costs = £3,000 + £5,000 + £2,000 = £10,000

Step 5: Social media ROI

By using the ROI equation the ROI of the fashion brand's sales campaign can be calculated as:

(Revenue – costs) / costs = ROI
(£52,500 – £10,000) / £10,000 = 4.25
ROI = 4.2

Social equivalent advertising value

Some brands find it difficult to attribute a value to their marketing goals. For example, perhaps you are a tourist board charged with increasing the visibility of your country as a holiday destination and encouraging people to choose it for their next trip away. As a tourist board you have a website but no means of confirming whether your website visitors have booked a flight or any accommodation – there is no tangible direct monetary allocation you can give to your website visitors. In this instance, another metric other than ROI is useful in order to compare your organic social media activity with other paid for advertising.

SEAV enables you to demonstrate the savings in advertising spend generated by having organic social media activity.

There are three steps in calculating SEAV:

- Step 1: Calculate the average CPC of generating a website visitor. This cost could be calculated using the cost from a single channel or a combination of channels. Typical channels to use for reference would be paid search (PPC), display ads or social media advertising.

- Step 2: Calculate the number of clicks to your website generated by your organic social media channels and any shares within them. You can do this by using unique tracking codes within your organic posts.

- Step 3: Multiply the average CPC from step 1 with the number of clicks from step 2 to calculate the advertising spend saved by using organic social media. This is your SEAV.

The example below shows how to calculate SEAV for a tourist board.

SEAV CALCULATION FOR A TOURIST BOARD

Step 1

The tourist board has generated 25,000 visitors to its website in the last month from organic social posts. It usually pays an average of £0.56 for each visit from PPC.

Average CPC = £0.56

Step 2

Total number of clicks to website:

25,000

Step 3

Savings in paid advertising spend or SEAV:

£0.56 × 25,00 = £14,000

Measuring social media activity in this way can increase its recognition with the C-suite and provide support for additional investment. In reality, just as SEO leads are stronger than PPC leads, a web visit from an organic social post is more likely to convert to a sale than those from paid advertising.

Net promoter score

Your NPS is an important indicator of the strength of your brand and its value to your audience as it demonstrates how likely someone is to recommend you. Brands with a high NPS score are able to build a loyal customer base and use them to support referral marketing campaigns. Knowing your NPS score, relative to your market sector, will give an indication of the relative strength of your brand and whether you need to work on improving it. If you have a strong NPS score you can confidently implement a referral strategy. Measuring changes to your NPS score over time will provide insight into the current strength of your brand.

How to measure NPS

NPS is a score between −100 and +100. You can calculate your score by surveying your customers and asking them on a scale of 0–10 how likely they would be to recommend you to a friend. Each score falls into one of the following categories:

- Scores of 0–6 are classified as Detractors – people who are likely to share negative experiences of your brand with others.

- Scores of 7 and 8 are classified as Passives – these people have no strong feelings about your brand and are unlikely to discuss you with others.
- Scores of 9 and 10 are classified as Promoters – these people are likely to share positive experiences of your brand with others.

The NPS score is calculated by dividing the percentage of Promoters by the percentage of Detractors. The Passives are not included in the calculation.

The examples below show how a negative and positive NPS score is possible.

NPS SCORE CALCULATION FOR AN ONLINE FASHION BRAND

A fashion brand has an ecommerce site and at the end of the sales process the customer is asked to give a score between 0 and 10 on how likely they are to recommend the retailer to a friend. In the last month 520 customers responded with the following results:

TABLE 7.2   Calculating a positive NPS score

Customer response	Number of responders	Percentage of responders
Detractors (score 0–6)	110	21%
Passives (score 7 or 8)	186	36%
Promoters (score 9 or 10)	224	43%
Total	520	100%

The overall NPS score can be calculated using the following equation:

Percentage of Promoters – percentage of Detractors = NPS score

43 per cent – 21 per cent = 22 per cent

The NPS score for this brand is therefore +22. It has a high proportion of Promoters in the make-up of its score and should look for ways to facilitate the sharing of their experience in social media. At the same time, the brand should look for ways to identify and address the issues that concern the detractors.

NPS SCORE CALCULATION FOR A HOTEL BOOKING SITE

Once a visitor has made a hotel reservation using this site, they are asked via a pop-up box to give a score between 0 and 10 on how likely they are to recommend the site to a friend. In the last two months they have seen the following results:

TABLE 7.3   Calculating a negative NPS score

	Customer response	Number of responders	Percentage of responders
Month 1	Detractors (score 0–6)	86	37%
	Passives (score 7 or 8)	120	52%
	Promoters (score 9 or 10)	24	10%
	Total	230	100%
Month 2	Detractors (score 0–6)	55	21%
	Passives (score 7 or 8)	186	73%
	Promoters (score 9 or 10)	15	6%
	Total	256	100%

The overall NPS score can be calculated using the following equation:

Percentage of Promoters – Percentage of Detractors = NPS score

In month 1 the score is therefore:

10 per cent – 37 per cent = –27 per cent, giving an NPS score of –27

In month 2 the score is therefore:

6 per cent – 21 per cent = –15 per cent, giving an NPS score of –15

Looking at the detail of the score changes over time shows that, although there is an improvement in the NPS score, it is driven by reducing Detractors rather than increasing Promoters. In this instance the hotel site should continue to focus on ways to improve its performance before embarking on a referral strategy in social media.

Benchmarking your NPS score

Once you have calculated your NPS score it is a good idea to benchmark it against other brands in your sector, as there is a great variation in score depending on the type of business you have. For example, consumers are much more likely to give retailers higher scores than internet service providers, and therefore the benchmark will give you a relevant way of assessing your own score. Every year NICE Satmetrix, the co-developers of the NPS methodology, produce an NPS benchmarking report that details how different sector scores compare (NICE Satmetrix, 2018).

INTERVIEW
Christophe Folschette, Partner and founder, Talkwalker

Background

Talkwalker provides companies with an easy-to-use platform to protect, measure and promote their brands worldwide across all communication channels. Using their AI-powered social media analytics platform, they turn big data into actionable insights, to enable brand monitoring, brand protection and brand promotion. Folschette is responsible for building awareness of Talkwalker on a global scale, and encouraging more businesses to embrace the opportunities that its social listening platform can give them. They currently have over 2,000 global clients across a wide range of industries and sectors including Duracell, Ogilvy, Hong Kong Airlines and AccorHotels.

How do you measure social media impact?

Ultimately, measuring your social media impact is based on your goal. Forget vanity metrics. These are the numbers that look nice, but are pretty fluffy, and aren't directly related to impact. Numbers like reach and engagement. Yes, they're useful in some respect, to understand how exactly a particular tweet or campaign did, but on a broad scale, they're not important to your CMO. Instead, look to tie your results back to your business impact metrics – the numbers that matter to your board. They're often related to your bottom line, like your sales or profit. These are the numbers that will make or break your business. Your overall marketing strategy, and indeed business strategy, should drive these numbers.

What do you think are the most important social media KPIs now – and will they change over the next few years?

I'm glad to say that people are moving away from the vanity metrics, and moving towards a data mature strategy that focuses their marketing strategy on the business impact metrics.

I think in the future we'll see brands mature further, with less siloed thinking. So, there won't be department strategies with individual measurements, but democratized strategies that align across the whole business to drive complete cross-company impact metrics.

What advice would you give on social media insights and measurement to a large global brand?

Think small. It's easy to look too broadly at your brand, and forget the individual aspect. With social data, you can look at the niche markets, the different demographics, the localized impact, and understand how consumers interact with you at various levels. This can open up new opportunities, new marketplaces, even new campaign ideas.

And to a small business?

Think big. The power of social media is that any brand has the opportunity to create global impact. Don't underestimate your capabilities, but take a full perspective of your audience, your global competitors, your marketplace, and aim big.

And to a B2C brand?

Be part of your consumer conversation. People are now expecting better brand interaction and transparency, so open yourself up to your consumers and be part of your social communities. You can't be aloof online, so find the message you want to promote and be the voice that promotes it.

And to a B2B brand?

Don't forget that business clients are real people too. All too often I see B2B messaging and social strategies with messaging that is dry and dull. The new generation of B2B successes, are the businesses that understand that their audience is human too, and are creating emotional, impactful marketing that targets them as individuals, not faceless numbers.

References

Fitzgerald, D (2019) Director of Communications, Marketing and Student Recruitment, University of Gloucestershire [Interview] (7 January)

Folschette, C (2019) Partner and founder, Talkwalker [Interview] (15 February)

Google (2018) Google Analytics social media. https://analytics.google.com/analytics (archived at https://perma.cc/HPJ2-2FEW)

NICE Satmetrix (2018) *NICE Satmetrix 2018 Consumer Net Promoter Benchmark Study*. http://info.nice.com/rs/338-EJP-431/images/NICE-Satmetrix-infographic-2018-b2c-nps-benchmarks-050418.pdf (archived at https://perma.cc/A6BG-J2Q8)

Talkwalker (2019) [Interview] (February)

8

Customer or celebrity?

Identifying and attracting the right influencers to advocate for your brand

This chapter explores how to identify and attract the right influencers to advocate for your brand. Case studies and examples are used to demonstrate how celebrities, experts, employees, fans and customers can be deployed for different influencer objectives and at various stages of the customer journey.

The importance of influencer marketing

Social media is a unique marketing opportunity, in part because of its ability to connect individuals to each other and to brands in a multitude of different interest driven communities. A mum of two young children who works in IT and loves to run could be a member of many different groups on social media, follow a range of brands and influencers, and have a diverse network of relationships with friends, school mums, work colleagues and family. The strength of the relationships in each of these communities will vary, but in each there is the ability for the mum to be an influencer and influence others in her networks, or to be influenced by others on what to buy, where to go, what to do and even how to think.

The influencer Sophie Radcliffe describes influencer marketing as 'a three-way relationship, between the brand, influencer and their community, built on trust' (Radcliffe, 2019). What is important here is trust, as without it there is no meaningful relationship or opportunity for influence.

What is an influencer?

An influencer is an individual who has built up an established credibility in social media, usually in a specific business area. They are able to persuade their following to try or buy different experiences or brands because of their authenticity and reach. Brands are attracted to working with influencers as they enable them to reach new audiences via a trusted third party.

Influencer marketing is particularly effective in reaching audiences who ad block or are hard to reach through traditional channels. For example, eMarketer report that in 2018, 43 per cent of UK internet users ages 18 to 24 used an ad blocker (Fisher, 2018). At the same time research showed that 61 per cent of consumers aged 18 to 34 have at some point been swayed in their decision-making by digital influencers (Influence Intelligence & Econsultancy, 2018). Even though influencer campaigns are ads, and feature the #ad to demonstrate this fact, influencers' social posts circumnavigate ad blocking tools as followers are actively seeking out the content the influencers share.

Influencer marketing is also particularly useful in helping brands reach new audiences or markets. The recommendations of the influencers act as an introduction, which can change their community's impression of a brand or make them aware of the brand for the first time. This association enables the brand to immediately gain access to large numbers of potential consumers.

In influencer marketing, different types of influencers are identified based on the scale of their reach and level of impact.

Niche influencers

These influencers are defined not by the size of their following, but rather by the narrow interest area or industry segment that they have an influence on. These influencers are associated with a specific industry segment or a small area within an industry segment. For example, Karina Garcia is a slime influencer who has more than eight million followers on YouTube and is famous for her recipes for bubble wrap slime and glitter slime (Wood, 2018). If Karina were to use your brand of glitter, contact lens solution or bubble wrap she could have a dramatic influence on your brand awareness and sales.

Micro influencers

These influencers have the smallest communities, typically fewer than 100,000 followers, but can have a very high impact on those communities because of the very focused and authentic content they share about mutually interesting issues and experiences. Micro influencers are selected because their audiences are a strong match for the brand's target audience, and because they have a genuine love of or interest in the brand. Multiple micro influencers are used at any one time to increase the collective reach and impact. Since 2018 they have become the most popular influencer choice for brands to work with, and 61 per cent of consumers say they produce the most relatable content (Influence Intelligence & Econsultancy, 2018).

Mid-tier influencers

Typically, these influencers will have a community of between 100,000 and 1 million, and although their reach is not as high as that achieved by top-tier influencers their engagement rates are generally higher. Mid-tier influencers tend to have a particular focus for their community. @challengesophie is a good example of a mid-tier influencer. She has over 100,000 followers across her Instagram, Twitter and YouTube channels, all focused on the area of adventure sports.

Top-tier influencers

These influencers are generally celebrities, for example Kim Kardashian, or have become celebrities because of the impact of their influencing, for example Zoella. They usually have over 1 million followers who will follow them for a range of reasons. They tend to have the largest reach but the lowest engagement rates of all the different types of influencers.

Authoritative influencers

These influencers are experts in their field of influence. They could be journalists, scientists, technologists, or from another field of expertise, but they are recognized in the industry sector as thought leaders and opinion formers. In the same way as niche influencers, they are defined by their area of influence rather than by the size of their community. Some authoritative influencers can be forums or websites such as moneysupermarket.com or Mumsnet. Mumsnet is particularly interesting as it offers brands the opportunity to build micro-influencer partnerships via the platform, as shown in the Dreams case study appearing later in this chapter. Here Amie Shearer talks about the power of influencers and Mumsnet.

INTERVIEW
Amie Shearer, Head of Influencer Marketing, Mumsnet

Background

Mumsnet was started in 2000 by Justine Roberts and is the UK's biggest website for parents, with around 14 million users per month. Best known as a website and discussion forum where users share advice and information on parenting and other topics, it is proudly 'by parents for parents' and is highly trusted by this key demographic. A leader in utilizing influencer marketing, Mumsnet has its own marketing division where it partners with brands who want to connect with and understand its community.

Shearer manages Mumsnet's network of 10,000+ influencers and develops research, brand awareness, lead generation and sales campaigns utilizing the members' blogs, vlogs and social channels. Immersed in optimizing influencer marketing, Shearer brings a wealth of experience in using influencers for research, ideation, endorsement, awareness and sales from working with brands such as O2, Danone, Disney and P&G.

What is special about the Mumsnet community?

Mumsnet is a highly trusted space. Trust is very important, so we make sure that we are completely transparent with our community, our influencers and the brands we work with. We have a good relationship with the Advertising Standards Authority, regularly checking campaigns with them on their hotline and running training with the influencers to make sure that they understand the advertising guidelines. A lot of our influencers are actually Mumsnet users; for example, Mother Pukka has had open conversations on the boards in the past about what it is like being an influencer.

Mumsnet believes in freedom of speech. The forum is anonymous, so people can talk freely on the board in a way they may not be able to do in real life. We have threads about partner abuse, miscarriage and other areas that make the anonymous element really important.

Mumsnet is first and foremost a community of users, and our priority is to let their conversations flow, although we do have a set of guidelines that are used to moderate the site. Users are supportive of this approach and they are quick to report trolls and other rule-breaking behaviour.

What is important when choosing an influencer?

The most important factor is that the influencer and their followers are a very good match to the brand and the project. If they are not, their content won't feel authentic or honest and will not work, no matter how high their reach is. Mumsnet have a database of influencers and can select a long list for consideration based on their age, location, the brands they follow, the performance of their channels in terms of engagements, reach etc, and many other factors.

Mumsnet also give every influencer a professionalism score based how they work with brands and if they are improving or in decline.

The second criterion ensures the influencer is strong in social media in the area you need your campaign to work. For example, if the campaign is working to improve SEO, long form blog content is more likely to achieve that goal than tweets and Instagram posts. But whatever the campaign objectives, it's important to check the quality and performance of the influencer's relevant channels and content, to make sure they'll be able to achieve your goals and help you access your desired target audience.

Sometimes influencers will be very specialized; for instance, they are very good at creating Instagram stories but not posts, so it is important to review their previous content to confirm their strengths match the brief requirements.

Finally, we like to provide the client with a shortlist of influencers appropriate to their brand/product and campaign. They then choose from that shortlist who the final influencers are they'll work with, just as they would any other creative or media buy.

How much freedom should an influencer have in representing a brand?

It's a balance. You want the influencer to be themselves, that is why you chose them. However, the campaign needs to meet the overall objectives. We share the important factors such as key messaging, the purpose of the campaign, product information, the hashtags, timelines or any brand mandatories in a brief, as it is a good way to make sure all parties are clear on what needs to be done. You don't want an influencer to be confused as to whether a campaign is about brand awareness or clicks through to sales, or to photograph the brand's product next to its competitor's.

How do you measure the success of an influencer campaign?

Influencer marketing is different from other types of marketing activity because it is a hybrid of media buying and creative content creation. To make it work you need to be able to track and measure the performance of the media buy as well as understand that the creativity in the content has a value in itself. The tone of voice, filming style, personality of the influencer etc has an inherent value, otherwise you wouldn't have chosen the influencer and their activity wouldn't work for the brand.

To measure the impact of any campaign, Mumsnet uses its data platform, which collates the pixel data from blogs, vlogs, Google Analytics, etc. For tools such as Instagram Stories, which haven't opened an application programming interface (API) yet (at the time of writing), screen grabs and more manual evidence is used to demonstrate reach and engagement.

How important are micro influencers?

Many agencies and brands are worried about working with mini-micro influencers, those with less than 100,000 followers, because they imagine that working with two to three influencers on a campaign can be hard work.

Admittedly, there are some challenges, but the benefits far outweigh them especially on projects where there is a long customer journey.

The industry average engagement rate for influencers is between 2.5 per cent and 3 per cent, and typically, as their number of followers increases over the 100,000 mark, their engagement rate drops. Mini-micro influencers have engagement rates upwards of 5 per cent. They also have much higher conversion rates to sale because their followers know them better and have a closer relationship with them.

In an ideal world, combine a big-name influencer at the start of a campaign to maximize reach and awareness of the overall campaign message, and follow up with mini-micro influencers to persuade and reinforce the message.

(Source: Shearer, 2019)

Key opinion leaders

These influencers tend to have large volumes of followers and can often be celebrities. They are a sub-set of top-tier influencers but are known to their community for being a genuine connoisseur of a particular topic, and as such their opinions on this topic are respected by their followers. Unlike other influencers, social media may not be their main channel of communication but when they recommend or endorse it is taken seriously by their community. Key opinion leaders (KOLs) differ from authoritative influencers because their expertise or talent may not be from the topic area they endorse. They are, however, known to be passionate about and interested in that topic.

In China, KOLs, and wanghongs are an essential part of any marketing strategy and a whole industry of KOL academies operates to incubate the careers of aspiring KOLs. In Chapter 10 Clay discusses the next level of KOLs – computer generated imagery (CGI) influencers. These virtual influencers, such as Lil Miquela (Joo, 2019) are especially popular with luxury brands, and although they play with the boundaries of authenticity they do 'offer brands more control… you can create the perfect influencer' (Clay, 2019).

Figure 8.1 shows the relative reach of different types of influencer and the level of fit their audience is likely to have with your brand. The closer the match between a brand's audience and an influencer's community, the higher the engagement rate will be when the influencer posts on behalf of that brand, and the larger the size of the community, the bigger the reach will be.

FIGURE 8.1   The relative size and brand fit of influencer communities

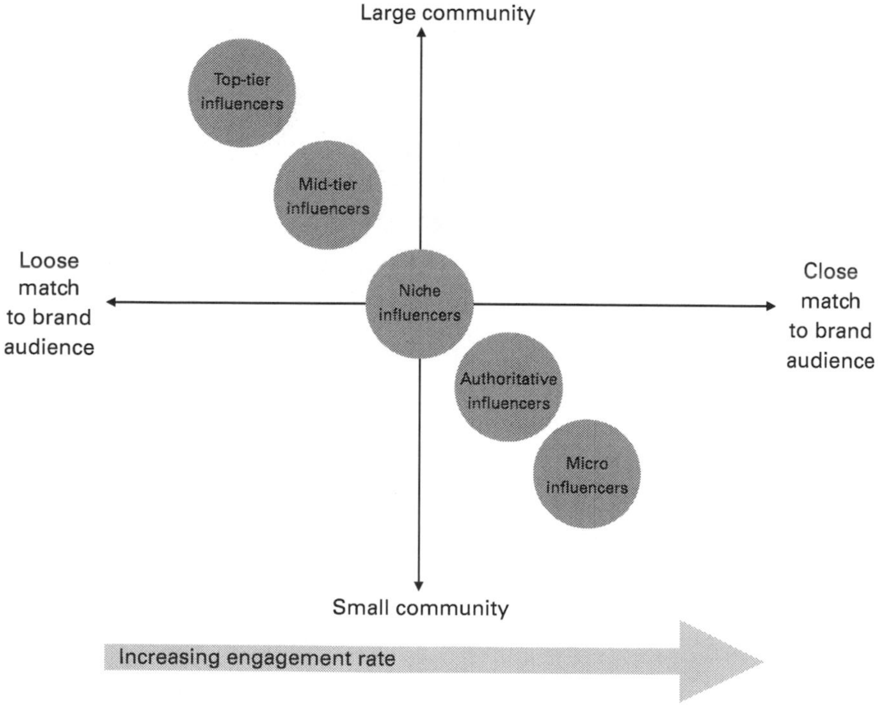

Therefore, when planning an influencer campaign brands will flex the proportions of different types of influencers to suit their objectives. Brand awareness campaigns are more likely to use top-tier influencers while campaigns that focus on conversion and sales are more likely to use mid-tier influencers. Micro influencers are particularly useful for building long-term relationships with brands and collaborating on unique content creation.

Customers as influencers

In Edelman's customer decision journey, discussed in Chapter 2, successful brands are able to build strong bonded relationships with their customers though facilitating enjoyable experiences and encouraging advocacy. Traditional influencer marketing focuses on paid-for relationships between

FIGURE 8.2   The relative size and brand fit of employees, customers and brand communities as influencers

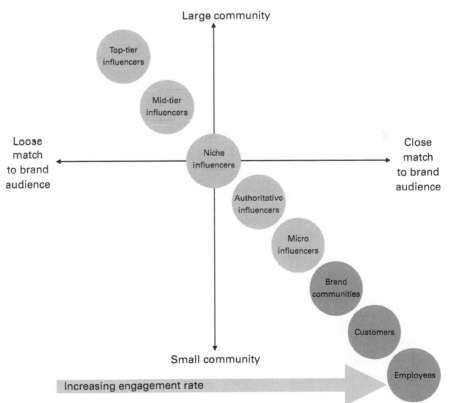

professional influencers and brands. However, it is just as important for brands to also consider their own communities, customers and employees as strong and important influencers.

If employees, customers and brand communities are added to the chart above, they are seen to be even more influential than paid-for influencers. This is because, although their individual reach is small, the people in their communities/network are likely to know them personally and well. Trust is therefore higher, relevancy is improved and engagement rates and level of influence are increased. In addition, the total reach possible, when the collective reach is combined, can be quite significant by considering these influencers as specific groups of either employees, customers or communities, in an influencer strategy deployment.

Core influencer goals

There are many different reasons why brands use influencers, but one of the most compelling reasons is probably because they can have a direct and positive effect on sales, as shown by research by YouGov for Social Media Week (Figure 8.3).

FIGURE 8.3   The selling power of influencers

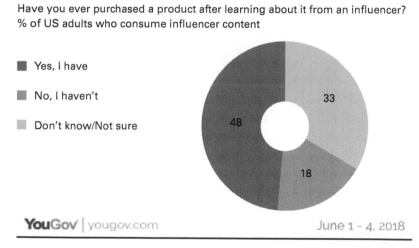

Selling power of influencers
Have you ever purchased a product after learning about it from an influencer?
% of US adults who consume influencer content

- Yes, I have
- No, I haven't
- Don't know/Not sure

33

48

18

YouGov | yougov.com   June 1 - 4, 2018

SOURCE Reproduced with kind permission of Social Media Week (2018)

In addition to sales, influencers are able to build brand awareness through their significant reach, generate unique and compelling brand content to help brands build engaged communities, and add value to the brand experience by providing unique interactions with the brand. Influencers can also be used to improve SEO through link building, improve brand sentiment or help change brand perceptions, and generate reviews to increase brand trust. When integrated into a wider marketing strategy, employees and customers also offer important influencer opportunities. The following case study for Dreams Beds demonstrates how they used influencers for a range of purposes in an integrated strategic approach across research, product ideation and co-creation, and marketing for sales.

CASE STUDY DREAMS
*Using influencers and Mumsnet users to co-create new products –
the Mumsnet Kindred and Spirit mattresses*

Background

Dreams Beds are the UK's most recommended bed retailer. In 2018 they partnered with Mumsnet to design, build and market mattresses in collaboration with parents. Knowing that parents often find it hard to get a good night's sleep, Dreams wanted to understand their problems and create the perfect mattress to help. A mattress created 'by parents for parents'.

The project had four parts running concurrently: research, ideation and co-creation, product testing, and influencer marketing.

Research

Families come in lots of shapes and sizes, and sleep in many different ways. Whether you are a single parent, co-sleepers, a family of one or six, a couple who never let the kids in bed or someone whose children join them in the middle of the night, all of these will affect your sleep as much as the firmness of your mattress. Quantitative research was conducted using surveys on the Mumsnet site to understand the range of family sleeping habits, mattress price points and buying habits, and the overall demographics of the parent mattress market.

In addition, Mumsnet looked at the way parents made decisions about buying a new mattress, the customer journey, who influenced that decision and the channels brands used to reach them.

Ideation and co-creation

Using the research insights Mumsnet and Dreams selected groups of parents and influencers to take part in the ideation and co-creation of the new mattresses.

The parents were Mumsnet users, selected to represent the range of parents found in the research. They included parents from different family sizes, with children from babies to teenagers, with one to five children and different sleeping habits and disposable incomes.

For the social media influencers we also took into consideration their size and the engagement levels of their followers, the social channels that they used and the level of interaction they displayed on the Mumsnet forum.

On the ideation day the parents and influencers were invited to the Dreams factory. In a focus group they discussed all aspects of sleep, what they looked for in a mattress, allergy considerations, firmness levels, and their understanding of the different types of mattresses from foam to springs. The group were given samples of all the materials and information on their benefits and areas of consideration. For example, memory foam isn't recommended for co-sleeping as babies cannot move themselves out of a pocket that might be made between the parents and can overheat. None of the parents knew this, and one of the parents in the group had a memory foam mattress and was a co-sleeper.

Dreams realized there were lots of things that parents didn't know and the research groups realized there were lots of considerations needed to build the perfect mattress.

By mixing fillers and structures, different mattresses were identified and the factory went off to build the prototypes for the groups to test. These included different price point versions, firm versus softer and a hypoallergenic version.

While the test mattresses were being built the group shared their thoughts on other mattress brands they knew and how they engaged with those brands. Facebook and banner advertising played a big part in the competitor' marketing strategies.

In addition, the group went into a bed store. This highlighted several pain points in the customer journey, such as the parents being worried about the kids jumping on the beds and making them dirty when trying out a mattress. Dreams wanted potential customers to try the beds, so realized that they needed more family friendly signage in store to promote this behaviour.

Product testing

When the test mattresses had been built, each member from the focus group received their own mattress to test and review, providing feedback via a survey and Mumsnet forum thread.

Influencer marketing

The strategy for this campaign is really clever because the marketing is embedded in every aspect and runs concurrently with the research, ideation and co-creation, product testing, launch and ongoing sales activity.

The research groups themselves were selected not only because they were parents but also because of their ability to influence, either as a Mumsnet user or a social influencer. On the research day, the social media influencers released teaser stories using hashtags that would be used when the new products were launched in store.

A month later the new mattresses were launched to the trade (Dreams Beds, 2019) and the Mumsnet/Dreams partnership to create a family friendly mattress was promoted by the social media influencers.

When the mattresses were ready to be launched to the public, each member of the research group received a mattress to try. The social media influencers created blogs and vlogs, going live about the family friendly mattress and the efforts that Dreams had made to make sure it was perfect for parents.

Content was seeded on Instagram, Twitter, Facebook and Mumsnet, and the Mumsnet users from the research group created a thread on the forum about the co-creation day, how much they enjoyed it, and the facts and information they learned about (such as the alert about memory foam and babies).

The content in the thread has an indefinite lifespan – every new generation of parents will need to know what to consider when buying a family friendly mattress.

Results

The project has been a phenomenal success, with all the sales targets being beaten, with 6,500 mattresses sold in the first year of activity. The holistic influencer strategy has resulted in some real wins for Dreams:

- The level of research and co-creation has resulted in products parents really want at a price they are prepared to pay.

- The mattresses passed Which? testing and won the Which? badge.

- The influencer involvement and sharing has increased trust in Dreams as a brand.

- The Mumsnet name on the mattresses further increases parent trust.

- The Mumsnet content page and thread continue to drive strong SEO and with strong click-throughs to purchase driving high levels of sales.

- The project won The Drum's Social Buzz Award for best use of a group/community 2018.

Overall there has been a three-way influencer effect, with users influencing by talking on the forum, social influencers driving reach and persuading their followers, and the Mumsnet brand endorsing the quality and suitability of the product itself.

(Source: Shearer, 2019)

Using influencers to build a brand presence

Influencer marketing strategies vary depending on the specific goals you wish to achieve but essentially, they fall into two areas – supporting your brand presence on social or, driving activity for campaigns.

It has become increasingly difficult to build and sustain a brand presence organically on social media, as the platforms become increasingly monetized, and the algorithms prioritize peer-to-peer engagement over brand-to-community engagement. Including influencers in your strategy can help address this issue but they need to be considered as a long-term relationship rather that a short-term solution, when used for this purpose.

Many types of influencers can be used to support brand building and the amount and proportions used should be budget and objective driven.

Top-tier influencers

Top-tier influencers are particularly useful in driving brand awareness and changing audience perceptions of a brand. Celebrities have a huge reach and, when they are also a KOL, such as George Clooney is for superior coffee and Nespresso, they can be particularly impactful.

Chinese consumers are particularly influenced by celebrities and other influencers, with 78 per cent of their internet users receptive to celebrity recommendations about brands in social media and 63 per cent receptive to micro-influencers and online celebrities (eMarketer, 2018).

For this reason, in China, KOLs are central to establishing brand awareness and maintaining brand engagement, with some, such as the fashion and beauty KOL Kakakoo, having millions of followers and now working as a brand partner with MAC lipsticks (Shea, 2019).

Authoritative influencers

In some market sectors journalist, scientists and experts have an important part to play in establishing brand authority and thought leadership. Automotive brands in the UK may look to building strong relationships with key journalists, such as Quentin Wilson and Peter Campbell, to support credible reputation building (Smith, 2017). Other sectors such as health, financial services, legal and technology are all heavily reliant on authoritative influencers.

Micro and mid-tier influencers

Micro and mid-tier influencers are particularly useful for building a continuous brand presence and creating highly engaged communities. These influencers should be selected because of their close alignment to your core target audiences and their relevance to the content pillars (as discussed in Chapter 5) that are central to your overall social media strategy. This will mean that, although different influencers are selected for each content pillar and audience, they will still be engaging with relevant communities and supporting your brand stories around the consistent themes you have identified as important.

Because the influencers and their communities are interested in the same topics as your brand, you can enable the influencer to collaborate on campaign ideas, generate content freely, and engage with their community as they decide.

A great example of this is Chivas Regal, who have built a number of long-term influencer relationships including the Instagrammer @theamateurmixologist (2019), and the YouTuber Dave Erasmus (2019). According to Warren Dell, Senior Brand Manager at Chivas Regal, the brand wants to 'immerse ourselves in the culture that surrounds our target audiences, and influencers enable us to bridge that gap' (Dell, 2019).

@theamateurmixologist helps Chivas Regal reach younger, and more female, audiences as the influencer uses Chivas18 to create authentic and compelling content around new cocktail creations. Dave Erasmus focuses on social impact and was therefore commissioned to partner the brand on their Chivas Venture project, which gives away $1 million each year to social entrepreneurs. Both examples are highly targeted at different Chivas Regal audiences, both enable the influencer to create their own content in their own way, both are still delivering authentic, engaging content about the core pillars within the Chivas Regal wider marketing strategy. Furthermore, because the brand is building a partnership with each influencer, the engagement of their community with Chivas Regal should continue to improve as an ongoing support to increasing and maintaining the brand's presence on social media. Ultimately, these long-term influencers could become true brand ambassadors for Chivas Regal (Dell, 2019).

In the following interview, Sophie Radcliffe, a mid-tier influencer, shares her thoughts from the influencer perspective.

INTERVIEW
Sophie Radcliffe, adventure athlete, influencer

Background

After a successful career in sales and marketing, Radcliffe began blogging about the adventures and challenges she took part in her spare time before quitting her job to follow her dreams (@challengesophie, www.challengesophie.com (archived at https://perma.cc/H5TD-B6QY)). Inspired by her personality and achievements, her following grew. An influencer, Radcliffe connects with her community on Instagram and Twitter and has partnered brands including Oakley, Adidas, GoPro and Special K. Radcliffe is also the founder of Trailblazers, a youth empowerment project.

What is influencer marketing?

Influencer marketing is a three-way conversation based on trust between the brand, an influencer and their community.

Social media is about inspiring people. Influencer marketing inspires people to change their minds about their existing habits. Because influencers aren't celebrities, they are real people who engage with their following, they make inspiration feel more accessible.

An influencer develops their own individual voice and lends their voice to things they are passionate about. In my case, I am passionate about my 6Cs and only lend my voice to them. My 6Cs are cause, champion, change, climate, collaborate and community.

What inspires you to be an influencer?

I've always had an ambition to do something meaningful with my life and as soon as I started building a community and platform, I knew I wanted to use my voice as a force for positive change in the world. I love building my own business and I love brand building and meeting and engaging with lots of people. Being an influencer enables me to do this while doing the thing I am passionate about – personal growth, championing the power of adventure sports, and building your own resilience and confidence. I believe that confidence can be nurtured – my community sees my vulnerability and how I overcome my struggles to meet each challenge. Hopefully, I help people break down barriers, knowing it is ok to be scared – that's normal, you can still do what you are passionate about.

Why does influencer marketing work?

Brands want their advertising to stand out from their competitors and brand advertising is focused on storytelling. When brands create adverts with influencers, they are creating real stories with real people and sharing these with communities that resonate and have a deep level of trust with the influencer. This is why influencer marketing works; it's authentic, creative and meaningful storytelling content that's shared with a community where there is already trust. It's like asking a friend for a recommendation for something you want to buy. People trust influencers they follow and like in the same way they trust a friend.

Do you have any tips for brands wanting to work with influencers?

There are five things brands really need to focus on when working with influencers:

1   **Community comes first:** Although influencers want to be paid, influencing is their job. Their community comes first. This means that any brand partnership has to fit with the influencer's community, values and ethos to be credible and authentic.

2   **Influencers aren't sales teams:** The influencer's personal integrity is at stake when they agree to work with a brand. This means that they may not work with certain brands for ethical reasons or won't want to be too salesy. For example, many influencers will not plug discount codes or quote sales messages.

3   **Long-term commercial value and integrity are important:** As the industry matures, influencers are recognizing that a single post payment model doesn't work in the long term. For example, making a single post as part of a car brand campaign may be profitable in the short term, but it precludes the influencer from forging a long-term partnership with another car brand in the future without sacrificing their personal integrity.

4   **The influencer is part of their community:** Competitions, free samples, insider information and other exclusives can be an important part of any influencer partnership as they enable the influencer to give something back to their community as well.

5   **Creative freedom is paramount:** The amount of creative freedom an influencer is given can really affect the price a brand pays and the performance of the activity. Influencers are not a media buy, it is their personality and

creativity that connects with their community. Clear briefs and contracts are really useful in setting the parameters and enabling the influencer to experiment and play within them.

What is your typical day like? Are you posting and commenting 24/7?

Time management and well-being are as important to influencers as in any other job. It is especially important to be aware of the amount of screen time in any day, so splitting the day into segments allows time for community management, content creation, brand partnership building, blog writing, event preparation, trip planning, client management and personal fitness, mental health and well-being.

What is next for influencer marketing?

Brands are starting to see the value of building long-term partnerships with influencers. This deeper commitment is a sign of the industry maturing and is important for many reasons including:

- Having a limited number of brands that an influencer works with increases their credibility and builds up authenticity in their support of those brands.
- Long-term relationships mean the brand and influencer invest in a deeper understanding of each other. Mutual support builds increased creativity and improved campaign performance.

(Source: Radcliffe, 2019)

Brand communities

Many brands have built up large communities on their own social platforms, which if managed effectively can become important sources of influence and engagement. Entertainment brands are particularly good at supporting brand communities and fandoms by providing exclusive access to stars, backstage footage and insider information to keep their fans talking and sharing content about the brand. As Williams discusses in her interview in Chapter 5, 'fans are looking for more personal feeling ways to make connections with the shows they love and we give them the space to be able to do that' (Williams, 2019).

Customers

For some sectors and brands, customers have become an essential part of their influencer marketing strategy. Marketing in the travel sector, for example, is dominated by user-generated content (UGC) as potential travellers are inspired by friends' travels on Instagram and Facebook, and check previous visitor reviews and sites such as trip advisor to confirm the quality before they book. This UGC acts as a form of social proof that the product or service really is worth buying. If your customers are visibly and consistently recommending your brand they will help to establish confidence and trust as well as a continuous presence in social.

Research by Edelman in 2018 showed that peers have the strongest influence in driving brand advocacy and therefore in supporting an impactful and positive presence for your brand (Figure 8.4).

FIGURE 8.4   Relative increase in the likelihood that each type of spokesperson will drive advocacy (regression analysis); data shown as an index

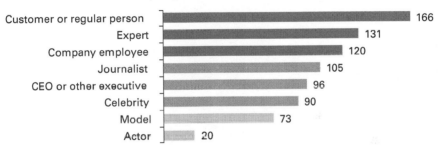

SOURCE Edelman (2018)

Busabout, a UK alternative travel company operating in Europe, the United States, South East Asia and North Africa, uses only UCG in its marketing activity (Whitby, 2018). The brand realized that they had thousands of tagged images and videos in YouTube, Instagram and Facebook, and that their audience loved to share on social media. In fact, 61 per cent of 18- to 34-year-olds want to share beautiful or important holiday experiences online (Whitby, 2018). They therefore decided to build a marketing strategy based on authentic customer experiences with the facilitation and encouragement of UGC at its heart. This strategy helped build and support Busabout's brand presence, reinforcing its honest, practical approach to travel through its customers' eyes.

Employees

In B2B organizations employees are often expected to be explicit and implicit influencers and advocates for their business, most commonly building up their personal LinkedIn network and using it to support commercial sales relationships, as discussed by Sweales in her interview in Chapter 6. Less common are explicit employee influencer strategies in B2B businesses. However, your employees will have a good understanding of your brand and ideally are committed to living your brand values and behaviours. If your employees are proud of what you do and how you behave they can, and should, be encouraged to share news and stories about your brand on their own social media channels. This type of influencer marketing can support employee recruitment and retention, but also underpin the customer service and customer relationship elements of any brand engagement.

Using influencers in campaign delivery

Influencers can also be used tactically to support specific campaigns and KOLs, and micro influencers can be particularly useful in delivering conversion and sales. In platforms with one-click ordering and payment such as WeChat, influencer conversion rates can be particularly effective. This is especially true as the platform also enables influencer related social commerce, by providing a discount to anyone who influences another person to buy by recommending products and services that they go on to buy within the platform. In her interview in Chapter 10, Clay refers to this as the 'WeChat ecosystem' (Clay, 2019), enabling integrated purchases, sharing and influencing without leaving the platform.

Choosing influencers to meet your strategy

There are three key factors to bear in mind when choosing your influencers – how close a match is their community to my target audience, what objectives will they help me meet, and how good a fit are they for my brand?

Community

The rise in popularity of the use of micro influencers is a recognition that your brand relevance will be significantly increased by using multiple micro influencers with communities that closely match your target audience, rather than using celebrities whose audiences can be broad and often less engaged.

Objectives

Influencer marketing requires a different mindset, as many of the benefits your brand will get from working with influencers goes beyond traditional KPIs such as cost per thousand impressions (CPM) and cost per view (CPV). Influencers are great at creating and co-creating content, coming up with innovative ideas to promote your brand and telling emotive and authentic stories. It is therefore really important to decide your objectives before you choose your influencers, and include some of these wider elements if they are important to your strategy.

Brand fit

Research by Zine shows that 75 per cent of influencers put more effort into posts for brands they like (Zine.co, 2019), and this effort will not only pay dividends in terms of the amount of posting and commenting by influencers, it will also affect the authenticity and credibility of the brand–influencer relationship. If one week an influencer is talking about Nike and the next week they love Adidas, their followers will wonder what they really think and how genuine they are. It is therefore really important to ensure your influencers care about your brand and are genuinely interested in what you do and how you do it.

Reviewing influencer profiles

Many influencers work with influencer marketing agencies and can provide detailed profiles of their communities across each of their social platforms. These profiles are a great way for brands to assess an initial fit. However, to make the final selection you should personally review their content and activity, and engage with the influencer to assess their commitment and suitability to working with your brand. A good starting point for this will be to look at each influencer's media kit. The excerpt in Figure 8.5 is a typical example of a section from an influencer profile included as part of their media kit and that might be used at the first stage of selection by a brand. The full media kit example can be seen at www.koganpage.com/sms.

FIGURE 8.5   An excerpt from the digital media kit offered to influencers by ZINE magazine

REACH INSIGHTS

Reach				
46 %	45.3 %	N/A	46.7 %	2 %
193,153	190,315	N/A	195,991	8,268
Impressions				
58.9 %	60.1 %	N/A	57.7 %	2.1 %
247,468	252,668	N/A	242,269	8,880
Engagement				Replies
3.9 %	4.9 %	N/A	3 %	3
16,590	20,465	N/A	12,714	

SOURCE Used with kind permission of Zine.co (archived at https://perma.cc/MGV7-FU8L) (2019)

Measuring influence

Reach and engagement are the most popular measures applied to influencer marketing campaigns, and as for all social media activity ROI remains a challenge for many brands to measure.

What is important is to ensure you are clear about your objectives and assess the value authentic brand building content has on your reputation and brand presence as well as the impact influencers can have on sales.

Fake or real followers?

Influencer marketing is already big business and is projected to be worth up $10 billion by 2022 (Gallagher, 2018), but it is still a relatively loosely regulated and sometimes 'wild west' landscape for brands to navigate. One reason for this is the lack of transparency over fake followers, with 31 per cent of influencers saying they have been 'gifted' fake followers or fake engagements and 45 per cent of influencers saying that they don't get asked by brands who work with them to prove that their followers are genuine (Zine.co, 2019).

As influencer marketing develops, the policing of the industry is becoming more robust and it is expected that tighter controls or proof will be demanded by brands on the real/fake follower issue.

TOP TIPS FOR USING INFLUENCERS

The following tops are useful for every type of influencer project:

- Select influencers with communities that match the characteristics of your own target audience as closely as possible.

- Ensure you influencer genuinely cares about and loves your brand.

- Invest in building a strong relationship with your influencers.

- Trust your influencers to create content and engage with their communities in their own way.

- Invite your influencers to collaborate on future directions and projects for the brand.

- Formalize the relationship with a contract and be clear about the amount of ongoing interaction you expect.

For many brands, using a specialist influencer platform can help identify and support a strong partnership between the brand and the influencer. Caroline Duong discusses her thoughts on this in the following interview.

INTERVIEW
Caroline Duong, Chief Executive Officer, Zine.co
(archived at https://perma.cc/MGV7-FU8L)

Background

Zine.co (archived at https://perma.cc/MGV7-FU8L) is an influencer marketing technology company that provides a complete set of tools for both professional influencers and brands. They exist to connect brands with global influencers who are a true match to their audience profile and therefore will care enough to authentically support the brand. By providing influencers with their own media kit, the influencer gains unique insights into their own effectiveness, which helps them to manage their profile and commercial opportunities.

What are your thoughts on the current state of play in influencer marketing?

Influencer marketing has exploded over the last three years and other markets are starting to catch up with the United States in terms of maturity. Because of the fledgling state of the industry there aren't a whole lot of agreed rules on the state of play. This has led to much discussion in the press about fake followers, lack of transparency between brands and influencers, and misunderstandings over brand–influencer agreements. Despite this, the opportunities for brands, consumers and influencers are really exciting as technology and innovation bring them together in new ways.

In the past, influencer marketing was primarily the responsibility of PR but, as it has moved into the marketing department, the need for accountability and measurability has increased and the areas of customer advocacy, influencer marketing and celebrity endorsement are becoming more distinct from each other and are working more effectively together.

How does your tech platform help brands?

Brands want to connect with customers in an authentic and engaging way, but managing a large influencer portfolio can be very time consuming and it can be hard to find the right influencers for your brand. For this reason, many brands use a limited number of influencers and keep re-using the same ones even if they aren't particularly effective.

We have over 50,000 influencers in our database, so our platform enables brands to select only influencers whose followers match their desired audience profile. In addition, our reach calculation gives brands the confidence that they have both volume and quality. Some campaigns have 50–70 influencers so you can really target the right audience but at scale.

How does your tech platform help influencers?

Influencers really care about their followers and want to be honest with them. We allow the brand to talk directly to the influencers to make sure they are the right fit, can build a relationship, and can work in the most creative way.

We see ourselves as the enabler, making sure everyone understands what has been agreed, and on what terms, and bringing a streamlined process, so they can concentrate on working effectively together.

How does your tech platform help consumers?

When a follower trusts an influencer they really appreciate the inspiration and advice that an influencer shares. The combination of selecting highly targeted influencers, and ensuring they are happy to endorse the products in a campaign, means that the consumer only sees brands that feel relevant and important to that influencer's profile. It feels authentic and real.

What is your top tip for brands thinking about using Influencer marketing?

Sometimes less is more. For example, some influencers might only have 10,000 followers but they are 90 per cent in the UK; another might have 10 times that number but they are all over the world. If you are a UK only brand, less might be more.

(Source: Duong, 2019)

References

@theamateurmixologist (2019) theamateurmixologist. www.instagram.com/theamateurmixologist (archived at https://perma.cc/58ML-UW29)

Clay, R (2019) Head of Influencer Marketing, Matter of Form [Interview] (6 March)

Dell, W (Senior Brand Manger, Chivas Regal) (2019) Understanding the value of influencer marketing, DMA Event, London

Dreams Beds (2019) www.dreams.co.uk/mumsnet-spirit-mattress/p/131-00638-configurable (archived at https://perma.cc/SP3R-QLFW) and www.dreams.co.uk/mumsnet-kindred-mattress/p/131-00639-configurable (archived at https://perma.cc/ZGQ8-ZNDM)

Duong, C (2019) CEO, Zine [Interview] (24 January)

Edelman (2018) 2018 Edelman Earned Brand Global Report, Edelman, New York

eMarketer (2018) www.emarketer.com/Chart/Internet-Users-Select-Countries-Who-Receptive-Select-Social-Media-Brand-Promotion-Tactics-May-2017-of-respondents/220147 (archived at https://perma.cc/44QS-3KFF)

Erasmus, D (2019) Dave Erasmus. www.youtube.com/user/daveerasmus (archived at https://perma.cc/ED8T-SYY8)

Fisher, B (2018) Ad blocking in the UK, 2018. www.emarketer.com/content/ad-blocking-in-the-uk-2018 (archived at https://perma.cc/WY3B-HSTF)

Gallagher, K (2018) www.businessinsider.com/the-influencer-marketing-report-2018-1?r=UK&IR=T (archived at https://perma.cc/4PHL-JWJK)

Influence Intelligence & Econsultancy (2018) Influencer Marketing 2020, Centaur Communications Ltd, London and New York

Joo, M (2019) Top 5 virtual influencers also known as CGI influencers on Instagram. https://popularchips.com/dailies/top-5-virtual-influencers-also-known-as-cgi-influencers-on-instagram/ (archived at https://perma.cc/69J8-U6RW)

Radcliffe, S (2019) @challengesophie [Interview] (26 February)

Shea, S (2019) www.dragonsocial.net/blog/fashion-beauty-influencer-kol-china/ (archived at https://perma.cc/6M7R-JZFL)

Shearer, A (2019) Head of Influencer Marketing, Mumsnet [Interview] (20 March)

Smith, B (2017) www.prmoment.com/blog/the-most-influential-people-in-the-uk-automotive-sector (archived at https://perma.cc/V4YW-KTZK)

Social Media Week (2018) The Influencer Marketing Report, Social Media Week, London

Whitby, P (2018) www.phocuswire.com/Busabout-revs-the-UGC-engine-with-Stackla (archived at https://perma.cc/RG9A-5BXK)

Williams, S (2019) Chief Operating Officer, Social Life [Interview] (5 February)

Wood, M (2018) www.marketplace.org/2018/09/10/tech/meet-woman-whos-making-millions-dollars-slime-videos-youtube (archived at https://perma.cc/2XAG-57FC)

Zine.co (2019) What's Next for Infuencer Marketing? Zine.co (archived at https://perma.cc/MGV7-FU8L) , London

9

Crisis and reputation management for social media

A clear guide for the unpredictable

An essential part of any social media strategy is planning for the unexpected. A brand's reputation can be significantly improved or harmed in social media, and this chapter includes key learnings from examples of success and failure. Interviews with social media crisis consultants on their planning and reputational management recommendations complement real examples to provide practical insights and advice.

How social media has changed reputation management

The immediacy and accessibility of social media has democratized mass communication, enabling organizations to engage directly with their stakeholders and interact with them in a cost-effective, timely and relevant manner.

Now, far from being simply an 'extra channel' to add to the marketing toolkit accessed via the 'digital manager', social media has grown rapidly into an amalgamation of all marketing channels where the role distinctions imposed by traditional marketing disciplines have blurred, demanding a more agile and integrated approach from organizations in managing content and information of all kinds.

In terms of reputation management, an increasing appreciation of the sheer reach of social media has seen quite dramatic changes in job functions, with online reputation management becoming a key activity. The role of PR for example, which focuses on building positive relationships with business or brand stakeholders, has been unshackled from the highly selective gate-keepers of public opinion in the form of the traditional news media and now has access to a multiverse of social media channels. Each of these channels branches out exponentially across all topics, cultures and online communities, enabling not only direct engagement with key audiences, but also the potential for super-fast and quantifiable word-of-mouth endorsements. In less than a decade, the PR's world has burst open to reveal unlimited creative opportunity, the holy grail of viral memes and masterminding the next way to 'break the internet' in a bid to build brands and reputations.

Social media, within which the official news media very comfortably sits and operates – many as re-launched web-based multimedia platforms – has disrupted the nature of information spread. The types of stories that constitute 'news' (ie something that someone, somewhere, doesn't want anyone else to know) are likely to originate online and be read, rehashed and shared by both news and social media propagators alike.

Interestingly, whilst social media may have eroded press *exclusivity* when it comes to mass communications, it has more than compensated by causing an unprecedented upsurge in public confidence in them as *trustworthy* sources. A YouGov survey on behalf of Local Media Works (2018) revealed the local newspapers were three times more trusted than social media as sources of local information. Seventy-four per cent of respondents trusted information in their local newspaper, both online and print (up from 58 per cent from a similar 2014 survey), whilst only 22 per cent of them invested the same trust in social media.

But that doesn't mean the power to influence is correspondingly affected. You may trust a news source and not believe something it reveals owing to your personal viewpoint. Equally, an unregulated source may have the power to influence because of a certain way it resonates with your belief system. And the press are perfectly entitled to recount what is being said on social media as 'legitimate' rumour, further muddying the waters.

For an example of this, look at how both entities covered the disappearance of the 3-year-old British girl Madeleine McCann in 2007. A wide range of social media platforms were (and still are) abuzz with claims, counter-claims and conspiracy theories that survive and propagate despite the people making the comments typically being unqualified to do so; they weren't there at the time, they have no first hand knowledge of the evidence and absolutely no experience of investigative work. Meanwhile, the real experts – Scotland Yard, CEOPs, Interpol, etc – who are arguably global leaders in this field seem to have faded into the background.

So perception appears to hold sway over professionalism. Leonardo De Vinci and the late Republican political strategist Lee Attwater expressed the same understanding of this aspect of the human condition across half a millennium with the former stating 'we base our knowledge on our perceptions' and the latter 'perception is reality.'

In effect, it's what people think that counts. And that means reputations that have been built over decades can often, inadvertently or maliciously, be brought down in a moment.

Understanding reputation management

Reputation is 'the beliefs or opinions that are generally held about someone or something' and 'a widespread belief that someone or something has a particular characteristic' (Oxford Dictionaries, 2019). Therefore, reputation management is shaping what your different stakeholders think of you, and endeavouring to maintain and enhance that shape over time through activity that simultaneously *promotes* and *protects* your reputation.

The upside of reputation management – promotion – and that 'belief that something has a particular characteristic' shares so much of its DNA with branding that it's commonplace for organizations to mistakenly believe that the two areas are really one and the same thing, ie promotion is, by default, protection and by assiduously promoting their brand they are throwing up an impermeable force field around their organization. But whilst promotion might help to build your reputation, it certainly won't be enough to protect it under duress.

In fact, reputation is a much more pervasive and endlessly mutable entity that can entwine itself around everything that your company, your culture, your brand and, in many instances, your people, are about. And in a world where everyone in your workspace, the shop you are in, or the street you are walking along, has a highly sophisticated camera and video recorder in the form of a smartphone in their pocket, one twitch of a thumb could see highly unflattering and wholly unregulated material instantaneously shared with millions of people.

So the process of protecting your reputation depends not simply on promotion, but on how you build and run your business, how you manage and engage your people and what you do to present yourself as an authentically capable, decent and trustworthy organization. Even if you're a hired assassin, your clients will still expect to deal with an honest, trustworthy and capable hired assassin.

Therefore, apart from developing, promoting and selling your products or services, you also need have an explicit *strategic intention* to protect your reputation, and this means that viewing your organization from a much higher (and usually external) vantage point than any one sector or market niche you may occupy.

Putting reputation management into practice

It is a surprisingly low-cost and simple exercise that starts with a very basic question: *How does this make us look?* Asking that before you implement any new initiative, whether it's a human resources policy or a product development costing millions, will inform the direction you will take and the decisions you will make. The same thinking applies to social media.

Although this sounds like an oversimplification, it is the test that real people will use to measure your organization by. Unfortunately, in the microcosm that is any given corporate entity, 'real world' rules and values are often applied differently or overlooked altogether in favour of company culture-specific operational, legal and financial considerations. The result can be the development of corporate policies that make absolute financial and 'business' sense but can be the instigators of a real reputation crisis when they are filmed and posted on social media.

A widely reported example of a business creating policies without asking 'How does this make us look?' is that of the United Airlines 2017 'involuntary deboarding' policy. This policy gave the airline the legal, operational and practical ability to remove passengers, at will, from their flights if a member of their crew needed to be taken to another location. The justification for the policy was to ensure they had crew where and when it was needed at all times, thereby reducing delays for all their passengers, even if they inconvenienced a few who were removed from flights against their will.

In April 2017 United Airlines crew on a flight from Chicago to Kentucky implemented the policy. A paying customer was randomly selected for involuntary deboarding in order to seat a member of standby crew. The customer refused to leave the plane and security staff were called to physically remove the man from the aircraft. The resulting footage – filmed in glorious, multi-angled detail by a number of passengers and shared globally, revealed the extremely violent scene which ended with the elderly man, bloodied and dazed, being stretchered off (Abad-Santos, 2017). This action was legal, but it didn't take into account 'How does this make us look?' It happened inside the cultural microcosm where legal, operational and financial are ticked and nobody thought about adding reputational to the list.

Social media offers real opportunities to get out there and defend yourself, but the tactical deployment of social media reputation management requires an ongoing strategic level approach that continuously considers the effect on reputation of all decisions.

When it all goes wrong: Crises and reputation

A crisis is any event that harms (or could have harmed) people, property and reputation and negatively impacts an organization's ability to undertake business as usual and/or the bottom line. Whether that's an unforeseen *force majeure* that stops production or some comment in the (social) media that sends sales plummeting, once that event occurs you are in crisis management mode, hopefully.

However, understanding where reputation and operation intersect and diverge is the key to getting that crisis management right for the long-term health of your organization and/or your brand(s). It's completely feasible that, if you do this well, there's a chance you could come out of the crisis in better reputational shape than you were at the outset. Why? Because your stakeholders get to see how capable, trustworthy and honest you are as a business.

So, an appreciation of crisis management is a leadership necessity. Many CEOs have already experienced a crisis and most expect to face one in the next three years. These findings suggest that managing crises may well become a new normal for all businesses. It's no longer a matter of if they'll hit; rather, it's a matter of when.

All of which confirms that a thorough understanding of Murphy's Law (anything that can go wrong, eventually will) should exist within every leadership team. The reality, however, is that even though companies understand what could go wrong, surprisingly few invest in crisis planning at all, and where they do they are irresistibly drawn to the immediate and practical operational, rather than somewhat hypothetical reputational, aspects. The result can be a leadership team high-fiving and hip-bumping for getting production back on track, only to find out relatively quickly that their stakeholders, rather than considering them operational geniuses, actually consider them laughably inept. So, whilst it is important to consider every operational (or legal or financial) part of the crisis plan, make sure you also ask how it would make you look if x happened, and what steps should be taken to mitigate that.

Here Amanda Wood shares her thoughts on preparing for and managing a social media crisis.

INTERVIEW
Amanda Wood, founder and consultant, AJW Corporate Communications

Background

Wood is a UK-based communications consultant specializing in change communications, employee engagement and corporate reputation. Having started her career in journalism, she has worked at a senior level within PR and communications for over 20 years, advising clients within the public and private sectors on both internal and external communications. Wood has worked predominantly within the construction, waste, energy and professional services sectors helping clients with crisis planning and reactive communications. Her focus is on ensuring her clients are able to confidently deliver a successful social and news media response following a crisis.

What are your top tips for managing a social media crisis?

Assuming you've got your well-rehearsed plan in place, there are a few things that should never be overlooked and others that will certainly make life easier:

1 **Show empathy and understanding.** This is especially important if your crisis involves a loss of life or injury. Be sincere, express sympathy and detail how you are helping and supporting those affected. Acknowledge and thank any services involved. Never overlook how people feel and never be afraid to show the human face of your organization.

2 **Use private social messaging to support instant and transparent communication.** Set up a 'virtual crisis HQ' as a Yammer group (or similar closed group platform) with your crisis management team. This provides a real-time log of what is happening and can be simultaneously updated by the team, ensuring not simply that everyone in the group is always fully briefed, but they are able to trim their approaches and access a record of events as they unfolded for later reference.

3 **Have a crisis management plan and trained staff ready to react immediately.** Your team needs to gain first mover advantage, because social media moves fast. For example, an Asiana Airlines accident at San Francisco Airport in 2013 was photographed by a passenger waiting for another flight and posted on Twitter within one minute, and generated 44,000 further tweets within 30 minutes. Ideally, your team will be onto this within half that time.

4 **Remember the public sees both your commercial and consumer activity as one.** Even if you have separate social media presences for marketing activity, any commercial activity should be respectful of the type of crisis that has occurred and not happily continue apace, oblivious to a potentially unfolding horror.

5 **Focus on established news media.** Remember that the established news media are more trusted as a primary source of information by consumers and social media commentators alike. If you can get your messages out here, the other forums will begin to self-moderate with the updated news.

6 **Help the media, and they'll help you.** Make journalists' jobs easier by providing speedy responses, access to spokespeople, regular information updates and quality images. If you are tempted to get adversarial, evasive or hard to find, they will get their information from other sources beyond your control.

7 **Never speculate.** It is unlikely that you will know the entire 'who, what, where, why, when and how' immediately, so it is fine to say you are trying to establish these facts, releasing them only when confirmed.

8 **Be honest.** There are many examples of companies who admitted their wrongdoing, apologized sincerely and made amends, actually coming out of the crisis with improved reputations. Those who take a 'post-truth' stance, cover-up and dodge responsibility fare much worse reputationally than if they had behaved with openness and honesty.

9 **Don't get angry.** A clear 'rules of engagement' policy for responding to critics that covers tone of voice and style of address is important. Anger, belligerence and outrage (even of the sub textual kind) reflect badly on your reputation. Great examples of 'how not to respond' can be found all over TripAdvisor in the vitriolic replies by some establishment owners to poor reviews. Whilst I'm willing to overlook the many different one and two star ratings based on badly folded towels and erratic thermostats, just one

psychotically vengeful response from the establishment's owner and I'm moving on to my next choice.

10 **Remember, people are entitled to their own opinions about you, but they are not entitled to their own facts.** You are always entitled to correct wrong information and present the correct version. Be wary, however, of correcting every little comment; it might be wiser to look for trends in the comments, identify the operational cause, and put it right.

11 **Always do a 'lessons learned' exercise after the crisis.** Work back from the effect it has had on your reputation, rather than forward from the event that precipitated it and you will see where the game was won or lost and the techniques that served you well (this will be easier if you set up that Yammer page).

12 **Use your common sense.** It is a valuable commodity during a crisis so use it, even where it may conflict with company policy. And, to be fair, there are many company policies that only make sense to those in the corporate microcosm but really won't stand up to scrutiny in the real world.

How do brands get a social media crisis wrong?

Whilst crises can occur as a result of a failure at any level of an organization, the blame for mismanaging the response to a crisis sits squarely on the shoulders of the leadership team. These failures fall broadly into two categories – those who never had a crisis management protocol in the first place, and those who did, but decided for whatever reason not to follow it.

Obviously, not having a plan means that when the crisis hits there is a delayed, wholly uncoordinated response that is often not led from the top, but fought at the coalface by communications teams struggling to get approval to act from their seniors. Often, leaders who maintain a 'command and control' stance abhor the thought of losing the end of the thread in the ensuing confusion and decide that the best way to stop the unravelling of their reputation is to clamp down on all outward messaging that isn't personally delivered or approved by them. The result is that control disappears into external hands – witnesses of the event, trade specialists, emergency services spokespeople and families of people affected – all of whom would have been immediately taken into the fold had the response protocol been there.

How do brands get a social media crisis right?

If brands are part of a culture that is honest, transparent, supportive, employee-focused and committed to their values, when a crisis tears a ragged hole in their organization it will reveal a predominantly highly functional, cooperative and supportive bunch of people keen to take responsibility and make it right. With a tight crisis communications protocol underpinning their response, they can start to lead on both the solutions and the messaging.

Really good crisis management views every crisis as a time to shine. Companies that ask themselves 'How can we come out of this looking good?' are more likely to actually *do* the right things as well as *say* the right things. Organizations that start with a 'How can we get out of this mess?' are likely to head off down the rabbit-hole of deceit and denial, dragging their tattered reputations behind them. Happily, in the court of public opinion, the nice guys don't always finish last.

How do you to turn a social media crisis into an opportunity?

Every crisis is an opportunity to learn, grow and improve over the longer term. However, from the very outset it's possible to ensure that the increased awareness of your company generated by the crisis is used beneficially.

Controlling the narrative around a crisis means gaining first mover advantage but it also demands you are prepared not just to respond to the facts of the crisis, but also ensure that key messages about your values as a company are reiterated. This could be ensuring, for example, that the audience understands the social equity your brand has built in the communities in which it operates, or simply reminding people of your organization's mission.

A well-managed crisis builds trust fundamentally because humans understand that other humans make mistakes and sometimes terrible things happen. If we can demonstrate that we are willing to acknowledge our mistakes and put them right we are entitled to forgiveness. That's the incentive for managing a crisis well.

How do you see social media affecting crisis management in the next three years?

Social media is fundamentally a force for good from a crisis management perspective. However, the speed of response that social media demands during a crisis has yet to be fully appreciated, and crisis management still has work to do with leaders to emphasize how early and how well they are expected to respond to any given crisis.

Social media demands snackable content, which means exactly that – quick bites of information that are easily read and absorbed. Anything too lengthy will be abandoned in favour of something more pithy elsewhere – and that might not be the right source. So, there is a need to keep the crisis communications moving, not simply to stay ahead of the curve but also to get all of those messages out there in a way that will best ensure they are received and understood. Link to the longer statement, but send the key messages it contains as separate communiqués.

With the increased familiarity that social media encourages between an organization and its audiences comes a similarly heightened expectation that brands and businesses are open, outward facing and happy to engage. The old fashioned, information managing, command and control hierarchies are no match for the social media age and we'll see corporate structures slowly morphing to reflect this more open and connected world.

How can brands use the news media to their advantage in a social media crisis?

The first thing to remember is that the press is viewed as a trusted source by the wider social media sphere so a good working relationship with them will ensure you have a route not just to get your stories out there, but to help rectify mistakes and nip rumours in the bud. True, they may be the carriers of messages you don't like, but that's where your crisis management expertise kicks in to redress the balance.

Companies that attempt a cover-up or some 'truth manipulation' via the press often overlook that it is an actual human being they have just lied to, and whilst journalists are no more amenable to being taken for idiots than anyone else, they alone have unique access to the means of reputational retribution! Furthermore, that same journalist will be sticking with the story from now on so your chances of turning the situation back to your advantage are slim.

On the flipside, if you are taking and returning their calls, going out of your way to ensure they get the information they need, are not leaving them out in the cold (figuratively or literally) and are treating them with friendliness and respect, they will appreciate it. Will this make your average journalists abandon their story and write a glowing testimonial about your company? No, not a chance, but it will ensure their coverage is balanced and fair. And that's all both parties need.

(Source: Wood, 2019)

How good crisis management can make a real difference

Almost exactly one year after the United Airlines social media crisis mentioned earlier, South West Airlines experienced a genuinely catastrophic event when an engine on a flight from New York to Dallas exploded, killing one passenger and forcing an emergency landing. The contrasting responses of these two companies shows how good reputation and crisis management can make a difference.

In the first 48 hours of their deboarding story breaking on all media, United Airlines ignored the injured man in favour of apologizing to the other passengers delayed as a result of his refusal to leave the plane. They seemed uncertain as to whether they had or had not 'reached out' to the victim and issued a memo internally standing by the staff involved and calling the victim 'disruptive and belligerent'. The memo was immediately leaked, and on social media direct comparisons were made to the airline's perceived behaviour and their current brand positioning of 'fly our friendly skies' (Abad-Santos, 2017). United Airlines apologized on day three of the crisis.

Southwest Airlines, in the 48 hours following their crisis, had pulled all of their advertising, put everyone on the flight in a hotel, issued a sincere and unreserved apology from the CEO, paid a no-strings $5,000 in cash and $1,000 travel voucher to each passenger and called, emailed and visited everyone with offers of counselling. They also put leaflets under hotel room doors with advice and counselling helpline numbers on them. The resulting social and media coverage portrayed South West Airlines as an airline of heroism, professionalism and customer service. They had thought about reputation and planned it in to any major incident response.

So, when it comes to managing your reputation through a crisis, it pays to be aware that the scale of potential reputational damage does not meekly reflect the severity of the crisis. In fact, the 'reputational impact' line on the graph is actively *disdainful* of how bad the crisis is and, prefers to judge you on how much attention you are paying it. That's how an incident involving the death of a passenger can win on reputation management, whereas another that injured a man can fail.

Crisis planning for your business

For the purposes of crisis planning, there are three types of crises:

- **Type 1:** Events that are specific to your type of business and for which you will be expected to have a well-rehearsed protocol. For example, contamination issues if you are a food manufacturing company or what to do during an escaped tiger scenario if you're a zoo. Failure to manage this type of crisis well will reflect extremely negatively on you.

- **Type 2:** Events that could reasonably happen to any type of business and therefore you should have a protocol to deal with it – eg fire, IT meltdown, death of an employee whilst doing their job, fraud or other serious criminal or terrorist acts. Similarly, because these are not in themselves unforeseeable events, you will be expected to have a plan to manage them well or take a reputational hit as a consequence.

- **Type 3:** Completely left-field and novel events for which nobody could plan – eg that escaped tiger turning up in your factory. Nobody would reasonably expect you to have a plan in place for this. Happily, if you have plans for types 1 and 2 you will have a usable framework for dealing very competently with type 3.

Crises are a real test of the quality of an organization's leadership, and having a well-established crisis management plan will be a key part of that leadership. This plan, actually more a well-rehearsed and tested process than a document that gets dusted off and read when something happens, involves a multi-disciplinary team, who are well versed in their respective roles, able to communicate instantly with each other in real time, and empowered to act. This means that, as well as being ready to respond when a crisis happens, they are involved *in advance* and asked to advise when a planned activity may prove controversial or potentially destabilizing reputationally. For example, any form of staff restructure, closure or product recall will demand input from your crisis management specialists to help anticipate what could happen and help you steer a reputationally sound path through the new activity and prepare for any negative reactions.

Although a crisis may break, and largely live, in social media your crisis planning needs to be developed across the organization. Involve your senior team (especially your internal and external communications and HR teams) in identifying what they feel are the operational and reputational vulnerabilities in their area of the business and include an external set of eyes and ears for objectivity and some 'real world values' input. Very often, this crisis planning audit turns up issues that are fixable before they ever become a problem, which is an added bonus.

The individuals involved in this process will be the core of your crisis response team: the CEO or most senior spokesperson available, area specialists (technical, legal, human resources, etc), social media monitoring and response team and press specialists. Depending on the business you are in, engaging key external stakeholders (eg industry experts, board members, government representatives, trade bodies, local emergency services and trade unions etc) might be advisable in the planning stage as they will certainly need to be in the information loop during any crisis that touches upon their area.

The majority of the crisis plan will be focused on the operational aspects of the solution; however, the crisis communications plan is arguably as important as the operational response and should be an intrinsic part of, not an addendum to, the overall plan. That's because this is where you not only put something right, but *are seen* to be putting it right. It's where your reputation is protected and potentially enhanced if it goes well.

The crisis communications plan

The crisis communications plan is the inward and outward facing reputation-protecting, and hopefully enhancing, side of your crisis response. It should include as its basic framework:

- the crisis team, including roles and responsibilities;
- key spokespeople, together with biographies and technical specialisms;
- key stakeholders (government, trade, etc);
- victims and survivors contact and support team,
- notification matrices: who should be notified, when, how;
- internal/staff communications channels and holding statements for immediate issue;
- pre-approved external communications channels and holding statements for immediate issue;
- key messages – the important must-communicate facts about the organization, its values and its heartfelt commitment to resolving to the crisis;
- more detailed, topic specific statements and content where possible to cover expected scenarios (ie for type 1 and type 2 crises);
- digital press packs including company background and relevant content;
- up-to-date media lists of key press contacts;

- potential off-site hosting facilities for members of the press and press conferences;
- quick media training refresher crib sheet for spokespeople, updated with key messages relevant to the situation and guides, where possible, to likely press angles.

As well as ensuring your key people are comfortable responding via the approved social media channels, some official media training for spokespeople is an absolute necessity. On screen charisma and a thorough understanding of the company and situation is great, but having the confidence to control an encounter with a skilled interviewer is key to not simply protecting reputation, but potentially enhancing it as well. Good media training will cover everything from expressing empathy and appropriate body language to tips and techniques to help you get your key messages into the interview. Anyone who simply answers the questions in a media interview is seriously missing an opportunity!

Crisis proofing: Leadership, culture and authenticity

The advent of social media has ensured that openness and transparency are facts of corporate life, and containing and controlling *all* of the messages emanating from your company is impossible. You have a staff of citizen journalists, opinion-owners and micro influencers and simply asking them not to tweet, gram or blog about your organization won't provide a watertight solution to the leaking of company secrets or the sharing of those little idiosyncrasies that are normal for your sector (but totally weird in the real world). Therefore, the most effective strategy is simply to build an environment that is always working for your reputation, not posing a daily threat to it. That means developing an organization that has clear values, behaves in line with those values and genuinely treats its employees well.

South West Airlines, whilst it is smaller in terms of assets and employees than United (approximately $25 billion and 57,000 people versus $45 billion and 88,000 people respectively), has an amazing internal culture. At the time of writing, a quick search online under the title 'South West Airways culture' revealed in the first 10 hits nine glowing reviews of their culture – including articles by Forbes and the Washington Post explicitly about culture and one hit clearly detailing the airline's purpose, vision, values and mission statement. That they have a great reputation with customers and employees alike and perform well in crises isn't a coincidence, it's a result of their culture.

That's because culture (as in a specific mindset born of shared values, attitudes, beliefs and behaviours) is *foundational* – everything grows from there, and whilst it's possible to have a toxic culture within a successful company, it's unlikely to go hand in hand with a great reputation and a rosy long-term outlook unless something improves. Culture is also pivotal in how the leadership and workforce respond in a crisis as well as whether certain types of crisis happen at all. This is especially noticeable with the growing numbers of disruptive technology companies like Uber, whose initial culture of brashness and disregard for convention may have provided the impetus for the initial rapid growth, but has eventually begun to draw flack for, well, not seeming to be very nice.

In fact, failure to apply the 'How does this make us look?' rule both internally and externally led to two separate social media crises for Uber in 2017 and reportedly contributed to their CEO stepping down because they didn't consider how the values they seemed to be portraying were playing out when up against those all-important 'real world' values. In the first instance, in January 2017, an opportunistic dropping of surge pricing, to exploit New York cabbies' JFK airport boycott to protest against Trump's Muslim country travel restrictions, saw the viral #DeleteUber campaign and a loss of 200,000 customers in one week. In the following August a damning 3,000-word essay about the firm's apparent institutionalized sexism written by a female employee went viral, effectively persuading a large number of customers to abandon the app.

So it pays to build your reputation from the inside out. The people that know you the best and are seen as the experts by the outside world are the people who work for you. Those same people will either stand up for you or throw you under the bus when it all goes wrong, so think of them as your primary and most influential audience.

Below, Kate Hartley explains how to best manage your reputation in a social media crisis and how brands that prepare are best placed to survive the storm.

INTERVIEW
Kate Hartley, co-founder, Polpeo, and author of *Communicate in a Crisis*

Background

Hartley is a communications consultant specializing in crisis communications and training. As co-founder of Polpeo, a crisis simulation agency, she helps clients plan for and experience how a crisis might spread through their organization and, importantly, trains them on how to communicate through the crisis and beyond.

What is a crisis?

A crisis occurs when something impacts on an organization's licence to operate, either literally a building burning down, or because consumers take away their permission by stopping buying from the brand because of a reputational event. In both examples, a crisis is not just an incident, it is something that can impact sales, reputation and share price.

People often confuse issues with a crisis. For example, Nestlé have been managing boycotts related to the sale of baby milk in Africa since the 1960s, but people still buy Kit Kats. This is because Nestlé are managing an ongoing issue, rather than facing a crisis. If unmanaged, the issue could turn into a crisis, but the company continues to operate.

Where does a crisis play out on social media?

At the moment, Facebook and Twitter are the main places we see the crisis appearing and being played out. Twitter is especially important to watch, as the wider media are active here and can amplify the crisis or help contain it.

We are starting to see Instagram as a place to complain, but LinkedIn plays a much less significant part in a crisis.

Is there a common type of crisis?

Today, because of social media, businesses are more visible. In addition, many organizations have focused on presenting themselves as brands with purpose who care about the supply chain, equality, diversity and the planet, in order to appeal to the Millennial and Gen Z conscious consumers.

However, businesses aren't perfect, as the ongoing list of corporate scandals and data breaches shows, and they need to be prepared for the potential of a boycott or campaign that will gain traction on social media.

Why should you prepare for a crisis?

You perceive any crisis – whether it's a physical threat or a social threat – in the same way. Your body prepares you to instinctively fight, flee or freeze.

By preparing and training for a crisis you learn to overcome those instincts, and embed best practices. You build 'muscle memory' into your business that will enable your team to manage the crisis effectively.

What are the key elements to remember when crisis planning?

- **Know when you are in crisis**, as opposed to when you're managing an issue. One of the hardest things is to know when you are in crisis. You need to know what 'normal' looks like. For example, a utility company may get thousands of complaints a week and that would be normal for them; for another business, this would represent a crisis. When building a crisis plan it is essential that you know how to recognize what is beyond normal for you.

- **Plan.** The more preparations you make the more likely you will be successful. Consider the different types of crisis that are most likely to happen in your sector or because of the wider environment.

- **Keep documents short.** In a crisis, people need to be able to quickly understand the process and important actions. Short and clear documents will assist rather than hinder, and are more likely to be read and followed.

- **Build resilience in the team.** Ensure your team are supported and know what to do.

- **Have clear roles and responsibilities, and communicate effectively.** Who is accountable? Who will activate the crisis plan? Who will lead the crisis? Who owns which channels? And who will phone the CEO at 3am?

- **Stress test the plan.** Rehearse the crisis, either through a full simulation exercise or a desktop scenario, to build muscle memory of what to do and find out where there are gaps in the plan. Often, simple things like a list of mobile numbers or logins can be forgotten and waste valuable time in a real crisis.

Why is resilience so important in a social media crisis?

Without training, people may respond badly in a crisis. With training, they gain confidence and have a process that can be followed to ensure effective behaviour. However, even with training a social media crisis is stressful, people can panic especially if they are tired or overwhelmed. They need support and help.

That is why it's so important to build resilience into your teams. Even in a simulated crisis environment we typically see that in the first hour or two people collaborate brilliantly, but by hour three they are starting to tire and begin arguing and feeling like they cannot cope. It's hardly surprising; if you are sitting on Twitter or Facebook and have had abuse hurled at you for three hours, you are bound to start losing patience. At some point, you'll crack.

Brands need to be aware of this and give team members time out or switch teams if they can. Everyone needs rest in order to do a good job.

How quickly should you respond to a social media crisis?

Before social media it was possible to control the narrative. Now, you perhaps find out about the crisis on Twitter. There's a tendency is to panic and the pressure is on to respond quickly.

In reality, you should pause, take a breath and check the facts before you respond. Once you have made a statement, people will remember it, even if you go back later and change it. But don't leave it too long to respond. If you don't get ahead of the narrative, someone else will do it for you, and they may not have your best interests at heart.

Most crises follow a common arc with four stages: pre crisis – spotting the issue and managing it; prodromal stage, where it is inevitable that the crisis will happen but you are not in full crisis yet; full crisis where you are focusing on damage limitation, and finally post crisis where you are looking at recovery. It is important to know what stage you are at and act accordingly.

How do you decide that a crisis is over?

People have very long memories. Data breaches from three to five years ago are still talked about today. This long tail is because social media extends the life of the crisis.

A crisis takes time to recover from and you may never be able to go back to business as usual. What is important is to have a post-crisis plan based on recovering your reputation and building trust.

Do you have any top tips?

Remember that some people will manipulate a crisis for their own ends. At some point in the crisis, there will be people spreading misinformation and rumour; there might be scammers trying to make money off the back of it; there will be campaigners and people who wear outrage like a badge; and others defending the brand. They all need managing.

It is important you are empathetic to your followers – understand what the crisis means to those directly affected. People tend to retreat behind a corporate statement, but in social media you are talking directly to the consumer and your language should change to suit the issue, consumer and channel. Empathy is hard, but people want an acknowledgement, an apology and clear action on what will happen.

How do you think social media crisis management will change in the future?

We'll all accept a great level of imperfection. Brands are a collection of people, and people make mistakes. Social media makes those very visible. If people want authenticity from brands, this will include imperfection. People will have to accept mistakes from the brands they engage with.

When brands do get it wrong, they need to be more open and transparent. Trust is very important in managing the crisis successfully, and it is critical to recovery.

(Source: Hartley, 2019)

References

Abad-Santos, A (2017) www.vox.com/culture/2017/4/11/15246632/united-airlines-drag-man-off-plane (archived at https://perma.cc/E5UM-EMKN)

Hartley, K (2019) Co-founder, Poleop and author of *Communicate in a Crisis* [Interview] (6 March)

Local Media News (2018) www.localmediauk.org/News/yougov-local-press-most-trusted-source-for-local-news (archived at https://perma.cc/A2GN-W94N)

Oxford Dictionaries (2019) Reputation. https://en.oxforddictionaries.com/definition/reputation (archived at https://perma.cc/E2NW-FJTN)

PwC Global (2017) CEO pulse on crisis. www.pwc.com/gx/en/ceo-agenda/pulse/crisis.html (archived at https://perma.cc/C78V-T48B)

Wood, A (2019) Founder and Consultant, AJW Corporate Communications [Interview] (27 March)

10

Thoughts on the future of social

What will happen next?

How do you stay abreast of the latest changes in technology and consumer behaviour? This chapter considers what might happen next in social. What will be the impact of artificial intelligence, virtual reality and voice, how will content be produced and what types of skills will marketers need to have? Interviews with leading practitioners bring an insight into their visions for social.

Innovation is moving at a terrific speed, and social is where the innovators spread the word, launch ideas and sometimes apply them. It's impossible to stay on top of everything, but this chapter highlights my views on what's next for social. They include:

- the integration of social;
- AI, bots and voice;
- social ecosystems;
- organizational agility;
- Facebook for now (outside of China).

The integration of social

Throughout this book I have discussed the important triumvirate of audience, brand and campaigns – the ABC of social. In the near future I don't envisage any diminishing of the importance of these three elements, in fact I believe they will become even more important as the lynchpins on which to build a fully integrated marketing and social media strategy.

As the population of younger generations grows and the behaviour of existing social media users becomes more sophisticated, brands will need to spend more time truly understanding their audiences and their needs and behaviours in social, across other channels and in the real world. This will become increasingly difficult, with more stringent privacy laws, the move to dark social and the rise of account resignations. However, by appreciating the integration of social in every aspect of our real and digital world lives, it will be possible to understand them and use that understanding to gauge where our audiences want our brands to be and how they expect them to behave. A sophisticated social audience can easily remove themselves from an unfulfilling or annoying brand experience or immerse themselves in a positive and rewarding engagement.

This means that brands that create and build a relevant and consistent brand presence that integrates with their wider business strategy will be poised to reach both their social and business goals. But, to do this, social will need to become an integrated skill set of every marketer and a 'core component of marketing' (Horry, 2019).

INTERVIEW
Toby Horry, Brand and Content Director, TUI UK

Background

As MD of the agency Dare, Toby Horry worked with brands from BMW and Diageo, to Nestlé and Ryan Air, in countless channels and markets. After joining Tesco, Horry re-structured and re-focused the social media team to support the rebuilding of the Tesco brand. Currently at TUI, he pursues an ambition to transform TUI into the most-loved holiday brand in the UK. Social and content play a huge role across his remit of brand, product, strategy and communications. Horry has worked on campaigns and led teams that have won multiple awards.

What are the priorities for social in the near future?

Make sure social doesn't live as a silo in the organization but is considered as a core component of marketing. In the next three years I think social media will come to be seen less as a specialism and more as something that any good marketer needs to understand.

What is the role of social media in brand building?

It is important that social is integrated into the brand, content and media strategy. My role at Tesco was about rebuilding brand trust, and I knew social had an integral part to play. Rather than treating social media very differently from other channels, I re-structured the team and integrated social media into the overall strategy.

For example, although we had a national TV campaign, there are many people who are much lighter users of TV. Social media, and particularly Facebook, enabled us to increase our reach to the non-TV audience, and also increase the impact of our campaigns for those who did see our work on multiple channels.

What do you think is the best channel combination?

I'm a firm believer in the IPA research [undertaken to analyse what makes marketing effective using the winners of IPA's Awards], which talks about five channels being the optimum media mix for the same message (IPA, 2017). Although there is overlap between the channels, reach is increased overall. For big, mass-market brands, TV will have a central role because it is able to reach both customers and non-customers, generating the best effect on brand longevity by continually filling the funnel. Social media acts as a support here. For smaller brands, with less cash to spend, social often takes a more significant role in a digitally led strategy.

What should be the balance of organic and paid media?

The mix is different by sector and by brand. On the surface, travel has a higher proportion of organic reach because consumers are more likely to share travel content than information about groceries. However, social did allow us to share a variety of content from the emotional hero video to the useful recipes and advice. And, by putting paid media spend behind the hero videos, we were able to support great content to get significant organic reach, such as Tesco's Fathers' Day Tannoy Takeover (Tesco, 2016a).

What's your view on using user-generated content?

At Tesco we involved customers in our brand content but didn't overtly seek UGC. We were putting significant media spend behind our activity and that meant a significant production spend with high production values. That said, internally, social content was seen as different from TV content, with more flexibility to move quickly and with less internal scrutiny. The 'surprise delivery' campaign for Tesco started on Facebook and only went onto TV because it was so successful (Gwynn, 2016; Tesco, 2016b).

Does social have any unique challenges?

Consumers increasingly use social media as a customer service channel, so it is essential brands resource it to manage the level and speed of responses expected by their customers. At Tesco, the more we posted, the more responses staff needed to deal with, and often the response had nothing to do with the post. It's a conundrum; we are trying to deliver a specific message and the customer responds by talking about mouldy apples, and you need to respond to that.

Tesco has one channel per platform which can lead to having lots of customer service conversations in the feed, which need to be isolated using the platform tools. TUI have multiple channels on each platform (for example they have a separate channel for customer service and for different holiday types such as skiing, summer sun, etc). This brings other challenges and especially the need to resource properly.

What do you measure in social?

Measurement is really important. It's not good enough to only measure impressions. At Tesco, we made sure that we had clear KPIs and targets for every campaign and built social media into our econometric model so that we knew the overall marketing effect. To measure against our goal of improving brand trust we used an ongoing tracking survey and were able to look at the differences between exposed and unexposed samples (customer groups who had either seen or not seen the marketing activity) to measure channel effects. Social is also great for measuring brand sentiment and providing immediate insights into how customers feel about the content we create and share. This sort of information can be time consuming and expensive to extract through more traditional research techniques.

What are your views on using influencers?

To be honest I think it can be a bit of a wild west. I'd want to be really sure that I could measure the effect they were having on my core objectives and KPIs. We are looking at the influencer strategy at TUI to ensure that it stacks up robustly against other marketing approaches.

(Source: Horry, 2019)

AI, bots and voice

I believe the next big impact will come from new technologies. The drive for the adoption of new innovations and technologies comes from two perspectives – consumers and brands. For consumers, shortening attention spans, expectations of instant gratification and intuitive experiences means that many are already eager to speak to bots rather than wait for someone to pick up a phone, or shout out their search requests rather than type them, and are comfortable with algorithms selecting content based on their previous behaviour rather than having to search through vast volumes of irrelevant content. For brands, these innovations feed either cost savings or leaps in creative thinking, both of which in combination can supercharge business success. For these reasons I think that adoption of AI, bots and voice will increase rapidly. Consumers are ready and it just needs brands to take the plunge. For those that have, they are seeing dramatic results; as Patel notes, although businesses spend less than half the time working on bots than they do on videos, bots are responsible for many more referrals to their websites. This is because videos keep your audience engaged within the social platform but 'you want visitors to go back to your site... and you can do this through chatbots' (Patel, 2019).

INTERVIEW
Kerry Harrison and Richard Norton, co-founders, Tiny Giant

Background

Tiny Giant is a marketing practice founded in 2018 by two award-winning advertising creatives, Kerry Harrison and Richard Norton. They work with a team of creatives and computer scientists to fuse technology and ideas in order to deliver creative AI projects, engaging content, chatbots, voice-first campaigns, and AI workshops. Their work is bold and challenges the interaction of what happens when creative ideas meet smart technology. They have already used this magic combination to create AI-conceived cupcakes and cocktails, Plath-inspired poetry and AIDA the first ever AI Guest Curator for the Cheltenham Science Festival.

What are your thoughts on the combination of AI and social media?

There are really two ways AI can help with social – improving efficiency and increasing effectiveness.

Efficiency isn't that exciting, but it does save money and time, which enables you to spend them both on more exciting projects. AI tools like Persado and Phrasee help brands generate the highest performing subject lines and social posts. Other companies are using AI to develop video content that is highly personalized.

Effectiveness is the more exciting area. It requires a shift in mindset for creatives and strategists. If we think of the efficiency area as the heavy lifting, letting the machine analyse subject lines and image positions, then the other side is about using the machine to inspire and stretch creative thinking to generate something totally new that will create cut-through and maximize engagement.

Is there a danger in combining social media and AI?

At the moment AI has no set rules of engagement. We really need to be thinking about the ethics of how we use it to ensure brands behave responsibly.

So, for example, social media is often weaponized by humans, when people use it to troll and defame others. What if unethical brands started to use AI to weaponize social media in order to change people's opinions? The machine will be bang on the money for knowing the exact words and images you like to see and what will encourage you to act.

Does AI always increase creativity?

We believe that the combination of minds and machines can boost creativity. We use AI as a way to augment human skills, so we can produce bigger, better and more creative outputs.

However, AI that focuses primarily on efficiency doesn't increase creativity. Going forward, we believe social media marketing will need to do two things to work. AI will enable micro-personalized content that is highly relevant to the individual, but it will also need human creativity and novel ideas to help make an emotional connection.

What is so great about bots?

Bots were slow to take off after the first jump on the hype curve. Even though there are over 300,000 on Messenger, only early adopters are using them, and mostly for customer service. But now, as the tech has got better and people are more used to the idea of a bot, we think they will really take off.

For customer service they can alleviate your customer service team by answering basic questions, and escalating to a real person if the customer is frustrated or has a tricky question. There are also some really innovative bots out there, like Woebot. Set up by an all-female team of cognitive behavioural therapists, the chatbot checks in with you daily and provides supportive CBT learnings. It doesn't replace a therapist but does help you feel more relaxed.

How do bots work with voice?

One in six US adults now have a smart speaker and the use of voice is growing exponentially. The potential of voice is really exciting. One bizarre but interesting example is the ongoing development of Grief Bots. They let you connect with your family beyond the grave by harnessing social data to build conversations with long-gone relatives. In a way, it's a kind of digital immortality. With voice, you could add their voice pattern and the bot would recreate how they speak –literally a conversation from beyond the grave.

As with new ideas and new technology, the initial cost is expensive. But, over time, it could become significantly cheaper as the concept scales.

How do bots support relevancy?

Bots work 24/7, so the information they have is delivered exactly when it suits you. As we become more keen for instant answers and tailored content, bots will increasingly be used to serve this purpose.

How do bots work on Twitter?

Twitter is a great environment for bots. We have made a few ourselves, including Eternal Love bot for Valentine's Day, which generated love messages that could be sent to loved ones, plus Pancakery bot, which generated weird and wonderful topping suggestions for pancakes on Shrove Tuesday.

Twitter bots are ideal for brands that want an interactive way to deliver content. This could include tweeting a bot for inspiration, recipe suggestions, jokes or punchlines, or supporting an event with real-time updates on the day's activities.

(Source: Harrison and Norton, 2019)

Social ecosystems

We need to be aware of the perhaps different motives of consumers, platforms and brands. The establishment social media platforms are mature business models creating vast revenues and aggressively defending their position from governments and competitors alike. In their ideal world they would like to keep us, their visitors, in their world as much as possible because the longer we stay the more money we make for them. In China, 'WeChat has evolved to become an ecosystem' (Clay, 2019), and I agree with Clay that other platforms, and especially Facebook, are moving in the same direction. The advantage for the platform is that consumers will discover, buy, influence, be influenced, pay and share all within their environment, thereby increasing time spent and engagement, and making it harder to defect.

This creates challenges for us as consumers – how much do we want one platform to know about us, and are we happy for them to 'control' our digital footprint? For brands, they are in danger of losing control of their owned media channels and customer relationships to powerful social platforms.

INTERVIEW
Rachel Clay, Head of Influencer Marketing, Matter of Form

Background

Clay is the Head of Influencer Marketing for the award-winning luxury branding agency Matter of Form whose clients include Breitling, The Rug Company, Elie Saab and Estee Lauder. The agency works with luxury brands across global markets in the arts, hospitality, fashion and retail sectors. Rachel is an industry expert and trainer on influencer marketing, with experience from working on both the brand and agency perspectives. Her knowledge of global social media marketing gives her an insight into the future of social media development in the west.

What does the Chinese social media landscape tell us about how social is likely to develop in the west in the next three to five years?

For many brands, especially luxury and retail brands, social media, and Instagram in particular, are becoming an ecommerce channel and the premiere online destination. This pattern is a mirror of the way WeChat works in the Chinese market.

WeChat has evolved to become an ecosystem, which has successfully created a range of services that live within in it and enable its visitors to conduct multiple experiences without ever leaving the WeChat environment. In China, WeChat has become the most important ecommerce channel for many retail brands. Supported by WeChat Pay, the bespoke payment system allows one-click ordering and one-click payment, which facilitates seamless social commerce. In addition, if you make a purchase in WeChat and share the link within WeChat messaging, you earn future discounts if any of your contacts go on to buy based on your recommendation.

It appears that Instagram is moving in the same direction and there are a number of key indicators for this:

- The 2019 announcement that the Facebook, Instagram and WhatsApp messaging services are being merged into one entity creates a single recommendation platform and keeps the user in one place for messaging.

- Shoppable tags are another step towards the single ecosystem. As Instagram's functionality increases, the need for retailers to support a website outside of Instagram decreases.

- At the time of writing Instagram appears to be introducing features that will enable it to function as a single ecosystem. Although the ecommerce tech already exists, Instagram has not fully integrated it into the platform. The expectation is that this is because Instagram is developing its own payment system and will introduce this in order to own the customer journey, rather than facilitating its users to move out of the Instagram world.

Why are influencers so important to a successful social media strategy?

Influencer marketing is important because they are central to how social media as a channel works. Social is just another marketing channel. In the beginning there were Hollywood films, then TV, radio, blogs, etc. Brands need to be present in the channels where their audiences spend their time. In 2018, Instagram reached 1 billion monthly users, and the volumes continue to grow, therefore your brand needs to be on Instagram.

Furthermore, because all content is prioritized by popularity, that is engagement, influencers are used to beat the algorithm in the same way as you would use content marketing to beat the SEO algorithm.

What will be the effect of CGI influencers?

The west is generally about three to five years behind the east in terms of social media development, so I would look at what is happening in China and Japan today to see what is next for the west.

In those regions the biggest influencers today are CGI influencers. Given the current trend for authenticity and transparency in brand-consumer relationships, the popularity of CGI influencers seems like anathema at first glance. However, based on the psychology that even though you will never meet an influencer you follow, you will build up a relationship with them via social media, it is possible to see how you can also build a relationship with a virtual influencer.

For brands, CGI influencers offer them more control. You can ensure that the influencer exactly meets the needs of your followers. In fact, for the first time, you can create the perfect influencer.

Can a CGI influencer be authentic?

These influencers do raise questions around authenticity, morality and ethics. However, so long as a brand that has created an influencer is honest and transparent about them being computer generated, their followers are likely to accept them.

One advantage is that fans can 'meet' their CGI influencers at events and choose their hair colour, outfits and the music they play. In a bizarre circle of influence, the fans can influence who and what the influencer is. Every innovation in this area demonstrates our acceptance of suspending belief. PokemonGo blended social and AI tech, and the 2019 Abba reunion tour is a sell-out, but the performers are Abba avatars rather than the real stars.

How is social media evolving?

I believe that soon many brands will have no need for a website and their Instagram page will be that destination. This has already happened for many bloggers who no longer need a blog.

Voice-based tech is the next big step change and the new marketing channel. Alexa is huge and offers innovative and fun opportunities; for example, Joe Wicks has an Alexa work out.

As innovations such as driverless cars offer new media opportunities, influencers will need to find their place in these environments and identify new ways to influence. Brands will want to pay for their destinations to be announced – what will be the answer when you ask your driverless car where to pop for a coffee on your way to work?

(Source: Clay, 2019)

Organizational agility

Many marketing departments (and organizations) operate in silos and still put the business needs before the needs of the customer. As social is embedded across every aspect of our lives, it also needs to be embedded into our business strategy and behaviours. To do this we need different and more diverse marketing skills and new ways of working. As brands move increasingly into customer-led relationships, content becomes ever more important. Relevant, engaging, timely, intuitive, creative content is a core building block of successful social media, but many organizations aren't able to deliver the level of agility required to really win with content. I predict that increasingly more agile multidisciplinary teams will be needed to create and distribute content in various forms, whether video, gif, bot, meme, text, song.... James Ainsworth's T-shaped teams are already moving in this direction.

INTERVIEW
James Ainsworth, Head of Content, Prophecy Unlimited;
Chair, DMA Social Media Council

Background

Ainsworth heads up the content arm of the award-winning agency Prophecy Unlimited, the customer journey agency. Working with global brands including BMW, Lexus, Barratt Developments, Confused.com and Danone, he runs a strategic content team that sits within the creative division of the agency. In addition, he chairs the DMA Social Media Council, supporting businesses and brands in the effective commercial use of social media.

Why do content and social media sit in the creative team in your agency?

When social media was an emerging discipline, it was part of our planning team, but, as the content capabilities have become more important to effective strategy development and deployment, we have moved it into creative.

We did this for two reasons.

First, because we can now very quickly translate our strategy into creative output. Social moves very quickly and has a huge number of different creative assets that can be deployed, from static to video, in a multitude of different sizes and specifications. To move this quickly and flexibly it is a real advantage to know what will work creatively.

Second, as social has matured and the platforms have adjusted their offering, organic social isn't cutting through. To make social media work you need a combination of a strategic understanding of the platforms as media channels and a creative understanding of what will work in each platform, the classic example being Facebook's algorithm, which penalizes the performance of an asset if it constitutes more than 20 per cent of text within the image. Data and targeting used to be the remit of the data or planning teams, but now creatives need to know how to beat the algorithm.

Can you describe how you deploy your T-shaped social media creatives?

Our team are true T-shaped marketers – each has a specialism as well as a broad understanding of digital marketing and strong strategic and creative skills. Our content team are as comfortable crafting copy for social posts and for longer-form blogs, making assets come to life with motion, and possess the knowledge and understanding of how to distribute content and get it seen.

What are the ideal skills of your T-shaped social media team?

In a perfect scenario the team would be made up of four members. The head of content is strategically minded but very quickly can see how to enable the strategy to work creatively and be reworked for different channels. The senior content manger understands the strategic approach but can also jump into Photoshop and Premiere Pro and create the content. It is a balance of strategy and creative. The content execs have either a copywriting or design/video specialism and complement each other's skills.

How is the content for social media changing?

Three years ago, 90 per cent of social media assets were static; now it is the opposite way around, with 90 per cent including some form of motion, from animation to gif to video.

Google prioritizes video in the search, therefore in video most content will start with an SEO query. Some brands, like B&Q, do a great job here. For example, if you type into Google a question about how to put up a shelf, B&Q will be at the top of the SEO list with their video of exactly how to do it. This video content works brilliantly in search but can also be used in social to answer questions and engage consumers.

How do you manage campaign delivery?

It's important to have a strategic approach that maximizes creativity, but it is also right to manage costs and streamline delivery. A monthly editorial-style posting plan functions well on both these aspects and works in this way:

- Agree the strategy with the client, the proposition, the creative direction, the customer needs being met, and the number of editorial elements each month – for example, on Instagram, creating nine functional building blocks of content using a combination of new original content, UGC and reused/repurposed content.

- Each month, assess the content available; for example, what already exists and can be reused?

- In the case of UGC, seek permission from the people who have originally created content on Instagram that would be great to include in the monthly campaign. This ensures there is a balance of authentic original unprofessional shots mixed with more structured, originally designed creative. Instagram shouldn't be just an ad space, it should be a slice of life.

- Involve the client in the content creation by sending story boards for the new videos, copy approaches, mock-ups of posts in Facebook and Instagram's own tools and the selected UGC.

- Fine tune and create content.

- Post and comment through the month.

(Source: Ainsworth, 2019)

Facebook for now (outside China)

For now, Facebook is here to stay, and is so pre-eminent and reaches so many eyeballs that it is hard for most brands not be there at all. What I would advise, though, is to monitor your audience and how they feel about each social platform. Gen Zs are spending less and less time there, and are much more interested in platforms that are more private and ephemeral; brands like Lush are opting out, 'tired of fighting algorithms and having to pay to appear in newsfeeds' (Kleinman, 2019); and governments are starting to flex their muscles over data and jurisdiction concerns. However, despite this you can still connect with younger audiences in this space, as the

University of Gloucestershire case study in Chapter 6 demonstrates, and brands are using influencers, communities and opted-in groups in Facebook's other environments (WhatsApp and Instagram especially) to continue to connect. So, maximize what you can from Facebook but be ready for where your audience most wants to be. In Will Francis' interview he provides some great tips for making sure you make the most of this ever-present channel – for now.

INTERVIEW
Will Francis, co-founder and Creative Director, Vandal London

Background

A consultant and educator on digital marketing and technology, Francis is an expert on using social media to launch, grow and support brand's marketing activity. He has used this expertise to build his own successful consultancy business with global brands including Google and Volkswagen. A commentator on all things social and digital, he contributes to reports from the BBC and Channel 4. As a consultant, Francis himself is the brand. He doesn't need hundreds of clients, but he does need to be found by the right people at the right time.

What is your approach to using social media for a small B2B business?

I use my social channels as points of discovery. This means I need to be where my potential clients are looking for people like me, and create valuable content to demonstrate why they might want to work with me.

High-quality content that you are passionate about, and is of interest to your potential clients, is valuable content. The more valuable your content is, the less likely it will be lost in the noise, hidden by an algorithm, blocked by an ad blocker or ignored by your audience.

To ensure I can maintain content quality, I only use a limited number of channels. I use LinkedIn, YouTube and Twitter, and they all point to my website where high-value leads are generated.

LinkedIn blogs and Tweets all show increased spikes in web traffic and initial conversations or meetings. Often, prospects will follow both my LinkedIn and Twitter profiles as I share different types of content on each.

What are your views on video content?

Video can be hard work; it takes time and equipment, but it is worth it. Many businesses under-use video, but it enables people to engage on a whole new level. They connect much more, and as a consultant you can use it to really represent your personality and approach at a very early stage in the buying process.

What do you think is going to happen next in social?

The landscape is moving very fast but I believe that it will move to an increasingly monopolized position. Zuckerberg wants to own the internet and our lives on it, and has long hungered after the position WeChat holds in the Chinese market.

In 2019, several changes in the Facebook group have indicated a move in this direction. For example, Instagram now enables shopping in platform through their own payment gateway, and the integration of the messaging apps of Messenger, Instagram and WhatsApp indicates the direction of travel. It isn't unimaginable that Facebook may bring out their own currency. Zuckerberg has shown an interest in blockchain for content verification, but the more of our lives that are spent within the Facebook universe, the more likely a Facebook currency becomes. [Note. After this interview Facebook announced the launch of its cryptocurrenncy Libra.]

How will consumers' attitudes to data privacy affect our use of social media?

People are more aware of their identity spilling out onto the internet than the data being held on them by platforms such as Facebook. In general, the average user thinks that Facebook are good at data management. When you use Facebook, it feels very robust and reliable. They hold oceans of data and the data leaks are the equivalent of a few drops on the shore from the Atlantic Ocean. There is so much more data that could potentially be leaked and so little that actually is. The tech and media heads are more worried than the public.

However, when it comes to identity and how we are losing control of where this goes on the internet, privacy here is another story. People are increasingly concerned, hence the rise of ephemeral content and channels such as Snapchat. Private, closed interactions are becoming more and more popular. I wonder when my 3-year-old will ask for all the photos of him on social media to be deleted.

This move to more private interactions also moves us away from a like-based economy on social. On Snapchat you can post candid and unpolished pictures because there is no vanity metric attached. It is a relief to not sit waiting for likes.

What are your top tips for using Facebook Ads?

1   **Multivariate testing** A hugely important piece of the puzzle that is all too often overlooked is multivariate testing. This isn't A/B testing, but rather A to Z and back again a hundred times. However good you are at marketing, it's highly unlikely you'll be able to predict which combination of image, copy, audience and placement will generate the highest return (lowest cost per conversion) so you must try everything. I use AdEspresso to generate these multiple combinations in seconds, and once the campaign is running I turn off combinations that don't work so well.

2   **Focus on cost per action, not cost per click** There is only one metric that matters if you're paying Facebook to drive people to your website to buy, subscribe or enquire about something – the cost per conversion, ie the actual cost of driving that action. How much the impressions and clicks cost can be indicators of ad quality, but they are close to irrelevant, so don't get hung up on them. There are lots of reasons an ad could be clickable, but unless it drives your desired action it's worthless.

3   **Don't be afraid to use emojis** Anything that can help format your copy, break it up, make it more instantly readable is a good thing. More brands are beginning to understand that emojis are just another way to do this, and not just something for kids. If you're running a high number of ad variants you should be experimenting with everything, including emojis in your copy, whatever industry you operate in.

4   **Use custom audiences** Core audiences – ones based on people age, location, interests, etc – are great, but you're still marketing in the dark and hoping for the best. These audiences are fine for large awareness-building campaigns, but if you're trying to drive conversions you absolutely have to be employing custom audiences, ie ones based on data. These can include:

a   website visitors;

b   email subscribers;

c   customers;

d   cart abandoners (people who almost bought);

e engagers on Facebook and Instagram;

f profile visitors on those platforms.

These are people who have in some way encountered you online, and are far more likely to become a customer than someone who fits a vague demographic profile. For this reason you should be focusing on custom audiences and getting maximum value out of these before spending money elsewhere.

5 **Experiment with copy** Many marketers forget to get creative with copy, going out with one, straight-to-the-point message. But with multivariate advertising we can try lots of different angles, and this is crucial because as humans we respond to different messages in different ways. Some people are motivated by a fear of missing out, some people want to save money, others respond to emotive content. Reach all of these people through writing about your brand or products in a variety of ways, and test the response. You might be surprised at the results.

6 **Now try it with video** All of the above will take you closer to those great results you're looking for. But have you tried running your ads with video? For most marketers the answer is no, because video unfortunately takes more time and equipment, and so doesn't feel viable. Fortunately the internet is now awash with a broad array of new apps and services that create professional-grade video very easily. Lumen5, for instance, turns a written blog post into video through AI and stock footage. Biteable creates TV-quality animated video packages with a few clicks. There's no excuse anymore for not running video in your social ads and marketing.

(Source: Francis, 2019)

Conclusion

So, social is here to stay. It's grown up and sophisticated and can make a dramatic impact on your overall business success. In fact, I believe that the more you integrate social media into your business strategy, the closer you will be to your customers and the more empathetic to their behaviours, needs, wants, joys and diversions. This in turn will give you a competitive edge. Go forth and create great strategies and, to help, use the strategy template to organize your thoughts.

A social strategy template document is available to download at www.koganpage.com/sms.

References

Ainsworth, J (2019) Head of Content, Prophecy Unlimited [Interview] (6 March)

Clay, R (2019) Head of Influencer Marketing, Matter of Form [Interview] (6 March)

Francis, W (2019) Co-founder and Creative Director, Vandal London [Interview] (20 March)

Gwynn, S (2016) www.campaignlive.co.uk/article/tesco-reunites-divided-families-christmas-last-minute-ad-campaign/1419518 (archived at https://perma.cc/AE5W-EXBA)

Harrison, K and Norton, R (2019) Co-founders, Tiny Giant [Interview] (13 March)

Horry, T (2019) Brand and Content Director, TUI UK [Interview] (15 January)

IPA (2017) *Media in Focus: Marketing effectiveness in the digital era*, IPA, London

Kleinman, Z (2019) www.bbc.co.uk/news/technology-47871948 (archived at https://perma.cc/4CUQ-SMBC)

Patel, N (2019) https://neilpatel.com/blog/social-media-trends/?utm_source=email&utm_medium=email&utm_campaign=email (archived at https://perma.cc/5LE3-H6X5)

Tesco (2016a) www.youtube.com/watch?time_continue=86&v=jiEo1-uzP5U (archived at https://perma.cc/9NCZ-RE4Z)

Tesco (2016b) www.youtube.com/watch?time_continue=11&v-UFaRkdJqvYs (archived at https://perma.cc/AWZ5-5K7B)

APPENDIX 1

Useful information

There are a number of resources that are extremely useful when building any social media strategy. These include research, trend reports, publications, marketing and advertising associations. Some examples of these, with the appropriate links, are included in this section.

Trend and forecasting reports

2019 Influencer Marketing: What's Next?
   https://resources.zine.co/2019-influencer-marketing-report-whatsnext
   (archived at https://perma.cc/T8LT-Y25B)
Adult Media Consumption and Behaviour Reports
   www.ofcom.org.uk (archived at https://perma.cc/T727-Q4W3)
Brand Z Top 100 Most Global Valuable Brands
   www.millwardbrown.com/brandz/rankings-and-reports/top-global-brands/2018
   (archived at https://perma.cc/V4W6-N5LM)
Global Digital Report
   https://digitalreport.wearesocial.com/download
   (archived at https://perma.cc/6GLZ-29CW)
GlobalWebIndex
   www.globalwebindex.com (archived at https://perma.cc/GB5Y-RFLT)
State of Social, 2019
   www.socialchain.com/scribe/social-chain-x-buffer-report-50-marketers-will-
   underestimate-messaging-apps-2019/
   (archived at https://perma.cc/5DH8-MDVU)
The Future 100: Trends and Change to Watch in 2019
   www.jwtintelligence.com/trend-reports/the-future-100-2019/
   (archived at https://perma.cc/HL5V-LRH6)
The Influencer Marketing Report
   https://socialmediaweek.org/blog/2018/07/free-download-yougov-social-media-
   weeks-influencer-marketing-report/
   (archived at https://perma.cc/2FF2-5YVC)
Webby Trend Reports
   www.webbyawards.com (archived at https://perma.cc/Q57R-4PFR)

World Advertising Research Centre (WARC)
   www.warc.com (archived at https://perma.cc/P23K-MCMJ)

Advertising, marketing, and social media information

Advertising Age
   www.adage.com (archived at https://perma.cc/46K8-WM32)
Adweek
   www.adweek.com (archived at https://perma.cc/AAZ6-8VEX)
Brand Republic
   www.brandrepublic.com (archived at https://perma.cc/WQK7-ZSUY)
Forrester Research
https://go.forrester.com (archived at https://perma.cc/6LWY-V275)
Future Strategy Club (FSC)
   https://futurestrategyclub.com
   (archived at https://perma.cc/5GVH-N4KG)
Hubspot Research
   https://research.hubspot.com
   (archived at https://perma.cc/FZ83-DE3D)
Interbrand Brandchannel
   www.brandchannel.com
   (archived at https://perma.cc/6CK9-VHBA)
IPA
   www.ipa.co.uk (archived at https://perma.cc/8JXP-JKF4)
ISBA
   www.isba.org.uk (archived at https://perma.cc/YSL4-M97Z)
McCrindle
   https://mccrindle.com.au (archived at https://perma.cc/L5RC-GB7W)
Market Research Society
   www.mrs.org.uk (archived at https://perma.cc/YB28-NQWM)
Mintel
   www.mintel.com (archived at https://perma.cc/JB6W-Q4MY)

Census data and statistics

Statista
   www.statista.com (archived at https://perma.cc/P4ND-AKV9)
UK Office for National Statistics (ONS)
   www.statistics.gov.uk (archived at https://perma.cc/V45Z-HE6T)

US Census Data
   www.census.gov (archived at https://perma.cc/4J9D-7ARE)

Social media blog, vlogs, WhatsApp threads and people to follow

Paul Armstrong
   www.hereforth.com (archived at https://perma.cc/A5MA-A9LY)
Peter Fisk @GeniusWorks
Scott Galloway @profgalloway
Simon Sinek @simonsinek
Social Chain
   www.socialchain.com/scribe (archived at https://perma.cc/C8LV-53WS)
Social Media Week
   https://socialmediaweek.org/news
   (archived at https://perma.cc/VUR3-NPM7)
TED Talks @TEDtalks
Tiny Giant Jams On your podcast medium of choice

Marketing and advertising associations

American Marketing Association (AMA)
   www.ama.org (archived at https://perma.cc/95GQ-TX8G)
Direct Marketing Association (DMA)
   www.dma.org.uk (archived at https://perma.cc/S8K3-DY75)
European Association of Communications Agencies (EACA)
   www.eca.eu (archived at https://perma.cc/26Y8-FVYD)
IAB Europe
   www.iabeurope.eu (archived at https://perma.cc/332U-VPDX)
Information Commissioner's Office (ICO)
   https://ico.org.uk (archived at https://perma.cc/RG3L-6ZSX)
Institute for Public Relations (IPR)
   www.instituteforpr.org (archived at https://perma.cc/624A-7F99)
Institute of Direct and Digital Marketing (IDM)
   www.theidem.com (archived at https://perma.cc/98J5-DBRW)
Institute of Practitioners in Advertising (IPA)
   www.ipa.co.uk (archived at https://perma.cc/29ZC-R8QR)
Internet Advertising Bureau (IAB)
   www.iabuk.net (archived at https://perma.cc/6AWQ-WRUL)

Social media awards and creative inspiration

BIMAs
    www.bimaawards.com (archived at https://perma.cc/HA2L-F8ZV)
Cannes Lions
    www.canneslions.com (archived at https://perma.cc/5MQC-YAND)
Caples Awards
    https://caples.org (archived at https://perma.cc/U4ND-K6JL)
Directory
    www.directnewideas.com (archived at https://perma.cc/CNW8-3A3E)
DMA Awards
    https://dma.org.uk/award (archived at https://perma.cc/V9FW-JS5N)
Webbys
    www.webbyawards.com (archived at https://perma.cc/J9QL-K6JX)
Whippies
    www.newswhip.com/2017/12/whippies-brands
    (archived at https://perma.cc/9WVX-2DC2)

Social media listening tools

Brandwatch
    www.brandwatch.com (archived at https://perma.cc/Z88X-QYUW)
Crimson Hexagon
    www.crimsonhexagon.com (archived at https://perma.cc/T6DY-WP67)
Fanpage Karma
    www.fanpagekarma.com (archived at https://perma.cc/LW5G UUKK)
Hootsuite
    www.hootsuite.com (archived at https://pcrma.cc/G7CN-2U5Z)
Talkwalker
    www.talkwalker.com (archived at https://perma.cc/QJ7P-QTDJ)

Social media listening tools

Bitly
    www.bitly.com (archived at https://perma.cc/B3Y5-M6B3)
Curalate
    www.curalate.com (archived at https://perma.cc/3ZRU-JU4V)
Google Analytics
    www.marketingplatform.google.com/about/analytics
    (archived at perma.cc/QK2W-C8QL)

Strategy creation insight and tools

Gartner

www.gartner.com (archived at https://perma.cc/3NKZ-4PER)

Simon Sinek Tools

www.startwithwhy.com (archived at https://perma.cc/SY4U-SASW)

APPENDIX 2

Social channels

The list below includes all the social media channels referenced in the book. While not exhaustive, the major channels are included.

TABLE A2.1   Social channels

Social media channel	Description	Country of origin	Link
Baidu Tieba	A communication platform hosted by the Chinese search engine Baidu. Similar to an online forum, it features millions of topic boards and interest groups with integrated social features.	China	https://tieba.baidu.com
Depop	A peer-to-peer social shopping app loved by the creative community. Users look for inspiration in category by scrolling rather than searching for specific items.	UK	www.depop.com
DZone	A global network of over a million developers, technology professional and architects to share information and connect with their peers. This type of social network is often referred to as a niche network.	USA	https://dzone.com

TABLE A2.1   *continued*

Social media channel	Description	Country of origin	Link
Facebook	The dominant global social network for connecting with family and friends and sharing photos, posts and videos. Facebook also own Instagram, Messenger and WhatsApp and are continually adding new features to the app. Facebook Business enables access to a sophisticated suite of advertising tools and targeting options.	USA	www.facebook.com https://business.facebook. com
Facebook Lite	A smaller version of the Facebook app, designed for use on low spec phones or where there are lower speed connections. The interface is more basic than the full Facebook app but most of the functionality remains, and the app uses a fraction of the data normally required.	USA	https://play.google.com/ store/apps/details?id=com. facebook.lite&hl=en_GB
Facebook Messenger	A free messaging app owned by Facebook and rivalling WhatsApp in popularity.	USA	www.messenger.com

TABLE A2.1   *continued*

Social media channel	Description	Country of origin	Link
Google+	Owned by Google, and initially seen by them as a rival to Facebook, the platform failed to gain significant traction and eventually a planned closedown was announced in 2018. The network developed to offer long-form, content-led discussion groups and was popular with a small, active community.	USA	https://plus.google.com
Instagram	A photo and video sharing network owned by Facebook. Features such as Instagram Stories, which were created to compete with Snapchat, are hugely popular and deliver high levels of engagement. Due to close links with Facebook, ads can be placed simultaneously on each network using either of their ad manager programmes.	USA	www.instagram.com https://business.instagram.com
Line	A free messaging app that also enables free voice, video calls and video conferencing.	Japan	https://line.me/en
LinkedIn	A professional networking and employment-led social platform owned by Microsoft. Users share CVs and business-focused content with their professional networks. It is a strong and popular channel for B2B marketing and sales, and recruitment.	USA	www.linkedin.com

TABLE A2.1   *continued*

Social media channel	Description	Country of origin	Link
Houseparty	A child/family-friendly face-to-face social app designed to share group video chats. It is aimed at including those too young for traditional social channels.	USA	https://houseparty.com
Musical.ly	A short form video app that enabled users to create their own music videos. The app was merged into TikTok in 2018.	China	www.tiktok.com
Odnoklassniki	A social network for classmates and friends to stay in touch. Used in Russia and former Soviet Republic.	Russia	https://ok.ru
Pinterest	A social network and bulletin board that enables users to create different boards and 'pin' content of their own or from the web. Followers can follow individuals or boards. The network is highly visual, popular with retailers and creative brands, and offers ecommerce features that support sales.	USA	www.pinterest.com
Poshmark	The largest social marketplace for selling fashion. Self-styled 'seller stylists' curate looks for their buyers.	USA	https://poshmark.com
QZone	The largest social network in China. Users can write blogs, keep diaries, send photos, listen to music and watch videos.	China	https://qzone.qq.com

TABLE A2.1   *continued*

Social media channel	Description	Country of origin	Link
Reddit	Breaking news, pictures, memes, Reddit is a discussion forum for members to chat about everything and anything. It calls itself the front page of the internet.	USA	www.reddit.com
Snapchat	A multimedia messaging app most renowned for its ephemeral video content and lenses, and popular with younger demographics. In 2018, Snapchat made some changes to the app's functionality to separate brand/commercial content from friend content. Although not universally popular, most of the updated features remain.	USA	www.snapchat.com
TikTok	A short form mobile video app that enables users to create their own music videos for sharing on social channels. It is karaoke for the digital age with lip syncing, dancing and comedy.	Singapore	www.tiktok.com
TinderU	Harking back to the origin of Facebook, TinderU enables students to find friend, dates, and study buddies who are located near them. A subset of the Tinder app, the focus is on creating hyper-localized communities by requiring an .edu email address to register.	USA	www.tinderu.in

TABLE A2.1   *continued*

Social media channel	Description	Country of origin	Link
Tudou	Originally a competitor of Youku, it now trades under the Youku umbrella and is a video streaming platform.	China	www.tudou.com
Twitch	An online video content livestreaming platform for gamers and game-related content. It is a subsidiary of Amazon.	USA	www.twitch.tv
Twitter	An online news and microblogging social network initially limited to 140 characters. In 2018 the character number was doubled and other changes have allowed additional media and links to be included without affecting the character count.	USA	https://twitter.com
Viber	A mobile messaging service for voice and video calls and sending private messages, photos and videos to small groups of friends/colleagues.	Japan	www.viber.com
Vkontakte	Although available in other languages, VK is mainly used by Russian speakers. It is a social media and networking site.	Russia	https://vk.com
WeChat	A mobile messaging service. Similar to WhatsApp but with significantly, increased functionality it is used for sharing private messages and photos with small groups of friends.	China	www.wechat.com

TABLE A2.1   *continued*

Social media channel	Description	Country of origin	Link
WeChat Pay	One of the most popular payment methods in China, WeChat Pay has the additional advantage of enabling one-click payment within WeChat for products and services bought within the platform.	China	https://pay.weixin.qq.com/index.php/public/wechatpay
Weibo (Sina)	An open microblogging social platform that is closer to Facebook in its functionality than Twitter. Sina Weibo has by far the larger following of the two Weibo channels.	China	www.weibo.com
Weibo (Tencent)	The Tencent version of Weibo, with a much smaller following. This version is based on the private messaging heritage of Tencent rather than the news media heritage of Sina.	China	www.weibo.com/tencent
WhatsApp	A mobile messaging service for voice and video calls and sending private messages, photos and videos to small groups of friends/colleagues	US	www.whatsapp.com
Yammer	Owned by Microsoft, Yammer is a private social networking services used within organizations. Accessed only via approved email addresses, the privacy is contained within the organization's domain.	US	https://products.office.com/en-gb/yammer/yammer-overview

TABLE A2.1   *continued*

Social media channel	Description	Country of origin	Link
Youku	Often referred to as the Chinese YouTube, it is a video hosting platform owned by Alibaba Group.	China	www.youku.com
YouTube	A video sharing website, YouTube was bought by Google in 2006	US	www.youtube.com

GLOSSARY

#ad   The ASA and CAP code require all influencer social media posts that involve some form of payment, or payment in kind, to clearly state that they are an ad. Ideally this can be done by using #ad at the start of the post or video.

above the line (ABL)   An advertising term used to describe traditional mass marketing channels such as TV, print, outdoor and radio. Typically, ABL ads do not have a response mechanism.

adblocking   Adblocking technology enables users on digital platforms to prevent ads being displayed or downloaded. The technology works on both mobile and desktop devices and is increasingly common in younger demographics.

Advertising Standards Authority (ASA)   The Advertising Standards Authority is the independent UK advertising regulator. Using the Committee of Advertising Practice (CAP) code, it determines which ads are in breach of the code. It can set fines, ask for amends to ads, or ban ads from being used. Social media posts by brands and influencers are considered as ads by the CAP code and the ASA.

affiliate marketing   This occurs when a company rewards another company for a referral. It is a financial transaction and is often managed by an affiliate network that connects brands with potential affiliates and organizes payments.

Alexa skills   Alexa is Amazon's AI voice assistant that enables you to perform voice-activated tasks using your Amazon Echo speaker. The skills are the apps that enable the voice assistant to connect to hardware and software in order to perform the task.

algorithm   A computer program used to follow a specific set of rules in order to organize and structure large data sets. The Facebook algorithm is used to decide the posts and adverts that appear in your newsfeed.

application programming interface (API)   An access point to an app that enables connection to a database. Many social media channels have an API that enables activity such as engagement, likes, etc to recorded on a database and translated into campaign results.

artificial intelligence (AI)   Sometimes called machine intelligence, AI is a technological development that enables computers to behave in a similar way to human beings. AI can utilize speech recognition, problem solving and planning and is used in social media for chatbots, creative optimization and many other automation initiatives.

astroturfing   In social media, 'astroturfing' refers to social ads by influencers that are masquerading as organic posts. Like the artificial turf, they look real, but are fake.

audience segmentation   The process of dividing up a brand's or business's audience into separate homogenous groups based on information such as their demographics, behaviours, location and spending patterns. By creating an audience segmentation, brands can target specific groups with products, services and content more relevant to their specific needs.

authoritative influencers   These influencers are experts in their field of influence. They could be journalists, scientists, technologists, or from another field of expertise, but they are recognized in the industry sector as thought leaders and opinion formers.

behavioural economics   In marketing, this is the study of psychological, emotional, cognitive and social effects on consumer behaviour. In recent years marketing has used insights into typical behaviour to focus advertising campaigns and the presentation of content.

below the line (BTL)   An advertising term used to describe direct to consumer advertising including direct response television (DRTV), direct mail, door drops and email. Highly targeted, BTL advertising usually includes a response mechanism.

biases   In behavioural economics terms biases, or heuristics, are the hard-wired behavioural patterns and responses most people will exhibit in certain situations. They are part of what is known as System 1 thinking, as defined by the father of behavioural economics, Daniel Kahneman. There are hundreds of different biases and some are particularly useful to marketers as they seek to encourage certain behaviour on behalf of, and in relation to, brands.

brand neighbourhood   A term used to describe the collection of brands most commonly used by a particular audience segment. The neighbourhood will include brands from the same sector as the business being analysed but will also include brands from other sectors. Typically, supermarkets, retail, automotive, fashion and tech brands are chosen to describe brand neighbourhoods as they provide good discrimination between different audiences.

brand purpose   A statement of belief, a brand's purpose defines what the brand stands for and how it wants to affect or change the world. It demonstrates why the brand exists.

branded links   This is a shortened version of a URL. It is written in plain English and features the brand name. Tools such as bitly support short and branded link creation. Some example short URLs are pep.si for Pepsi, fb.me for Facebook and movi.es for Netflix.

business-to-business (B2B)   When a business sells its products and services to other businesses.

business-to-business-to-consumer B2B2C   When a business is one step removed from their actual consumer and sells to a third party, who will then sell on to the end customer.

business-to-consumer (B2C)   When a brand sells its products and services to individual consumers.

c-suite   The board of directors or trustees who have overall responsibility for running an organization. The board will typically consist of a chief executive, finance director, sales and marketing director, IT director, HR director and other roles specific to the business sector and functions.

call-to-action (CTA)   The copy that defines the action required by the reader. This could be to buy now, follow now, like now, sign up now, or a variant on this theme.

CAP   The Committee of Advertising Practice (CAP) code sets the standards and regulations in the UK for non-broadcast advertising, sales promotion and direct marketing. The Advertising Standards Authority (ASA) independently regulates UK ads against the CAP code. Social media posts by brands and influencers are considered as ads by CAP and the ASA. Details of the code can be found on their website – www.asa.org.uk (archived at https://perma.cc/F2QL-WUJ3).

catchment area   This is the area from which a business or service draws its customers. For a bricks and mortar store or sales outlet this might be defined by a drivetime distance around the store or by a selection of local postcodes that meet the customer demographic. When a business has multiple outlets, the catchment areas can overlap.

CGI influencers   Computer generated imagery (CGI) influencers are virtual social media influencers who have been created to influence on behalf of brands. Generally originating in Japan, China and the United States, these virtual models have huge followings and share 'their thoughts' on fashion, life and feelings.

challenger brand   A term coined by Adam Morgan in his book *Eat the Big Fish*, which describes brands able to perform above the usual expectation of their resources because of their ambition and ability to change the way decision-making happens in their category.

chatbot A chatbot is a computer programme that uses AI to replicate human interaction. It can be speech or text based.

click-through rate (CTR)   A commonly used social media metric representing the number of people who have clicked on a link to your website or other content compared with the number of people the link was displayed to.

community   Social media communities are groups of individuals united by a common interest or brand and connected via social channels. Influencers often refer to their followers as their community.

Competition and Markets Authority (CMA)   In the UK, the CMA prosecutes brands and individuals if they falsely represent themselves as consumers, or do not make it clear when content is an ad. Many celebrities and influencers have been breaking the law in this area and the CMA is starting to investigate and prosecute offenders.

consumer-to-business-to-consumer (C2B2C)   Used to describe the situation when a business acts as a conduit for one consumer to make a sale to another.

content marketing   A form of marketing that does not overtly sell products. Rather, it attracts consumers to the brand by providing relevant, useful and timely information that provides value to the consumer by answering a specific need. That need could include entertainment, education, support, inspiration or information.

content pillars   Content pillars are a way of structuring different topics or themes of content into groups that appeal to specific audience segments. The content can be very varied in its type and include blogs, memes, vlogs, ebooks, case studies, reviews, videos, podcasts and many other elements, but the pillar is used to focus the purpose and theme of each different element.

cost per click (CPC)   The cost of a social media post divided by the number of people who click on the link within that post.

cost per lead (CPL)   The cost of your social media activity divided by the number of leads that activity generated.

cost per thousand impressions (CPM)   The cost of your social media activity divided by one-thousandth of the number of impressions that activity generated.

cost per view (CPV)   The cost of your social media activity divided by the number of views that activity generated.

crisis   A crisis occurs when, for example, something impacts on an organization's licence to operate, either literally such as a building burning down, or because its consumers take away their permission by stopping buying from the brand because of a reputational event. In both these examples a crisis is not just an incident, it is something that can impact on sales, reputation and share price.

cryptocurrency   A form of money, cryptocurrencies are virtual or digital currencies used in exchange for goods or services on digital platforms. Bitcoin is an example of a cryptocurrency.

customer engagement   In marketing, this term is used to describe the depth of a customer-to-brand relationship. It denotes the level of trust and the frequency, length, and type of interaction. At its best, customer engagement is instigated and maintained by both the brand and the customer via multiple marketing, social media and experiential channels and events.

customer relationship management (CRM)   The use of technology, strategies and processes to manage an organization's interactions and relationships with its customers in order to improve customer orientated goals such as customer service, lifetime value, loyalty and customer satisfaction.

customer value ecosystem   An approach to business strategy that enables an organization to increase its service and product offerings by understanding the value their customers place on their relationship with the brand and the broader needs the brand fulfils for them. This enables a brand like Nike to engage with its customers on their fitness, health and political opinions.

customer value exchanges   Social media can be used to add customer value to every stage of the brand-to-customer relationship. Examples of content that adds customer value are entertaining, inspirational, educational, convincing, informative and supportive content.

dark social   Refers to the social sharing of content that cannot be tracked with the usual web analytics tools. Private messaging apps, email and texting are the most commonly used dark social sharing methods.

demographics   These are variables that describe the characteristics of a population or group. They include information such as age, gender, income and marital status. This information can be used to describe audience segments for marketing purposes so long as the relevant legal permissions have been obtained.

detractors   The percentage of people who, when asked how likely they are to recommend a product or service, would score the likelihood as between 1 and 6 out of 10.

direct messaging (DM)   Social platforms enable you to send private messages to your connections. On Twitter you can send DMs to people even if they are not following you.

discussion forum   Also known as a discussion group, online forum, or discussion board, a discussion forum is an online bulletin board where you can leave messages and receive replies, or just read the threads of other conversations.

ecommerce   Electronic or internet commerce describes the buying and selling of products and services on the internet. This activity is facilitated and enabled by the transfer of data and money.

endowment effect   A behavioural economics bias, or heuristic, which describes the fact that people value things they own more than things they don't.

engagement pods   These pods can occur on any platform and happen when a group of users bands together to help increase engagement on each other's social content. The pods can be useful for boosting the content's position in the platform's algorithm but it isn't a true reflection of genuine engagement with the content.

engagement   In social media, engagement is used to describe the interaction with social media content such as likes, shares and follows. Increasingly, brands have started to rank engagement in terms of meaningful interactions (comments and conversations) over passive interactions (likes and shares).

ephemeral content   Short-lived, impermanent content. Embodied by Snapchat and Instagram Stories, this type of content typically has a high level of engagement but is the opposite of the more traditional timeless content brands more usually aspire to create.

EU E-Privacy Regulation   Planned changes to the current E-Privacy Regulations will create a standard across Europe and will specifically detail how GDPR is implemented online and potentially increase data regulations.

fake engagement   Even harder to detect than fake followers, fake engagement can be conducted by bots, other influencers or engagement pods and occurs when the engagement is purely happening to boost engagement levels rather than because an individual is genuinely interested in the content being presented.

fake followers   These are fake social media accounts that have been set up in order to follow other accounts. Some influencers and brands have bought thousands, and even tens of thousands, of these followers. Networks like Instagram try to find and delete these accounts but it can be hard to identify a fake account from a genuine one.

fandom   A community built around a shared enjoyment of an aspect of popular culture such as a TV show, movie, book or performer.

focus group   A form of qualitative market research where a group of people from a particular target audience or segment are gathered together to discuss a product, service or idea. Their feedback is used to provide insights into product development, packaging, creative approach and other aspects of sales and marketing.

followers   In social media, a follower is someone who chooses to see all of another user's or brand's social media posts.

frequency   This is the number of times the same person sees your post. If the frequency is too high it can cause people to become annoyed and unfollow your page or hide your posts.

General Data Protection Regulation (GDPR)   New data protection regulation which applies to any organization utilizing data on European citizens from May 2018 onwards. Information on the regulations can be found on the Information Commissioner's Office (ICO) website. Alternatively, the Data Marketing Association (DMA) website has guidance on the regulations' impact on marketing.

Generation Alpha   The generation born since 2010, they are the children of Generation Y.

Generation X   The generation born between the mid-1960s and the 1980s. These are the parents of Generation Z.

Generation Y   Born in the 1980s and 1990s, Generation Y are the children of the Baby Boomers and are often referred to as the Millennials.

Generation Z   The generation born between the mid-1990s and up to the early 2000s. Estimated to make up 25 per cent of the US population and 30 per cent of the global population, they are bigger than the previous cohorts and are increasingly important consumers and employees.

gifs   The acronym stands for Graphics Interchange Format and is used to describe the process of storing multiple images in one file, which allows images to appear with simple animation.

help or hygiene content   This is the content that is always available, easily found, and is created to fulfil particular customer needs.

hero content   The highly sharable, awareness generating content that provides the backbone of any content marketing campaign.

heuristics   In behavioural economics terms, heuristics, or biases, are the hard-wired behavioural patterns and responses most people will exhibit in certain situations. They are part of what is known as System 1 thinking, as defined by the father of behavioural economics, Daniel Kahneman. There are hundreds of different heuristics and some are particularly useful to marketers as they seek to encourage certain behaviour on behalf of, and in relation to, brands.

hub content   This content is used to encourage engagement and introduce consumers to different aspects of the brand. It is a form of outbound content.

hype curve   The curve is a graphical representation of how a new idea or technology moves through different stages of conception, early adoption, maturity and widespread adoption. Gartner have created a branded tool for this known as the hype cycle.

impressions   This indicates the number of times a piece of content or a post has been seen in social media. An individual may see the same content numerous times and each occasion will be counted in the total number of impressions.

inbound   This is the marketing activity that draws consumers to, and engages them with, your brand by meeting their specific needs. It is sometimes referred to as 'pull' marketing. Inbound activity is a continuous presence and takes time to build. It uses activity such as your website, SEO, content marketing programmes (blogs, whitepapers, how to videos) and CRM programmes such as email newsletters and customer magazines.

influencer marketing   A methodology for integrating influencers into a marketing strategy by matching influencers to brands and monetizing the access to the latter's communities.

influencer   A social media influencer is an individual who has established a large following, usually in a specific business area, on social media. They are able to persuade their followers to try or buy experiences or brands because of their authenticity and reach.

inmail   This is the messaging function within LinkedIn that sends messages directly to people you are connected to. If you are not directly connected, the LinkedIn Premium service allows you to pay for messages to be sent to targeted individuals.

key opinion leaders (KOLs)   These influencers tend to have large volumes of followers and can often be celebrities. They are a sub-set of top-tier influencers but are known to their community for being a genuine connoisseur of a particular topic, and as such their opinions on this topic are respected by their followers.

key performance indicators (KPIs)   These are the most important measurements in any campaign or project. These measurements will determine the success or failure of any social media activity. KPIs can be set at a business, project or campaign level. Examples of social media KPIs include reach, sentiment, cost per lead, cost per sale, return on investment (ROI), and sales equivalent advertising value (SEAV).

lifetime value (LTV)   This is an average, calculated value usually assigned to a customer segment or group. It is calculated by assessing the average length of time a customer remains an active purchaser with your brand – it could be a day, a month or several years. The time period selected is then used to calculate the total customer spend in that period. This is the LTV.

LinkedIn groups   These are private groups within the LinkedIn platform that enable groups of individuals to discuss topics of mutual interest outside of the public feed.

links   This is the code that directs traffic from one piece of content to another. You could link your Instagram post to your website or to your Twitter feed. A link strategy will formalize the hierarchy of your links, and tools can be used to create shorter, more manageable links.

loss aversion   A behavioural economics bias, or heuristic, which describes the fact that people are more willing to take risks to avoid losing something they already have than they are to gain something new.

meaningful interactions   A term used to describe a relatively high level of social media engagement, such as comments and conversations.

meme   A video, image or phrase that is often funny and is copied and shared, usually with variations, on the internet.

micro influencers   These influencers have the smallest communities, typically fewer than 100,000 followers, but can have a very high impact on those communities because of the very focused and authentic content they share about mutually interesting issues and experiences.

mid-tier influencers   Typically, these influencers will have a community of between 100,000 and one million, and although their reach is not as high as that achieved by top-tier influencers, their engagement rates are generally higher.

millennials   The generation born in the 1980s and 1990s, Millennials are the children of the Baby Boomers and are sometimes referred to as Generation Y.

mumsnet   A website for UK parents, Mumsnet hosts discussion forums where users share advice and tips on a range of family and work-related topics. Mumsnet also has an influencer network that provides access to over 10,000 vloggers, bloggers and social media influencers.

Net Promoter Score (NPS)   A measurement of how likely an individual is to recommend your product or service. NPS scores can be positive or negative and are calculated by calculating the percentage of promoters and detractors and taking the latter away from the former.

neutrals   The percentage of people who, when asked how likely they are to recommend a product or service, would score the likelihood as either 7 or 8 out of 10.

niche influencers   These influencers are defined not by the size of their following but rather by the narrow interest area or industry segment that they have an influence on. These influencers are associated with a specific industry segment or a small area within an industry segment.

niche social channels   These types of channel are often used to gain high visibility for a brand with a specific audience. They offer smaller volumes than the larger networks but because they are dedicated to a particular area (eg knitting, tech, cycling, the environment) the audience is highly engaged and responsive to relevant content. These channels can therefore drive a significant volume of high quality traffic to your website.

non-governmental organizations (NGOs)   Not-for-profit organizations that operate independently of government. Typically, NGOs work in areas of political and social change. They can operate internationally.

outbound   This is the marketing activity that is used to guarantee volume and reignite conversations. It is sometimes referred to as 'push' marketing. Typically, outbound marketing will use paid for media opportunities such as traditional and social ads, display, affiliates and PPC. Volumes can be achieved quickly and managed by controlling the amount of spend and type of activity used.

paid search (PPC)   Pay per click (or cost per click CPC) describes the advertising model used by brands to buy prominent page positions on search engine and other websites.

passive interactions   A term used to describe a relatively low level of social media engagement, such as liking and sharing.

PESTLE   Standing for political, economic, socio-cultural, technological, legal and environmental, PESTLE analysis enables a business to understand how external factors impact upon its ability to create and meet its overall strategic goals.

Photoshop   Part of the Adobe product suite, Photoshop is a graphics editing and publishing tool widely used by creatives in social media content creation.

pixels   In social media the various platforms enable the use of specific snippets of code (pixels) that can be added to a brand's website. These pixels track conversions from ads within the social media platform and support remarketing and audience definition and targeting.

podcast   A free audio service that enables internet users to listen to digital audio files on a variety of devices. Typically, a podcast will be a series of shows around a specific content area. When you subscribe to a specific podcast you will automatically receive each new episode and can listen to them at your own convenience.

power of the group   A behavioural economics bias, or heuristic, which describes the fact that experiences that happen as part of a group deliver heightened levels of emotion for the individuals within the group.

Premiere Pro   Part of the Adobe product suite, Premiere Pro is a video editing and publishing tool widely used by creatives in social media content creation.

Pride   Gay pride or LGTB+ pride is a positive stand against violence and discrimination towards the LGTB+ community. It promotes and celebrates sexual diversity and gender variance.

private media   A form of social media that is used to share information, images and videos between small private groups, usually through encrypted applications such as WhatsApp and WeChat.

prodromal   In social media the prodromal stage of a social media crisis occurs when it is inevitable that a crisis will happen but you are not in the middle of the crisis yet.

profile   A profile or pen portrait is a description of a particular audience or customer segment. It typically contains information about the demographics, characteristics, preferences and behaviours of the segment. The information in the portrait is used to demonstrate what sets the group apart from the other segments.

promoters   The people who, when asked how likely they are to recommend a product or service, would score the likelihood as either 9 or 10 out of 10.

qualitative research   Used to describe forms of market research, such as focus groups, that provide information and insight based on the views of small numbers of people. Often the insight is in discussion form and it is never a statistically significant representation of a specific audience's views.

quantitative research   Used to describe forms of market research, such as questionnaires, that provide numerically measurable insights and information on the views of representative samples of consumer groups. Ideally, the group sizes are statistically significant.

reach   This is the number of individual users who have seen a particular post or piece of content. If an individual sees the content more than once, only the first occasion will be counted in the reach calculation.

relevancy score   This score is allocated by Facebook to your social ads and indicates how relevant your ad is to your audience. The score ranges from 1 to 10, where 1 is irrelevant and 8–10 is highly relevant. The higher the score, the more likely Facebook will serve the ad to that audience. By increasing your relevancy score, you can effectively improve the performance of your posts and reduce the cost of your ads.

return on investment (ROI)   This calculation measures the revenue generated in relation to the amount of money spent to create the revenue. ROMI is also often used, and refers to the revenue return on marketing investment.

Rundle   A term coined by Scott Galloway, Professor of Marketing at NYU, to describe a monogamous recurring revenue model, such as Amazon Prime, where customers are locked in to a recurring payment model because of the value it brings. Galloway links this model to increased stock valuation prices and commercial success for businesses that adopt it enjoy.

search engine optimization (SEO)   The strategies and techniques used by brands to ensure the highest page position in response to relevant questions posed by consumers on search engine websites.

segmentation variables   The characteristics that can be used to identify and describe different audience segments. They are typically of four different types – demographic, geographic, behavioural and psychographic,

sentiment   A measure of brand opinion on social media where a social listening tool analyses the comments about a brand and grades them as positive, negative or neutral.

shares   When an individual user shares content from a website, social channel or other platform with other individuals. In social media sharing is generally regarded as a passive form of engagement.

shoppable tags   Sometimes known as product tags, these tags enable a one-click to purchase solution. When you click on the product image, which is set up for product tagging, you see a product description and the cost, and with one click you can buy in the platform. In 2018, Instagram allowed in-platform payments for the first time.

small to medium sized enterprise (SME)   A term used in business segmentation to define businesses with fewer than 500 employees.

SMART objectives   An acronym for the specific, measured, achievable, realistic and timebound goals that enable an organization to measure its progress within a strategic cycle.

social commerce   This is a subset of electronic or ecommerce. It describes situations where social networks are used to facilitate ecommerce transactions. Instagram's shoppable tags are an example of social commerce.

social equivalent advertising value (SEAV)   A measurement used in social media when ROI is difficult to calculate. This measure enables a monetary value to be given to the social media activity by equating results achieved organically with those from paid marketing. For example, if a native social media drives traffic to a website the SEAV will be the money saved by not having to pay for marketing activity to drive the same number of leads.

social listening   The process of monitoring and interpreting the conversations and behaviours of social media audiences.

social media   Web based applications and networks that enable the public sharing of, and collaboration around, information, images and videos.

social proof   A behavioural economics bias, or heuristic, that describes the fact that people make decisions based on social norms. That is, they like to behave as others do and will feel more comfortable doing something that they know is popular.

statistical significance   A measure of how likely a result is to deviate from a simple random variation. When conducting market research, or testing different marketing approaches, random groups of customers are used for the tests. Their behaviour or opinions are assumed to represent the way the remainder of the group will behave when faced with the same circumstances. However, to be confident that the remainder of the group will mirror that of the test group, it is important to use a test group that is large enough to provide a statistically robust result. The higher the level of statistical significance, the more likely the remainder of the group is to behave in the way that the test group did.

System 1   A phrase coined by Daniel Kahneman, the father of behavioural economics, to describe the automatic, subconscious way our brain behaves in many standard situations. These replicable patterns of behaviour are known as heuristics or biases and can be used in marketing to predict how consumers will behave, and to encourage preferred patterns of behaviour.

System 2   This is the other way our brain behaves. In contrast to System 1 thinking, this is a term used to describe considered, logical decision-making. System 2 thinking takes longer and is harder for our brains to complete, so is less frequent than System 1 thinking.

T-shaped marketer   Modern marketing professionals are often described as T-shaped. They will have a broad understanding of digital marketing disciplines and a detailed in-depth understanding of one area. For example, you could be a T-shaped planner, creative, social strategist or media buyer.

tentpole content   In the movie industry, a tentpole movie is a large blockbuster film that is expected to support other less well performing productions. In content marketing, tentpole content is used to describe hero content, as it forms the backbone of any campaign and supports the other content being utilized.

thread   In an online discussion forum or group, a thread is the sequence of responses to an initial post. By reading a thread you can understand how the conversation has developed and can join in or leave at any point.

top-tier influencers   These influencers are generally celebrities, for example Kim Kardashian, or have become celebrities because of the impact of their influencing, for example Zoella. They tend to have over a million followers who will follow them for a range of reasons.

touchpoint   In marketing, touchpoints are used to describe the places where brands and consumers meet. Some touchpoints happen in the real world, for example visiting a store, others are digital, such as website visits, social media likes or video views.

troll   Social media trolls deliberately post inflammatory or controversial comments in order to start quarrels and upset people in online communities.

uniform resource locator (URL)   This is the unique identifier of every piece of content on the internet. Because URLs can be long and complex, and include large groups of random letters and numbers, tools to shorten them and assign relevant names are frequently used.

unique tracking codes   These codes can be attached to custom URLs and are used to track the source, media and campaign of marketing activity. They are used within Google Analytics.

user-generated content (UGC)   UGC is content that has been created, and often distributed, by fans or customers of the brand. It is considered to give a more truthful representation of the brand and is trusted by consumers over brand-generated content.

virtual private network (VPN)   A private, encrypted and safe way to access the internet.

VMOST   Standing for vision, mission, objectives, strategy and tactics. A VMOST approach to strategic planning can ensure that everyone in your organization is aligned in achieving the same overall goals.

Wanghong   The romanization of the Mandarin pronunciation for online celebrity, it describes Chinese influencers who have become famous because of their internet presence. They differ from KOLs, because KOLs have a level of knowledge or expertise that forms the basis of their reputation and right to influence on a particular topic.

INDEX